ABOUT THIS PLAYBOOK

This Playbook gives you quick and easy visual steps for every popular task in Cricut Design Space®. Just follow along with the steps and you'll be good to go!

Each of these "cheat sheets" show you exactly what to click and what to do for easy, fast results everytime.

By learning in small steps, you avoid the overwhelm that usually comes with trying to get control over something that is confusing and hard to remember.

I've organized the pages in this Playbook by the way we access Cricut Design Space, using color coding so you always know whether you're on the right page. Here's how it works:

Hi! I'm Jennifer!

Cricut®-colored pages are for Design Space on Mac/Windows

Sky-colored pages are for Design Space® app in iOS (iPhones/iPads)

Gold-colored pages are for Design Space® app on Androids

If you have any questions about using the Playbook, email me at hello@jennifermaker.com.

For more Cricut ideas and inspiration, join me at jennifermaker.com

Happy making,

Jennifer

Key to Playbook Pages:

- Steps are in green
- Tips are in blue
- Notes are in yellow
- Warnings are in pink

ISBN: 978-1-64737-005-3. Updated version 8.5 - updated January 2026.

Printed in the United States

PLAYBOOK INDEX

HOW TO INSTALL CRICUT DESIGN SPACE (MAC)

Cricut Design Space is the free software you'll use to make amazing things on your Cricut. To install Cricut Design Space on your Mac desktop or laptop computer, go to design.cricut.com and click the Download button. Design Space for Desktop will allow you to work both online and offline. Follow the directions below to install it on your Mac.

Step 1: Download the installer at design.cricut.com

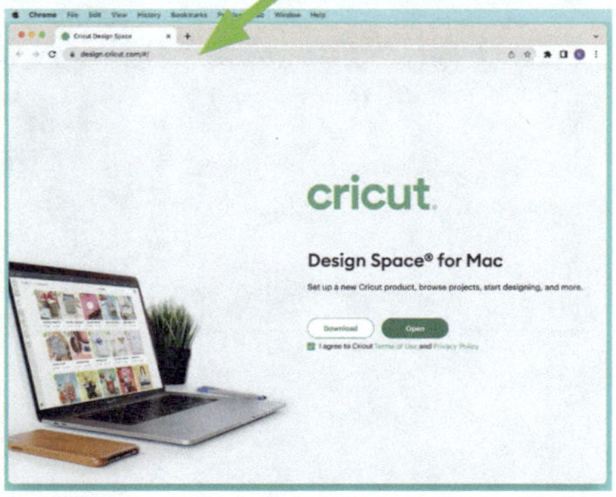

Step 2: Open the downloaded file and drag (click, hold, & move) the Cricut icon over the folder, then let go of the mouse.

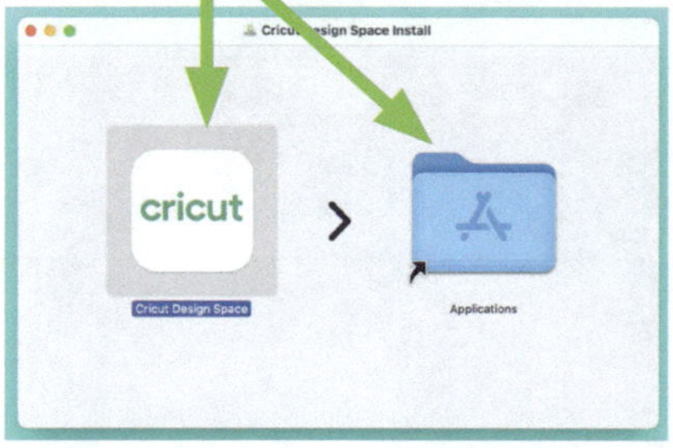

Step 3: Open your Applications folder and double-click the Cricut application to launch it.

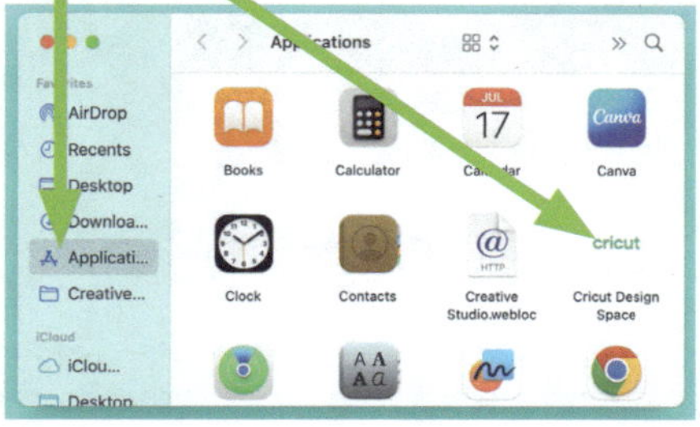

Note: If you get this warning, you can click "Open." This warning is notifying you that the app has been downloaded from the internet. By clicking open you are confirming that you want to open it.

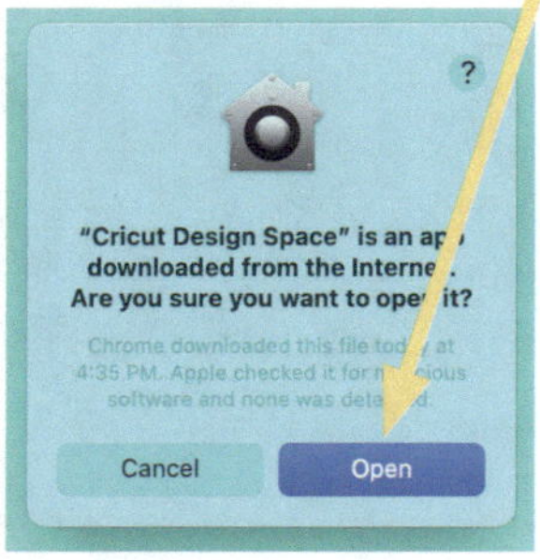

Step 4: If prompted, sign in with your Cricut account email and password. (If you're already signed in, you're logged in automatically.)

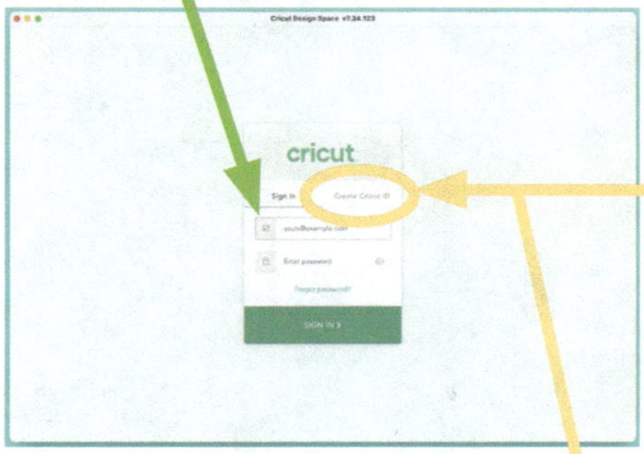

Note: If this is your first time using Design Space, click here to create a free account.

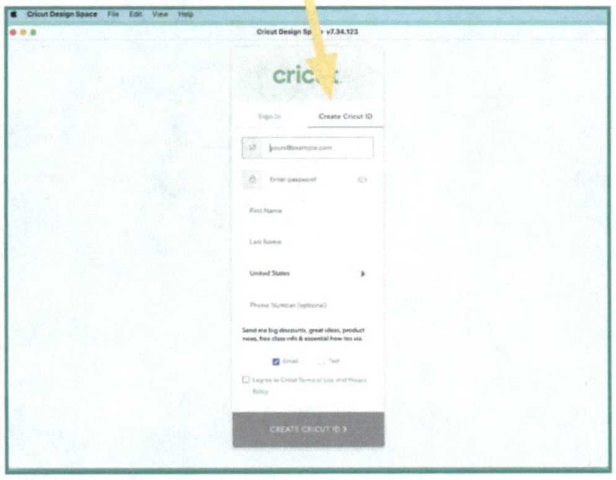

Tip: If you are completely new to Cricut, go to cricut.com/setup and you will be guided through a welcome sequence to cut your first project. If you'd like to revisit this, click your name in the upper right corner and choose Settings, Machines, then click Start next to New Product Setup.

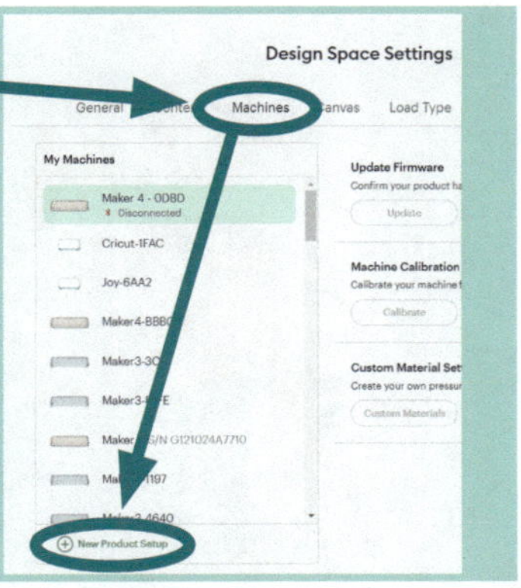

HOW TO INSTALL CRICUT DESIGN SPACE (PC)

Cricut Design Space is the free software you'll use to make amazing things on your Cricut. To install Cricut Design Space on your Windows desktop or laptop computer, go to design.cricut.com and click the Download button. Design Space for Desktop will allow you to work both online and offline. Follow the directions below to install it on your PC.

Step 1: Download the installer at design.cricut.com and select your machine.

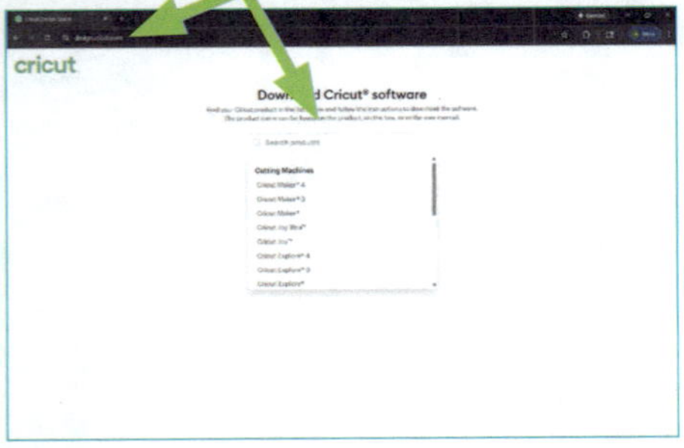

Step 2: Open the downloaded file and wait for it to install onto your hard drive.

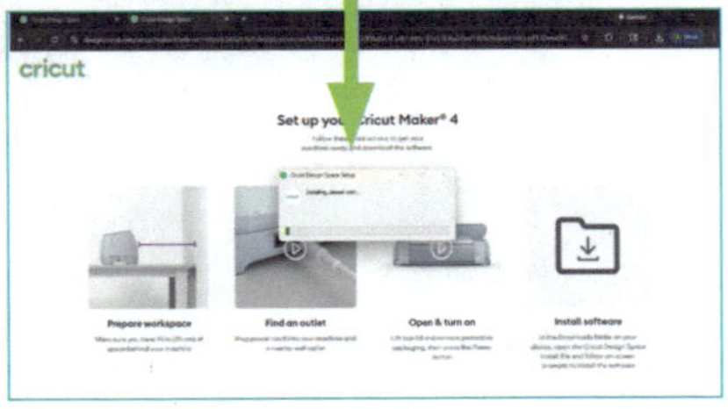

Step 3: Once installed, Cricut Design Space will automatically open and you'll see this screen.

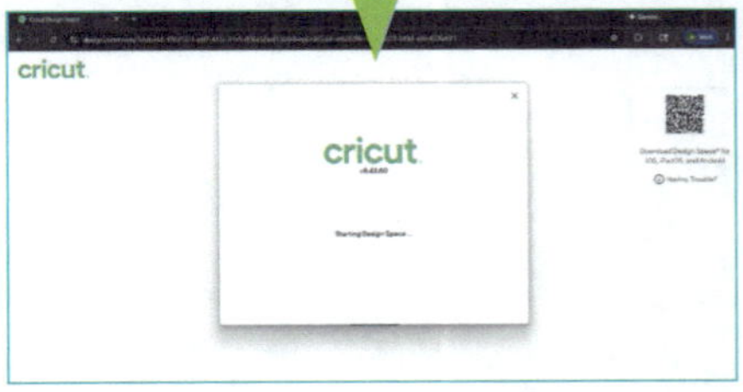

Step 4: If prompted, sign in with your Cricut account email and password. (If you're already signed in, you're logged in automatically.)

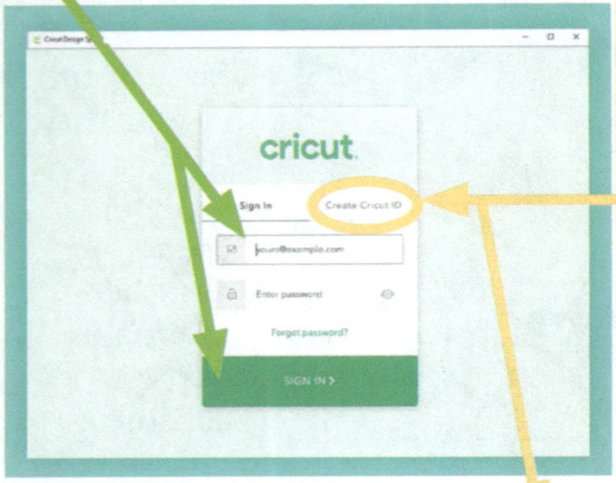

Note: If this is your first time using Design Space, click here to create a free account.

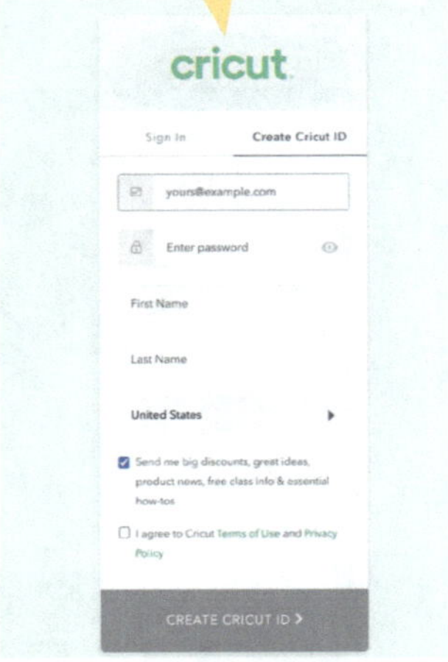

Tip: If you are completely new to Cricut, first go to cricut.com/setup and you will be guided through a welcome sequence to cut your first project. If you'd like to revisit this, click your name in the upper right corner and choose Settings, Machines, then click Start next to New Product Setup.

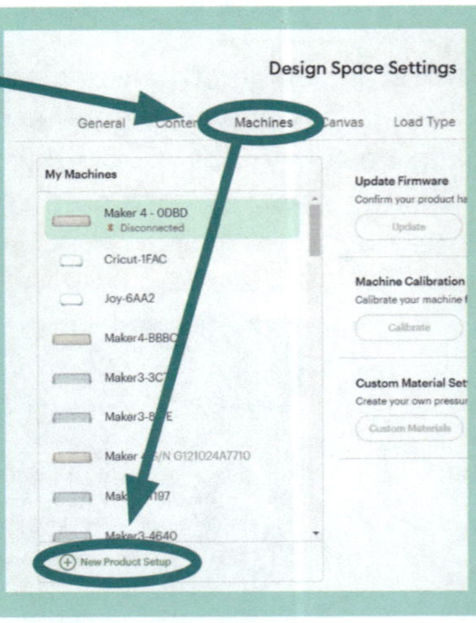

Once Cricut Design Space is installed on your PC, an icon will appear on your desktop as well as in your taskbar. Just double-click the icon to go to Cricut Design Space again. If you cannot find the icon for Cricut Design Space, click the bottom-left Start button on your desktop, tap "All Apps" in the menu and look for Cricut Design Space.

HOW TO OPEN AND START A NEW PROJECT

Step 1: Open Cricut Design Space on your Desktop by double-clicking its icon in the dock/taskbar or type design.cricut.com in your web browser to get a page with a button to open the desktop app.

MAC

PC

OR

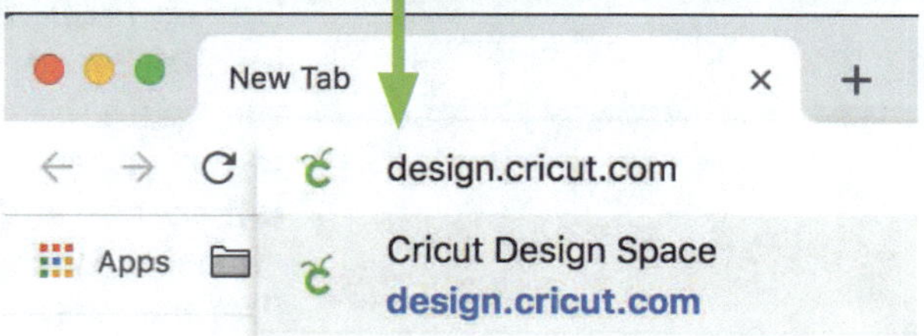

Step 2: If prompted, sign in with your email and password. (If you're already signed in, you will be taken to the next step automatically.)

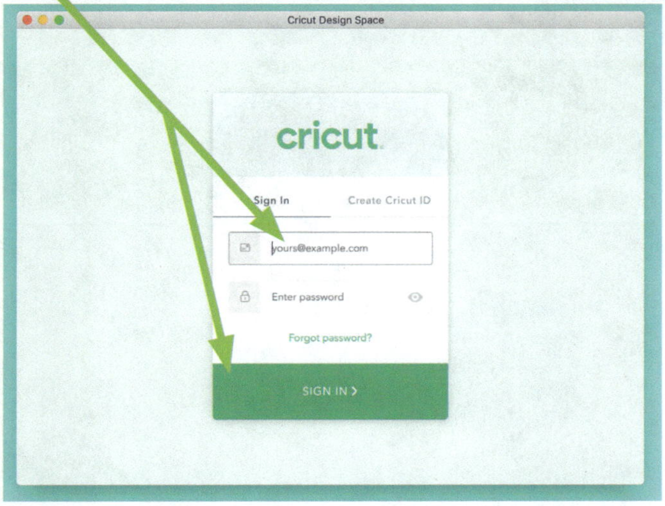

Step 3: Click the New Project button in the upper right corner or Canvas in the upper left corner next to Home.

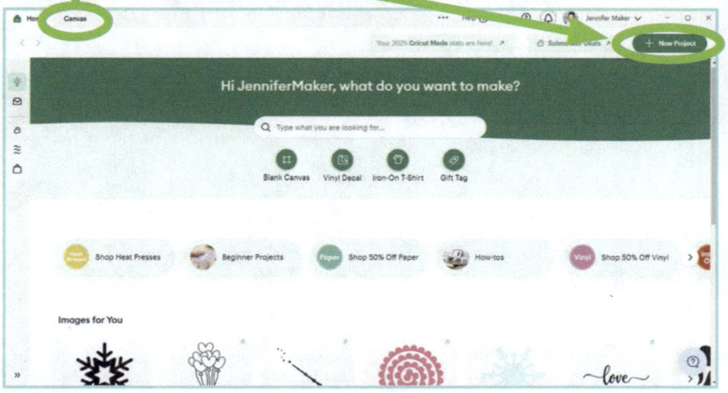

Step 4: If this menu appears when you click "+ New Project," click the Blank Canvas.

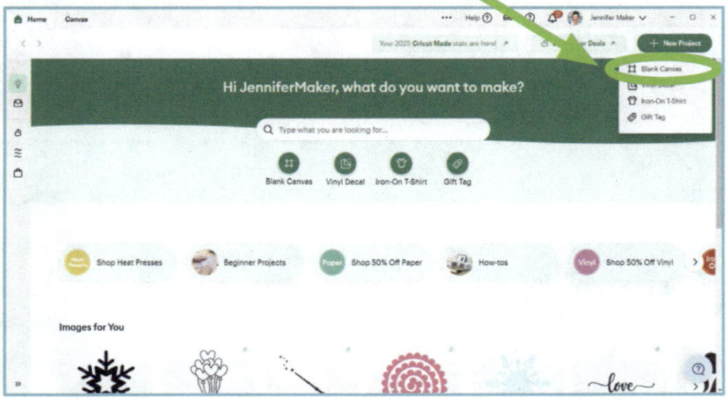

You will get a new Canvas, ready for you to add images, shapes, text, and projects!

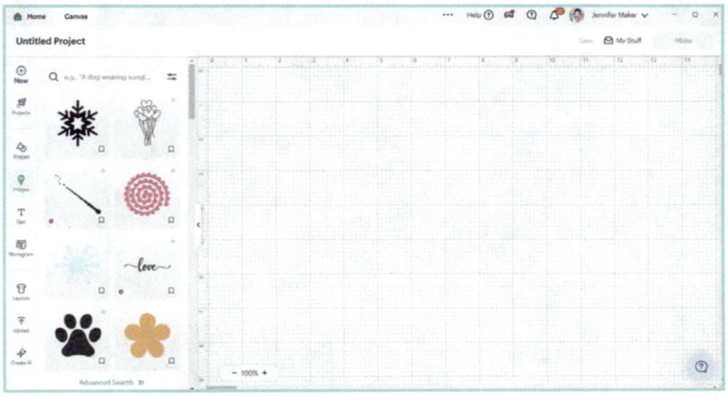

HOW TO CONNECT A MAC TO CRICUT VIA BLUETOOTH

Step 1: Open System Preferences in your Dock.

You can also find System Preferences by clicking on the Apple menu in the upper left corner and choosing System Preferences.

Note: Your Cricut must be within 10-15 feet of your Mac to connect with it. If your Cricut needs to use a Wireless Bluetooth Adapter (Explore and Explore One), make sure it is inserted.

Step 2: Click the Bluetooth icon to open it.

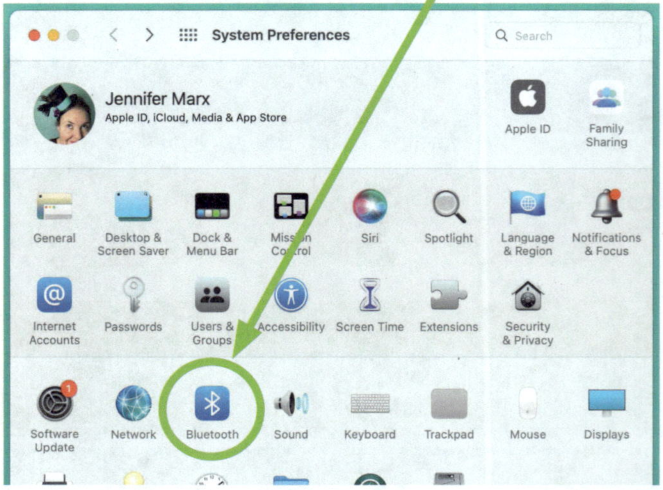

Step 3: If Bluetooth is off, click Turn Bluetooth On.

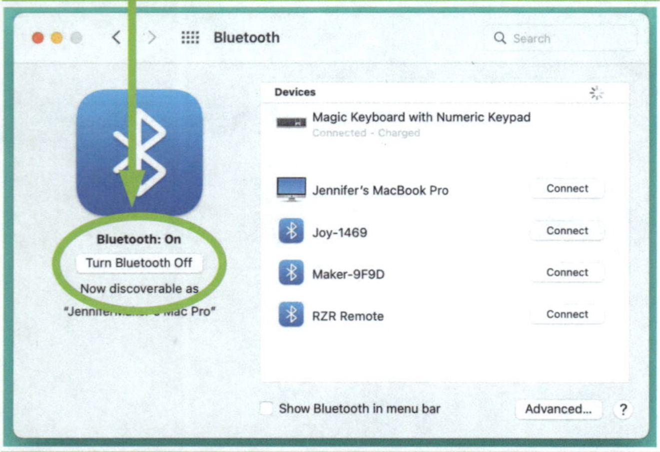

Step 4: Locate a device that includes a Cricut name and click Connect or Pair. If you don't see it listed, make sure your Cricut is turned on and no other Bluetooth device is connecting to it.

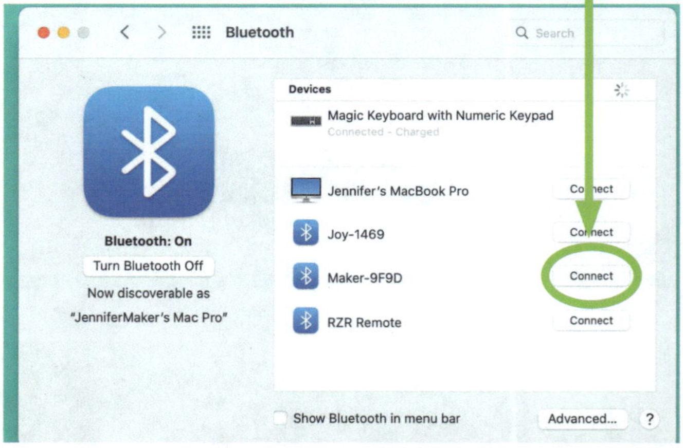

Step 5: If prompted, type 0000 (that's four zeros) as the passcode and click Connect.

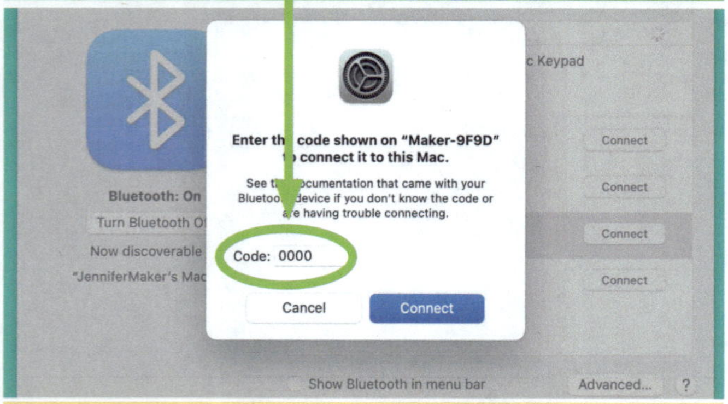

Once connected, you can select your machine from the drop-down menu in Cricut Design Space.

Your Mac will not always show "Connected" unless Design Space is communicating with the Cricut during a cut.

HOW TO CONNECT A PC TO CRICUT VIA BLUETOOTH

Step 1: Open the Control Panel app.

Find it by typing "Bluetooth" into the Search icon at the bottom of your window.

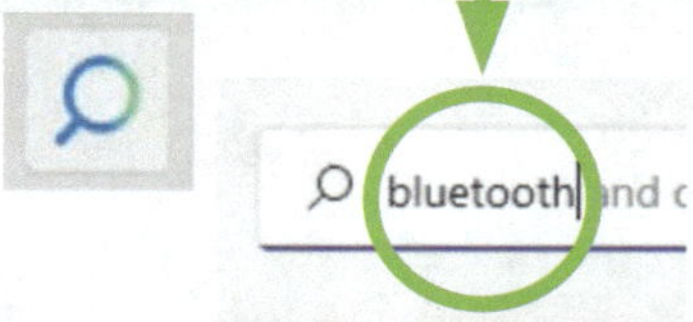

Note: Your Cricut must be within 10-15 feet of your PC. If your Cricut needs to use a Wireless Bluetooth Adapter (Explore and Explore One), make sure it is inserted.

Step 2: Click on Add Device.

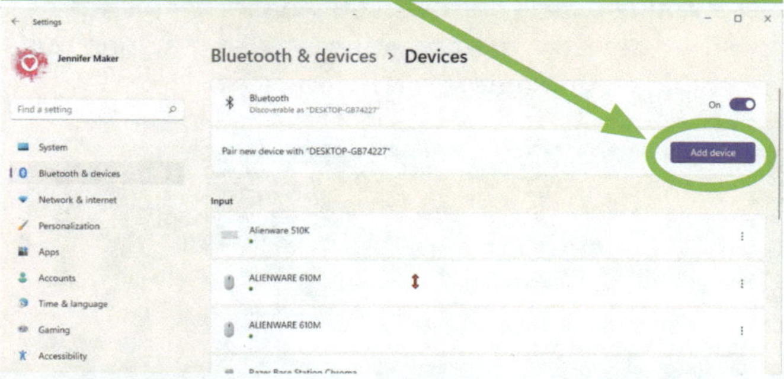

Step 3: Choose Bluetooth.

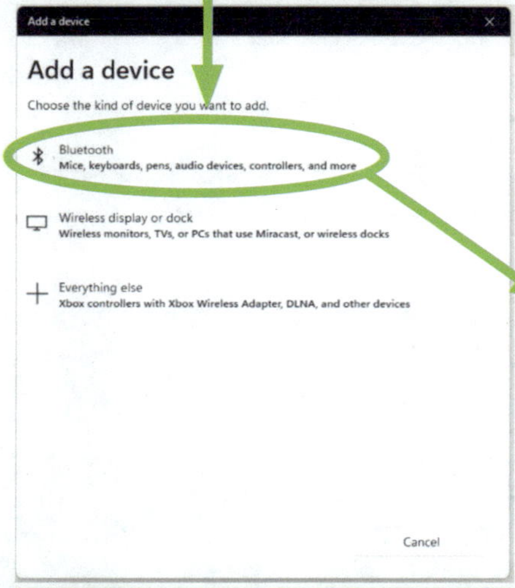

Step 4: Find your Cricut and select it.

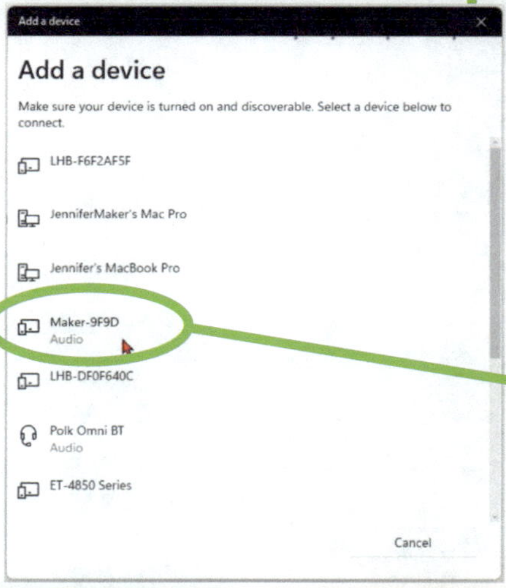

Step 5: Type 0000 (that's four zeros) and click Connect.

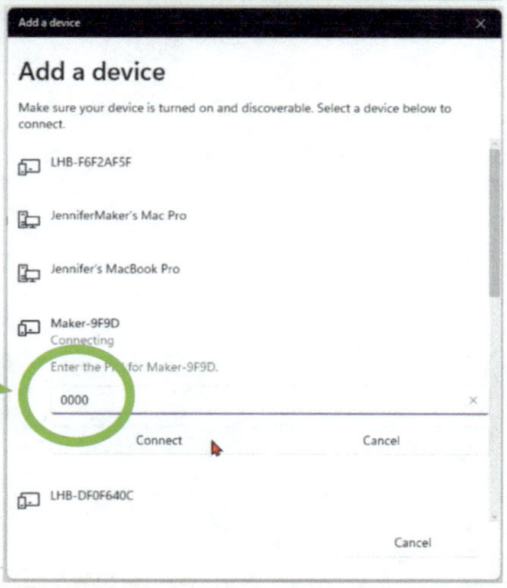

Step 6: Allow your PC time to setup the Bluetooth connection to your Cricut, then click Done.

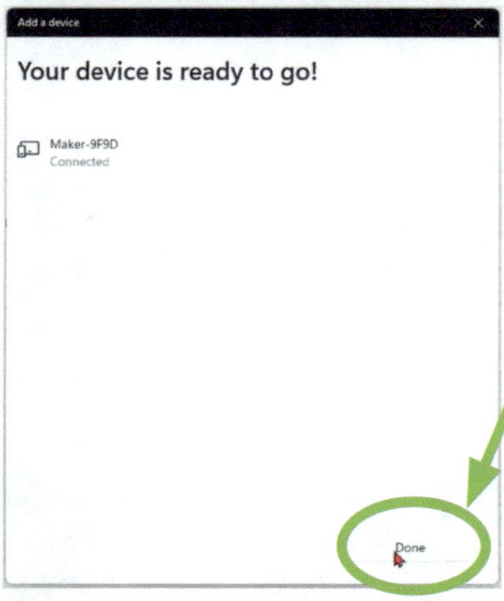

Once paired, it will appear in your Bluetooth & Devices window.

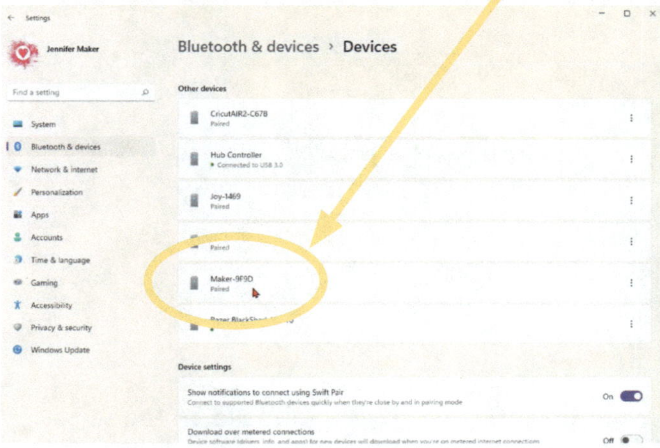

Once connected, you can select your machine from the drop-down menu in Cricut Design Space.

HOW TO ATTACH TO KEEP THINGS TOGETHER

Did you click Make and find all of your elements re-ordered and out of place? Fix this and keep everything exactly where you want with the Attach button. Use Attach to hold your cuts in the same position relative to each other on the machine mat. The Attach feature also helps you affix a draw, score, or foil layer to a cut layer.

Step 1: Add all of your elements to Cricut Design Space, including text, SVG designs, score lines, write lines, etc.

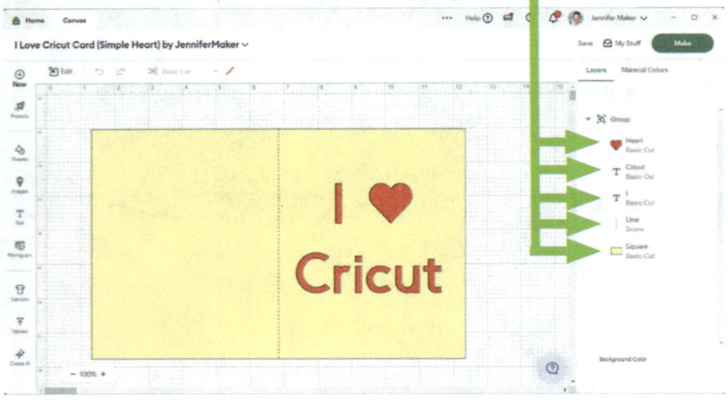

Step 2: Ungroup any groups. To do this, click on any layers called Group and click the Ungroup icon.

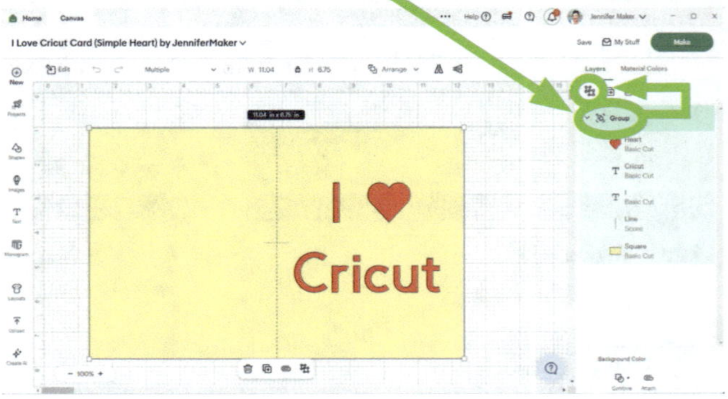

Step 3: Select any layers (two or more) you want to attach together (hold down the Shift key while you click to select multiple layers), then click Attach in the lower right corner.

Attach

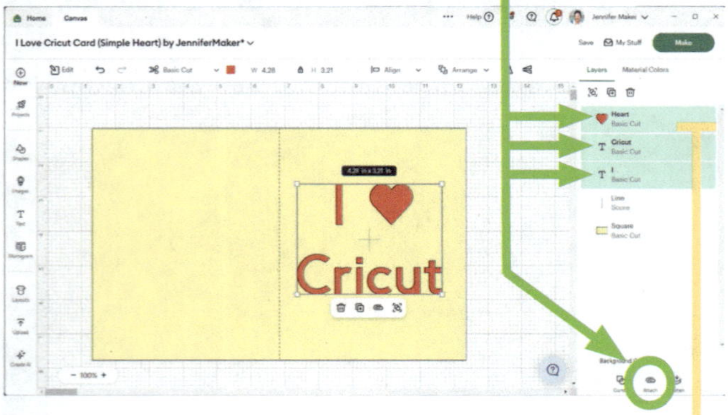

Note that attached layers will take on the same color. So only attach layers that you really want to be the same color!

Tip: If you are having a problem attaching layers, try ungrouping layers first.

Score lines must be attached with the appropriate cut layer in order for them to score on the right layer, as shown below.

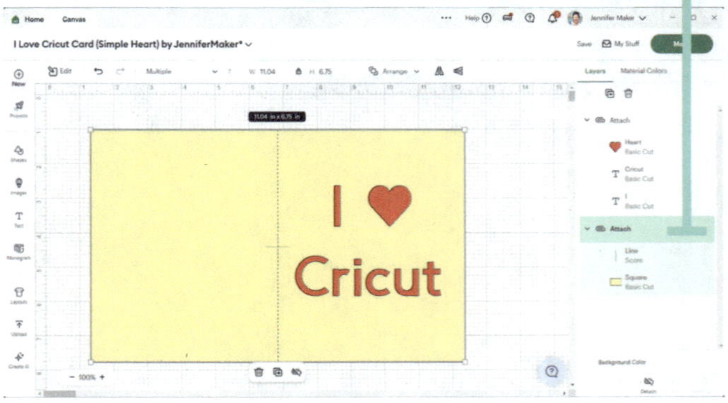

Tip: Layers may change or re-arrange when attached. To update your layer order, select an Attach layer, click on Arrange, and select a new order.

Practice this at jennifermaker.com/i-love-cricut

HOW TO GROUP AND UNGROUP

Grouping lets you keep objects together in your design but not necessarily on your mat (you still need to use the Attach function to keep things together on the mat). Sometimes projects and uploaded images will be grouped when you open/insert them, and you'll need to ungroup them so you can make changes.

HOW TO GROUP:

Step 1: Select each layer in the Layers Panel you want to group together. Alternatively, you can click and drag a rectangle to select objects.

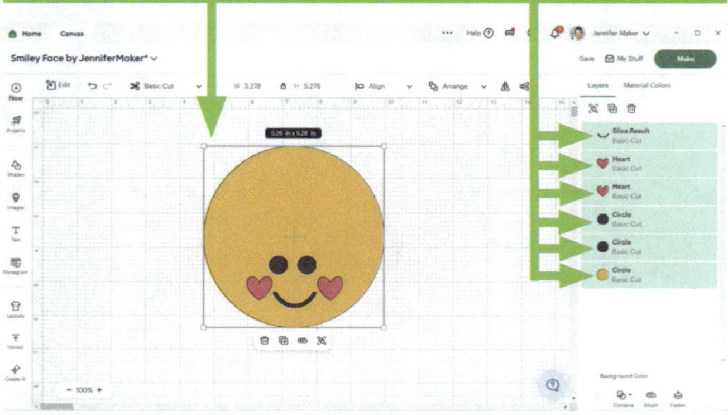

Step 2: With all objects you want to be in a group selected, click the Group button at the top of the Layers Panel.

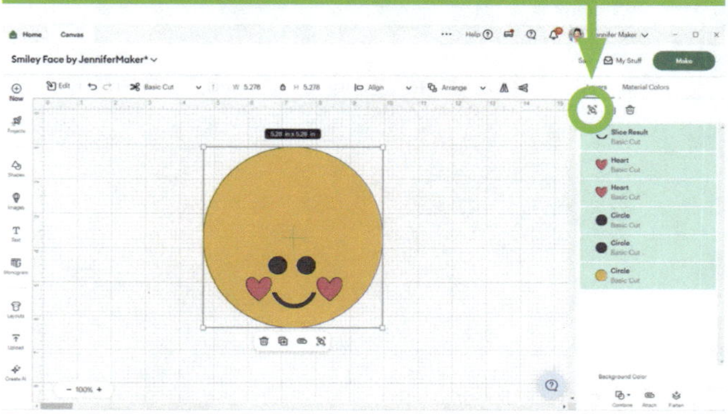

Tip: Once your objects are grouped, they will be nested under a new line item in your Layers Panel called "Group." > Group

HOW TO UNGROUP:

Step 1: To ungroup, start by looking for the word Group in your Layers Panel and click it.

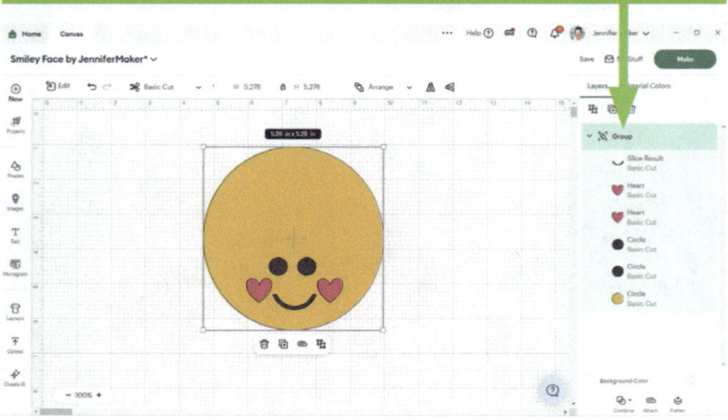

Step 2: With the group selected, click the Ungroup button at the top of the Layers Panel.

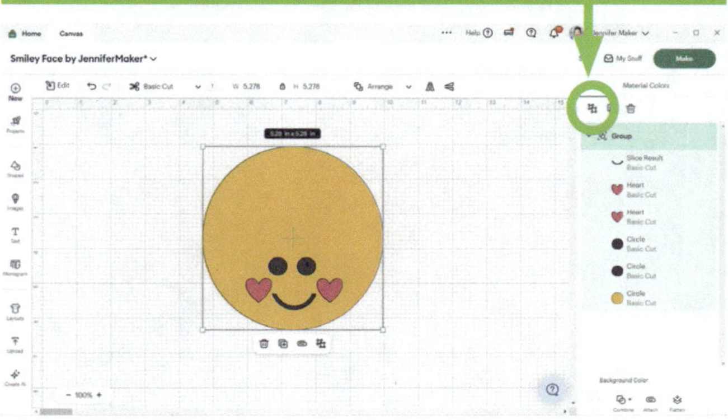

You often need to ungroup before you can attach objects. Sometimes, a project or image set has multiple groups. So if you want to attach and are having an issue, look for ALL groups and ungroup them first.

Practice this at jennifermaker.com/smiley-face

HOW TO WELD LAYERS TOGETHER

Need to join elements to create a new image? Do it with the Weld tool! The Weld tool can simplify a design, keep the letters of a word connected, and combine shapes to create new designs.

Step 1: Insert any images you want to weld onto your Canvas.

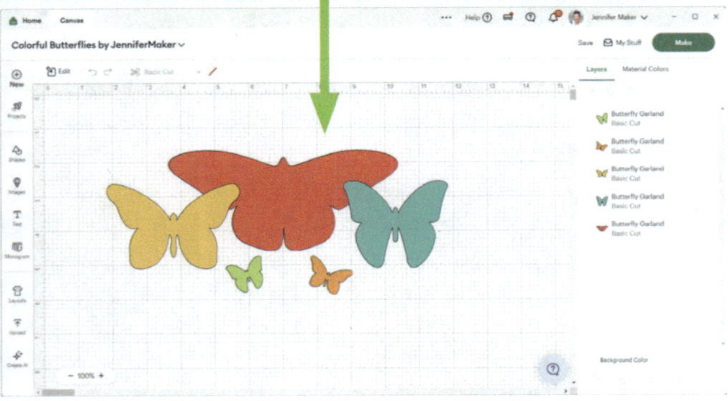

Step 2: Select all images to be welded together, then click Combine in the lower right corner, then Weld from the menu.

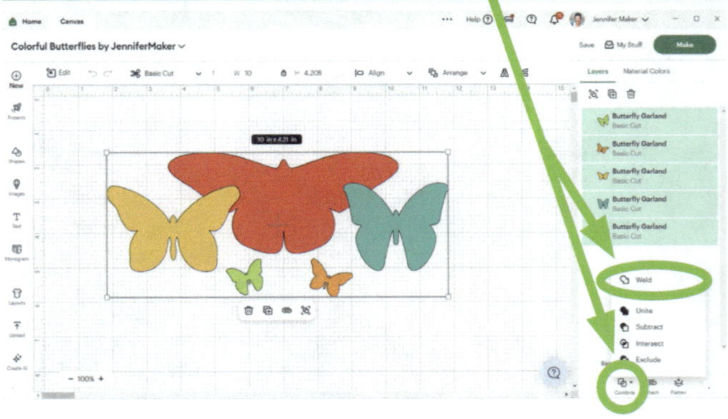

Note: If you are trying to create a single image with Weld, make sure all elements are overlapping.

Tip: You can select items within groups to weld by clicking on their names in the Layers Panel while holding down the Shift key.

Once your images weld, they will change to the same color and a new image appears in the Layers Panel.

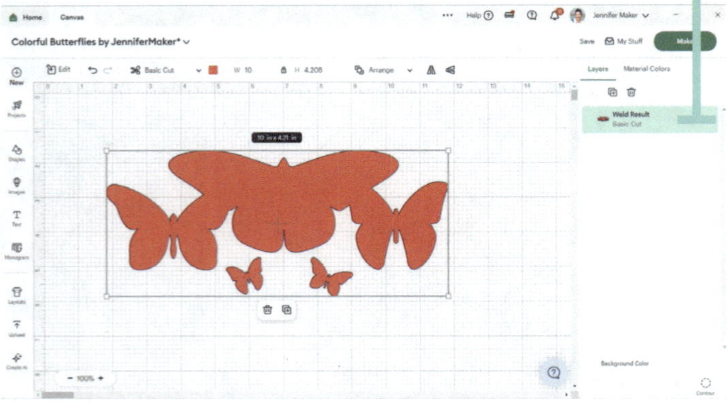

Note: You can unweld ONLY if it is the current project on your Canvas and you recently welded it. In this case, you can click the Undo button until you unweld the image(s).

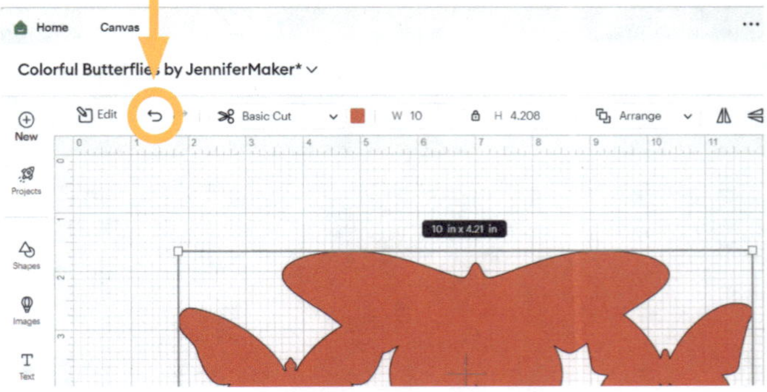

Weld is like permanent glue. Use Weld when you want to eliminate the cut lines between two images or letters. Weld keeps your project together on the Canvas and when you send it to the mat to cut. But beware, there is no Unweld button (only Undo). Weld is permanent!

Practice this at jennifermaker.com/butterflies

HOW TO UNION, SUBTRACT, INTERSECT & EXCLUDE

Need to join elements to create an image? These tools are similar and can be found when you select Combine! The Unite tool is similar to Weld (page 11) but it is not permanent! Your layers will still be accessible individually! Subtract is similar to Slice (page 13) but it does not leave you with remaining pieces; it subtracts the bottom layer and top layer. Intersect takes two overlapping layers and combines them, leaving only the parts that intersect. Exclude is the opposite of intersect; it takes two overlapping layers and cuts what overlapped, leaving behind what did not overlap.

Step 1: Insert your images onto your Canvas so that they are overlapping.

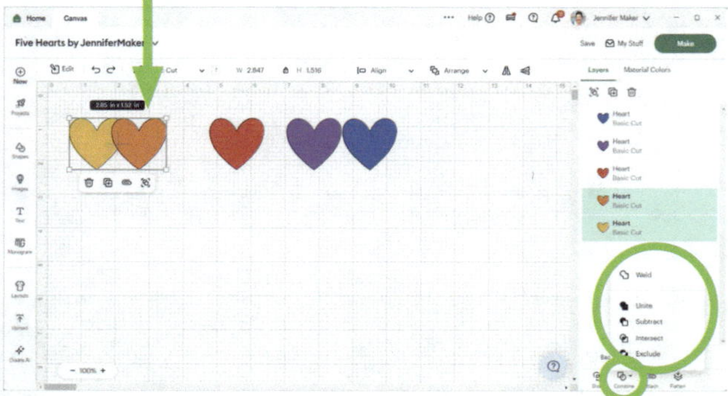

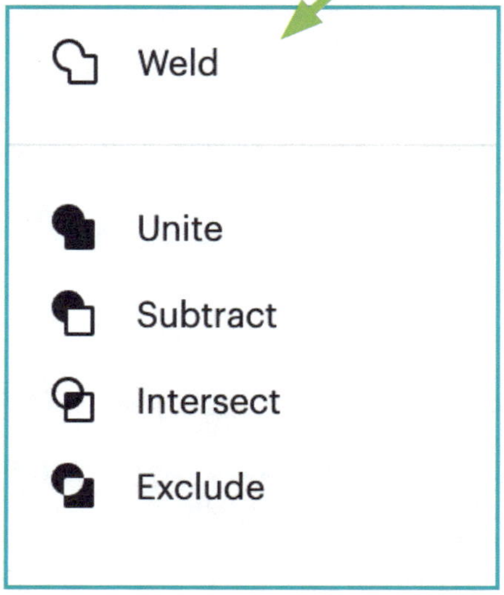

UNITE: Select your images and click Combine > Unite. This action combines the items together.

SUBTRACT: Select your images and click Combine > Subtract. This action subtracts the two layers from each other.

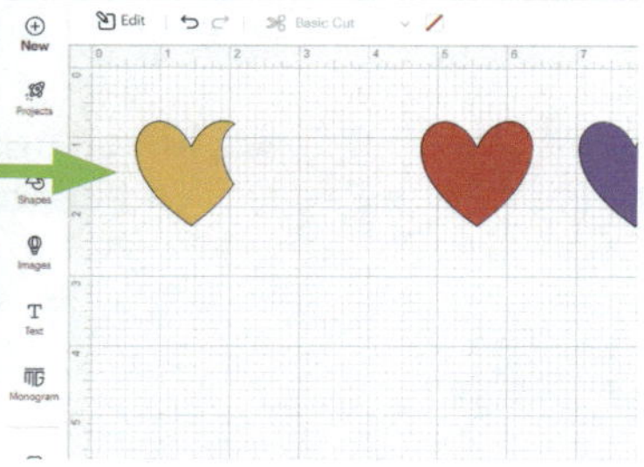

INTERSECT: Select your images and click Combine > Intersect. This action leaves only the parts that intersected between the two images.

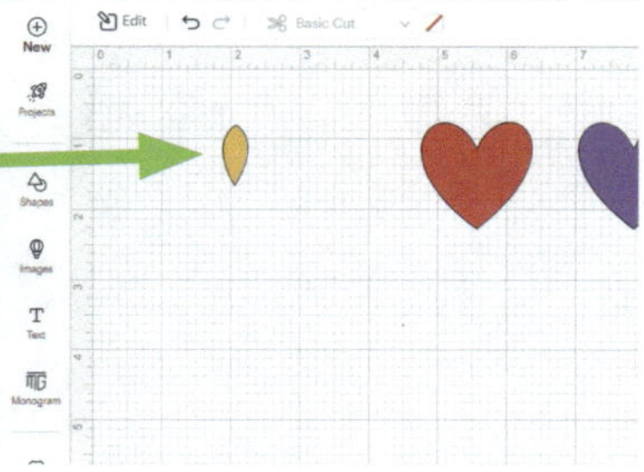

EXCLUDE: Select your images and tap Combine > Exclude. This action removes the parts that intersected between the two images.

Tip: If you don't like how the action operated on your images, press the undo button and try a different one!

Practice this at jennifermaker.com/five-hearts

HOW TO SLICE (CUT ONE IMAGE OUT OF ANOTHER)

Want to cut out parts or even make your own custom designs? If so, Slice is the tool for you! Slice lets you cut out parts of another object. If you keep slicing, you can make some pretty amazing designs!

Step 1: Insert your images onto your Canvas so that they are overlapping.

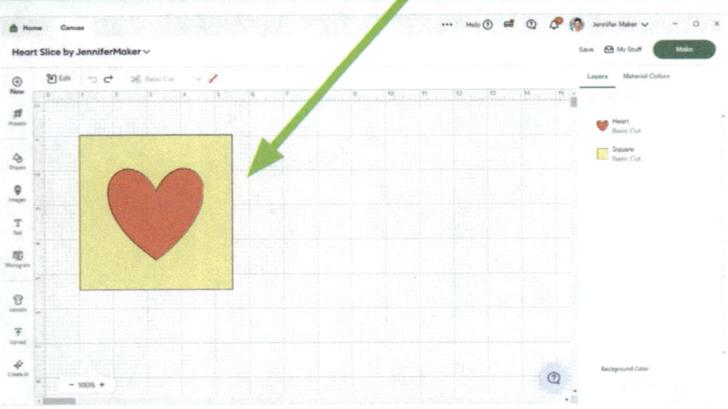

Step 2: Select just two layers (hold the Shift key as you click each layer), then click Slice.

Slice

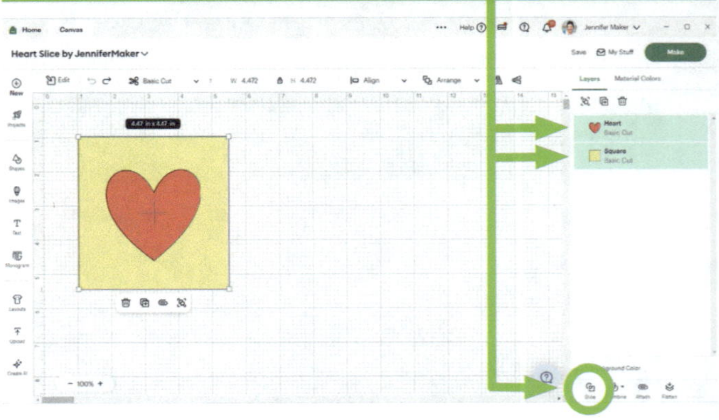

After you click Slice, three or more new layers called "Slice Result" will appear.

Step 3: Move, hide, or delete the layers you do not want, then you're good to go!

Slice Tips:

- You can Slice both images and text.
- You can only Slice with two layers. If you have multiple images you want to Slice out of another, use the Weld tool on the multiple images first. (Images need to be touching to be welded.)
- Layers in groups can be Sliced if you select just the individual layers, not the entire groups.
- If you use Slice with hidden layers, all hidden layers will be removed.
- If text is multi-layered and one layer is hidden, you can use the Slice tool. However, if you ungroup text from its shadow layer, it becomes an image and will no longer work with the Slice tool unless the text is ungrouped to individual letters.

Practice this at jennifermaker.com/heart-slice

HOW TO REMOVE PARTS WITH CONTOUR

Need to erase parts of an existing design? Don't want that word or that element, but can't ungroup or hide a layer? Use Contour to remove existing parts from projects.

Step 1: Choose an image with elements you'd like to remove, then click the Contour tool in the lower right corner of the layers panel.

Step 2: Click on the elements you want to remove. If you want to remove all elements (contours), click the Hide All Contours button. If you have trouble clicking elements you want to remove, use the zoom feature in the lower left corner.

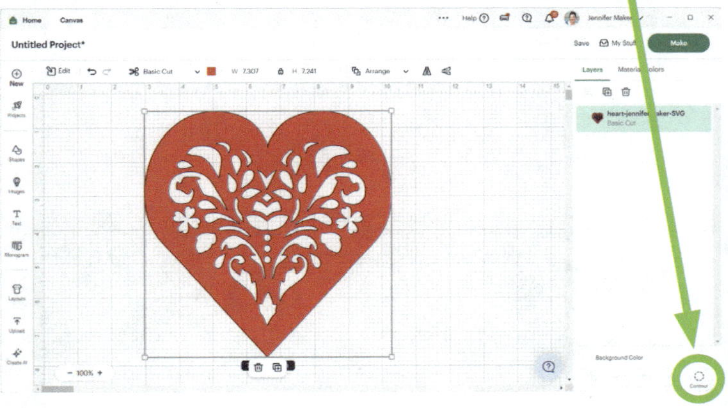

Step 3: Cut out elements that appear darker are those that you'll keep. When your image looks how you want it to, click the X in the upper right hand corner to return to your Canvas.

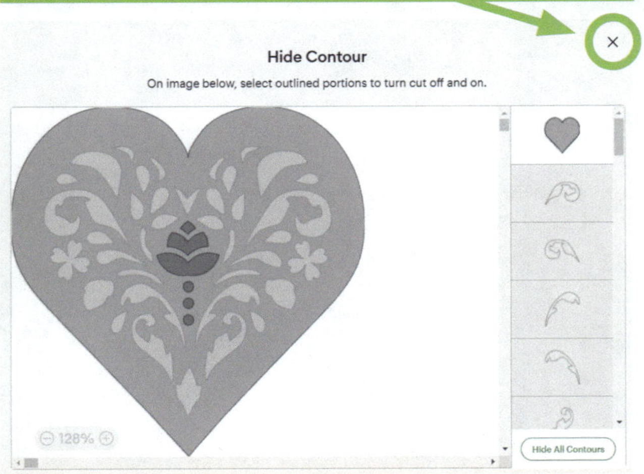

Step 4: Confirm that your image looks the way you want it. If you need to make more changes, just click the Contour tool again.

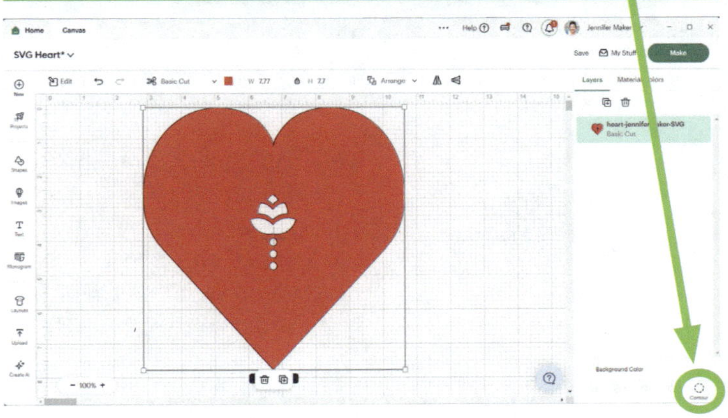

CONTOUR (REMOVE BITS)

Tip: Contour isn't permanent so long as you don't Weld or Flatten a layer! If you decide later you want a Contoured image to go back the way it was, or simply edit it further, all the hidden parts are retained!

Practice this at jennifermaker.com/svg-heart

HOW TO CURVE TEXT

Step 1: Select the text and rainbow, then click Align and Center Horizontally.

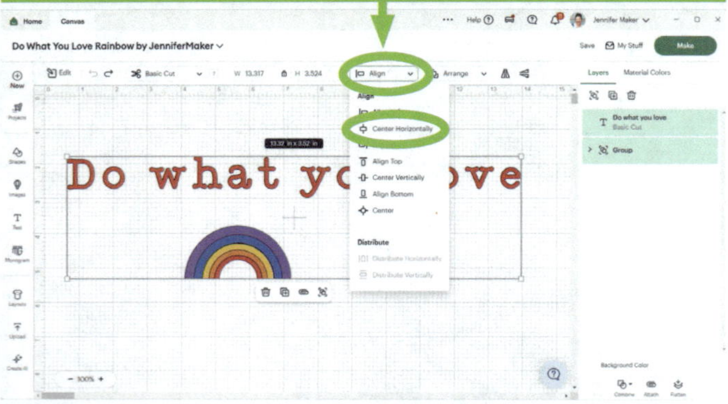

Step 2: Select the text and click the Edit icon. Scroll down in the Edit menu to find and click Curve.

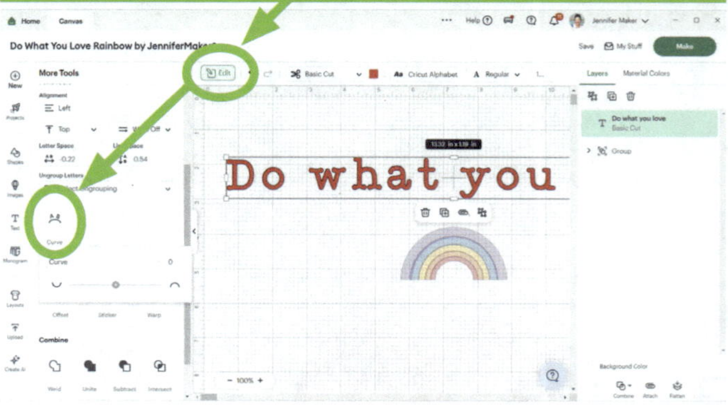

Step 3: Slide the slider to the right for a downward curve. The more you slide, the tighter the curve. You will need to resize the rainbow to fit with the text.

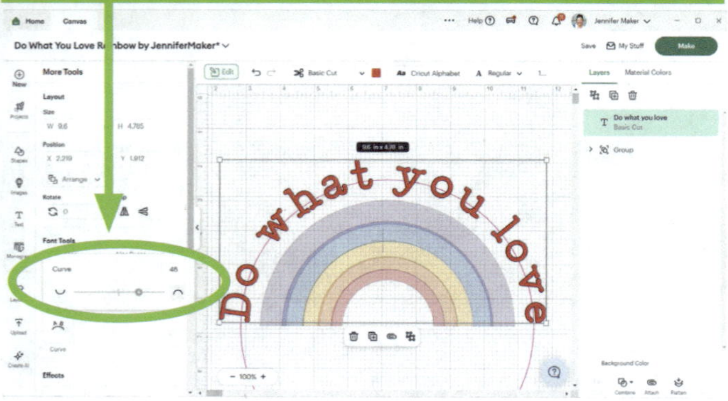

Step 4: Slide the slider to the left for an upward curve. The more you slide, the tighter the curve.

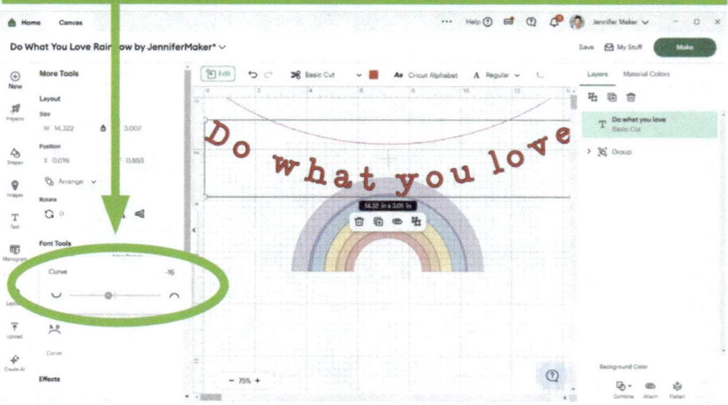

Tip: You can change the font, color, size, line spacing, etc. at any time (so long as you don't Flatten or Weld it) thanks to this Curve text feature!

Practice this at jennifermaker.com/rainbow-love

Desktop

HOW TO WARP TEXT, SHAPES AND IMAGES

Use the Warp feature to style your text into fun shapes! There are currently 30 unique warp styles to choose from. Note: There are some fonts that cannot be warped, as well as Print Then Cut images. Design Space will notify you if the font or image cannot be warped. Warp is only for Cricut Access members.

Step 1: Select the Shapes icon and add a rectangle to the Canvas. Resize it to make it wider.

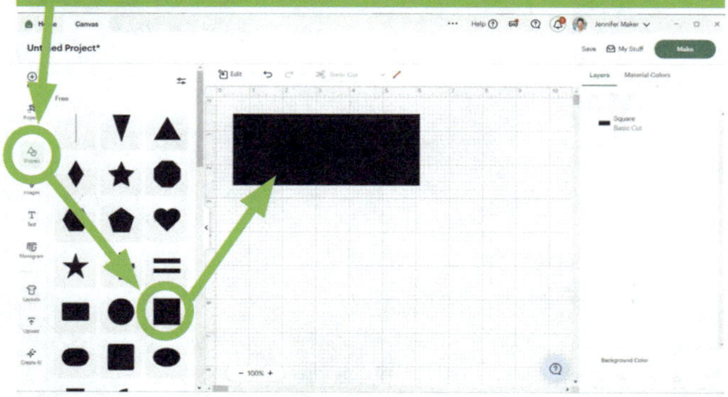

Step 2: Select the Text icon and type some text on the Canvas.

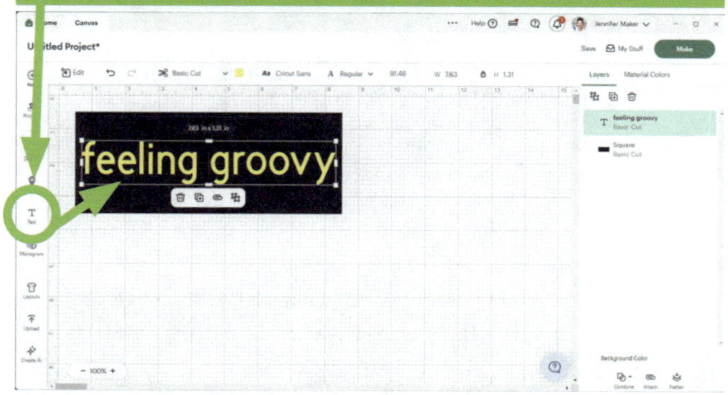

Step 3: Click on the Edit icon in the top menu bar.

Edit

Step 4: Scroll down in the Edit menu to find and click on Warp.

Step 5: Click on one of the Warp options. Then use the Adjust toggle bar to set the intensity of the Warp.

Step 6: Your text and shape will change to the warp style you chose!

WARP TEXT

HOW TO ALIGN AND DISTRIBUTE OBJECTS

Step 1: Add two or more items to your Canvas that you want to align or distribute evenly.

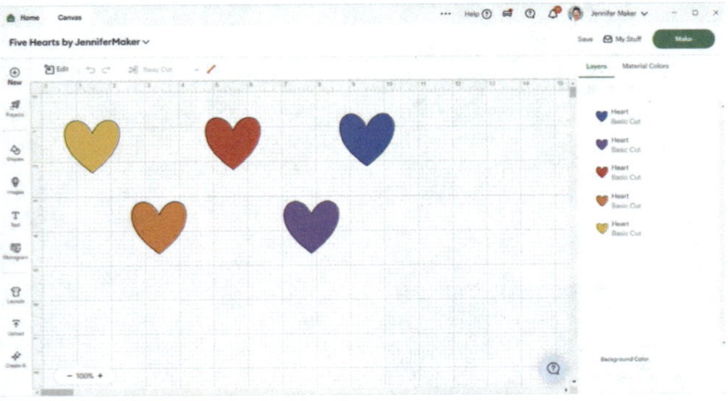

Step 2: Click and drag a selection box around all items you want to align and/or distribute.

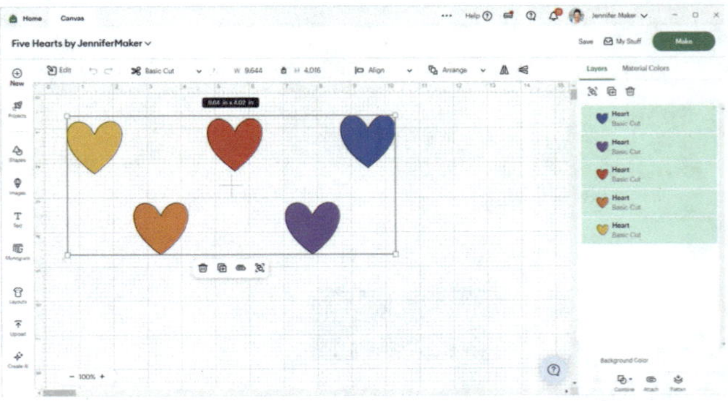

Step 3: Click on the Align tool in the toolbar and choose Align Top.

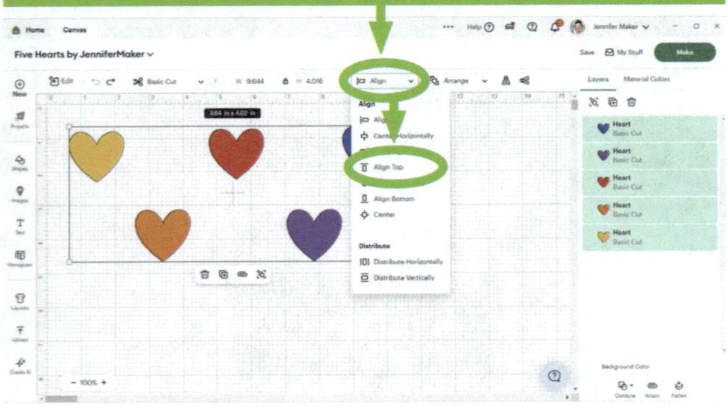

Step 4: All selected items are aligned with the topmost object. Now let's space them evenly.

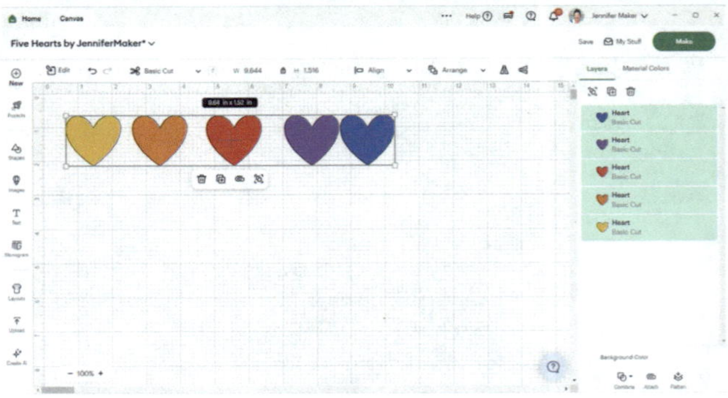

Step 5: Click the Align tool again and this time choose Distribute Horizontally.

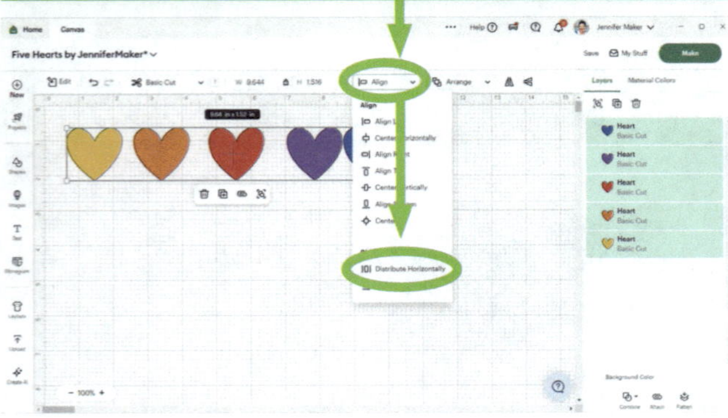

Step 6: Note that all the hearts are now in a perfect row with the same spacing.

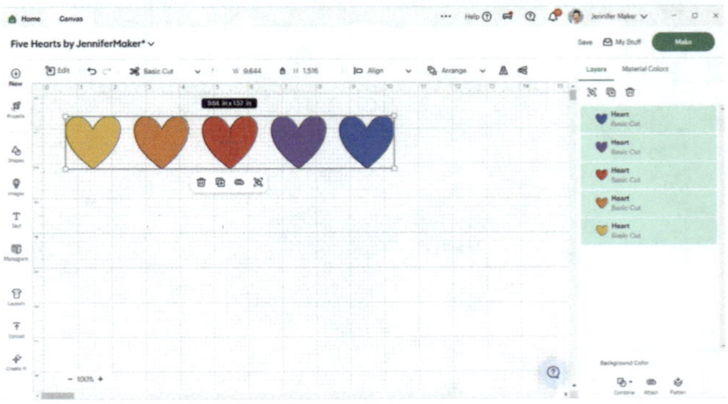

Practice this at jennifermaker.com/five-hearts

HOW TO KERN & CHANGE LETTER SPACE

Kerning is when a font's letters are arranged in a pleasing way rather than spaced oddly. Kerning is automatic for many—but not all—fonts in Cricut Design Space. Here's how to identify which fonts will kern for you automatically and what to do when you need to fix a font that is not kerned.

Step 1: Click Text, choose Cricut or System fonts, confirm that Kerned Fonts is checked, then choose a font.

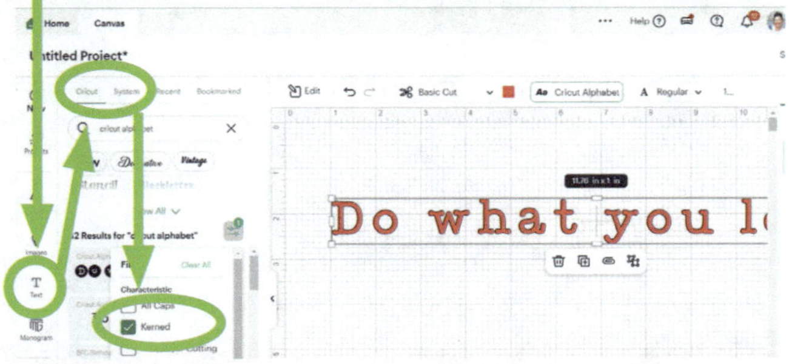

Step 2: Type your text and see it kerned! Compare the not kerned line (top) with a line that is kerned (bottom) to see the difference!

Note that text in older projects may not automatically be kerned. To fix this, click on the text, and then if it is a kerned font, it will automatically kern the text.

Kerned fonts are automatically welded after you click Make, so there is no need to weld manually unless you ungroup your text or change the letter spacing.

If your font isn't kerned, here's how you can manually change your letter spacing:

Step 1: Identify text that is not kerned. See how the letters in the text box below do not fit together well?

Step 2: Select the text, click the Edit icon, scroll down, and click the down arrow in the Letter Space box until the letters look better.

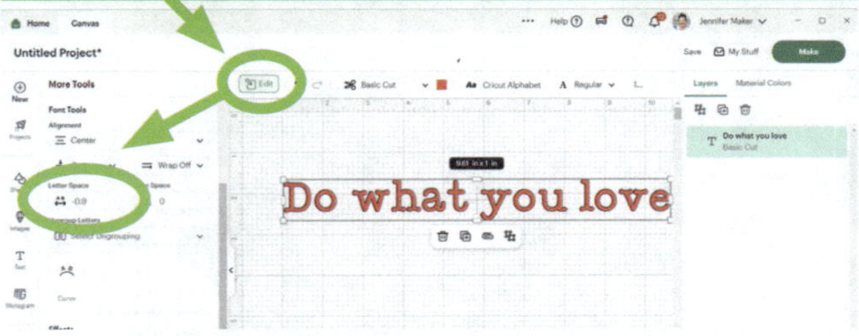

Step 3: The letter "w" is too far away from the "h" – select the text, click the Edit icon, scroll down, then click Ungroup to Letters.

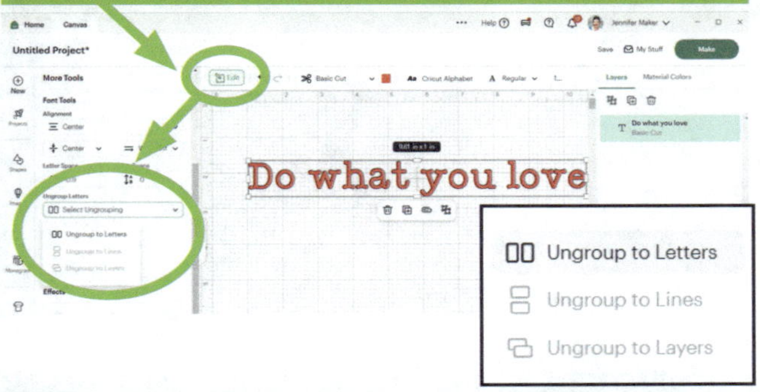

Step 4: Select just the letter "w" and move it to the right, holding down the Shift key to keep it in line. When you are done, select all letters and click Attach to cut them together. If your letters touch, click Combine, then select Weld instead.

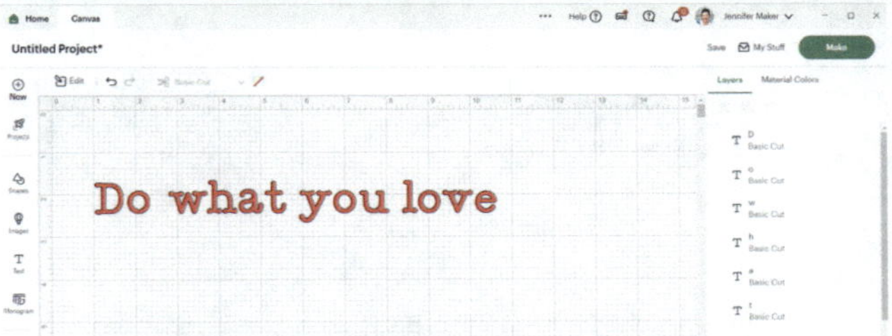

Practice this at jennifermaker.com/rainbow-love

HOW TO WELD TEXT AND KEEP LETTER CENTERS

Welding text can be a little tricky. Typically, you weld script fonts (which can have overlapping letters) so words cut out as single units. Sometimes when you weld, the centers fill in—here's how to fix that:

Step 1: Click Text, type in script text, change your letter spacing so they are overlapping a bit (see directions on page 18), click Select All, then click Combine > Weld.

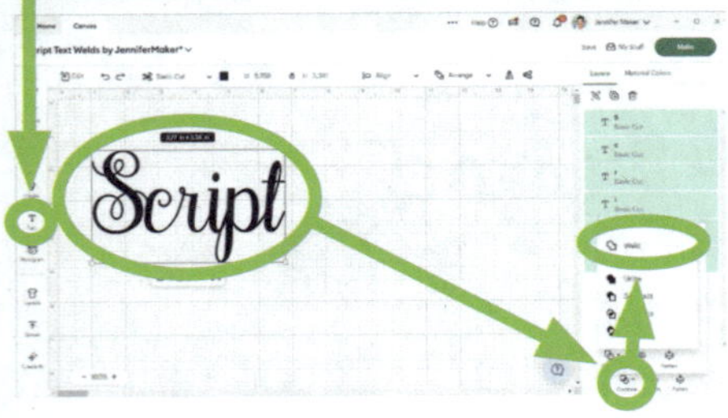

Step 2: If you get a center filling in (like in the letter "p" here), click Undo, then Resize from a corner to make your text MUCH larger, then click Combine > Weld again.

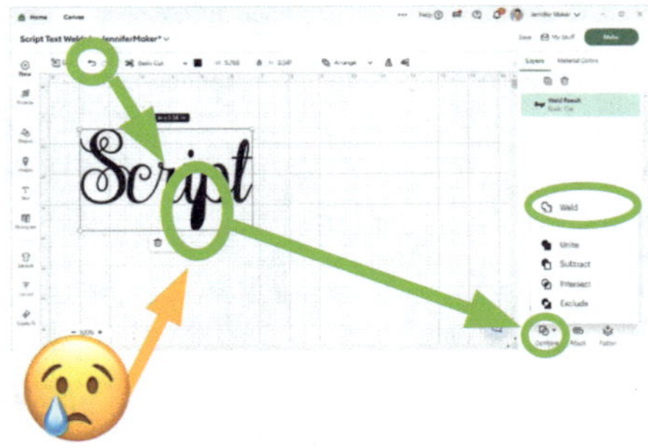

Step 3: Repeat step 2 until you can weld and the letter center does not fill in (you may have to get REALLY big), then resize back down to the right size.

Another thing that can happen with text is that letter centers (the interior white space) can disappear when you cut them out. But you can connect the spaces and keep the centers! Here's how to fix that:

Step 1: Click Text, type in your text, and look for letters with interior white space (counters), like these letters (A, B, D, O, P, Q, R, a, b, d, e, g, o, p, q) and numbers (0, 4, 6, 8, and 9)

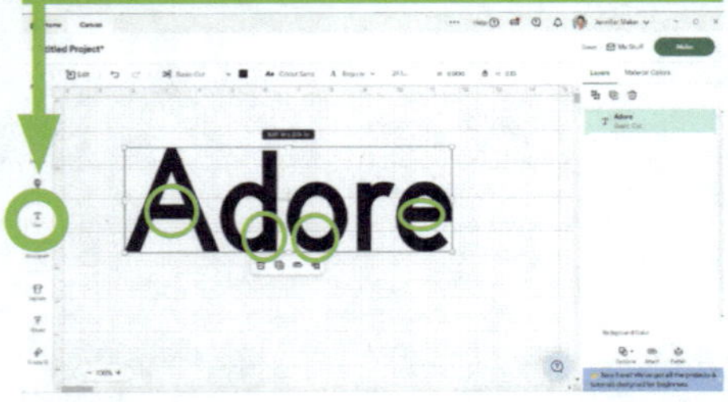

Step 2: Click Shapes, select a square, and unlock it and resize it so it forms a rectangle about the width of the letter's strokes.

Step 3: Click and drag the rectangle over a letter with interior white space so it's connecting the space inside to the space outside, like this:

Step 4: Select the word and the rectangle, then click Slice.

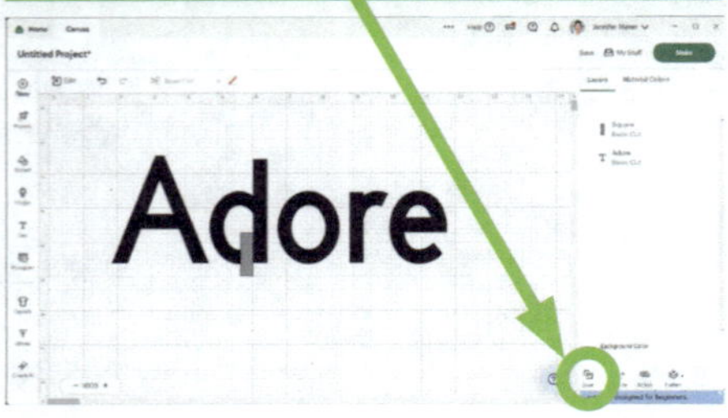

Step 5: Delete all layers except the word layer.

Repeat steps 2-5 for all letters as needed.

Practice this at jennifermaker.com/script-text and jennifermaker.com/adore-text

Desktop

HOW TO OFFSET & KNOCKOUT TEXT

Offset and inset is a feature of Cricut Design Space that allows you to create outlines around or within text and images. Here's how to use the offset feature to make a knockout design.

Step 1: Click Text, type in your main word using a bold font like Cricut Sans Bold. Unlock it, resize it to make it taller, and click Combine > Weld.

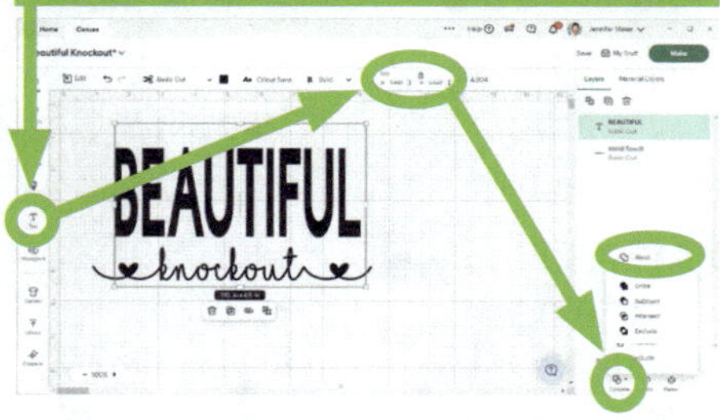

Step 2: Click Text, type an accent word in a script font, like I Love Glitter. Adjust lettering as needed, unlock it, resize it, and click Combine > Weld.

Weld

Step 3: Select the accent word layer, click the Edit icon, click Offset, and slide the distance bar to the right about .1 inch. Click Apply.

Step 4: Select and separate the new offset layer, which you can see looks similar to the accent layer but is thicker and bolder.

Step 5: Position the offset layer over your main word, select both layers (and only those two layers), and click Slice.

Slice

Step 6: Delete the Sliced out layers by selecting and clicking the Delete button. In this image, I moved the layers to see better.

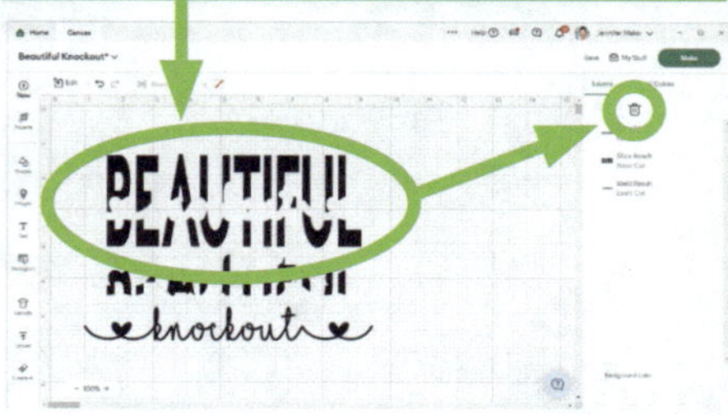

Step 7: Click and drag the accent word inside the empty space Sliced out of the main word. With the accent word selected, click the color box to change the accent word color if desired, and click Make!

Practice this at jennifermaker.com/beautiful-knockout

HOW TO
FIND & BOOKMARK FONTS

There are many fonts available in Cricut Design Space! Here's how to find them easier and faster in Cricut Design Space.

Step 1: Open your project (or start a new one) and click on Text on the left side.

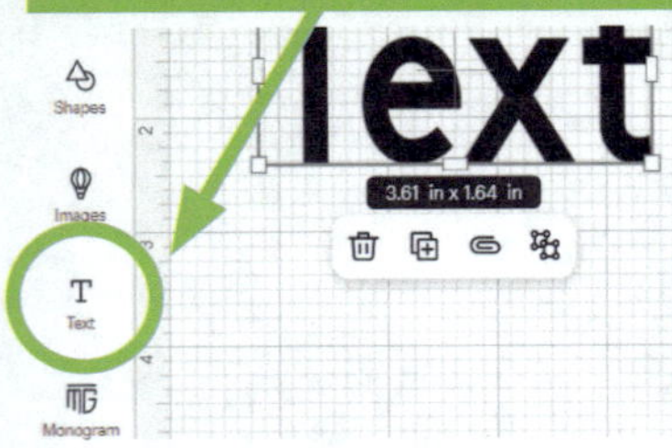

Tip: If you already have text on your Canvas, just double-click the text instead.

Step 2: Click the drop-down font menu in the top menu bar.

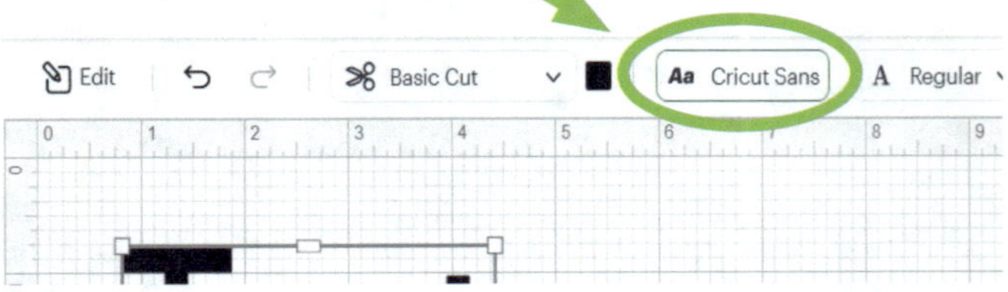

FIND FONTS

Step 3: Choose a new font from the list that appears. By default, you will see only Cricut fonts, in alphabetical order. Click System to see your installed System fonts instead.

SEARCH: Type in the "Search Fonts" box to look for fonts by name. I recommend typing just the first few characters of the font name and then clicking the Magnifying glass icon for the results.

BOOKMARKS: Find any Cricut or System fonts you've bookmarked in this tab. Note that system fonts will only appear in this list if you're on the device in which you bookmarked them.

MISSING FONTS: If you don't see the font you know is there, uncheck the "Kerned" box to see ALL Cricut fonts. A "kerned" font is one with extra data for better letter spacing. Kerned fonts look better!

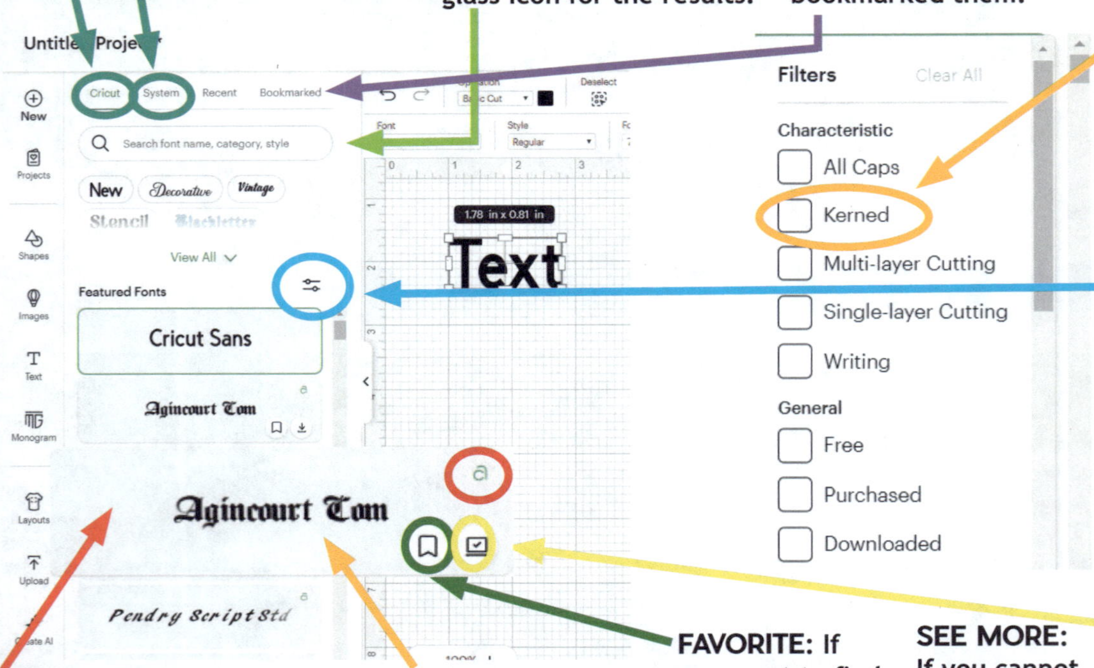

FILTER: Click on "Filters" to further refine your search, such as finding only "Writing" fonts. Note that only Cricut fonts can be filtered.

IDENTIFY: Font name, type(s), and price appears in each box. If you see a price, $6.99 the font must be purchased before you can use it on your Cricut machine. A green ⓐ symbol indicates that it is a Cricut Access font.

PREVIEW: A font preview appears here so you can see what it looks like. You're free to select it and see it in your own text on your Canvas without being charged for it.

FAVORITE: If you want to find this font again faster, click the Bookmark icon, then click the Bookmarks tab at the top to see your favorites!

SEE MORE: If you cannot see the entire alphabet and all of its numbers, hover over a line with your mouse and it will scroll for you to see.

OFFLINE: To design in Offline mode, click on the Download button so it is available even when you do not have an Internet connection.

HOW TO CHANGE THE FONT FOR EXISTING TEXT

Step 1: Open your project and double-click the text you want to change the font for. Alternately, you can right-click the text and click "Edit Text."

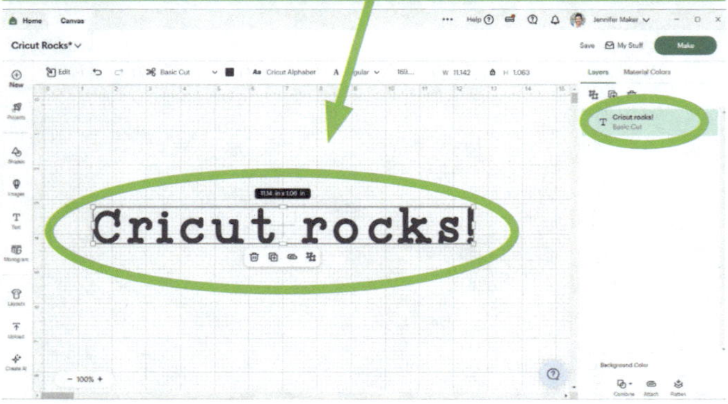

Step 2: Click the drop-down "Font" menu in the top menu bar to open the font menu.

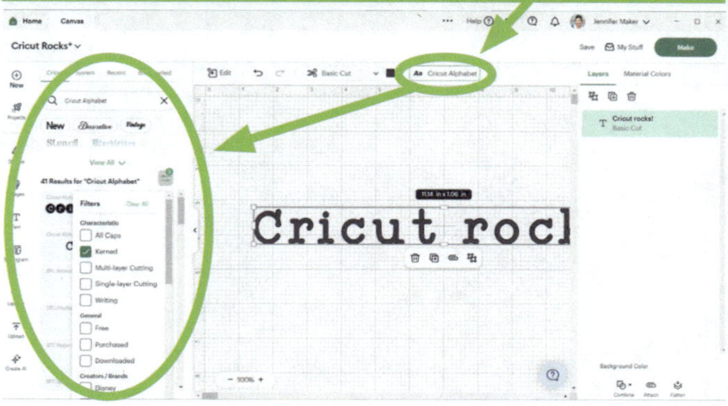

Step 3: Choose a new font from the list that appears. If you don't see the font you know is there, uncheck the "Kerned" box under the Filters button to see all Cricut fonts available or click on the "System" tab.

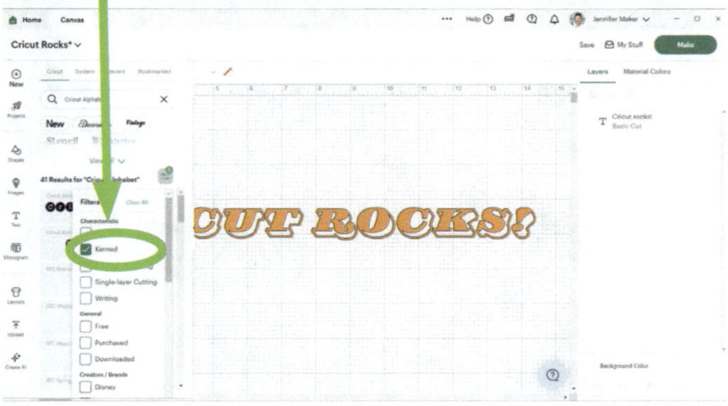

Once you have clicked on a font, click outside the font menu. Your font changes!

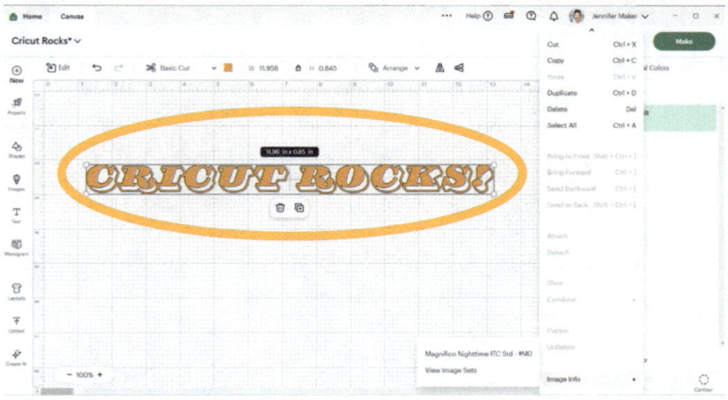

While you can't change a font you've welded (unless you're able to Undo and unweld it because you haven't saved and reopened your project), there is a way to tell WHICH font you used so you can re-create it. Locate the weld layer with the text, right-click on the layer name, and choose Image Info at the very bottom. A box will appear that shows you what font was originally used.

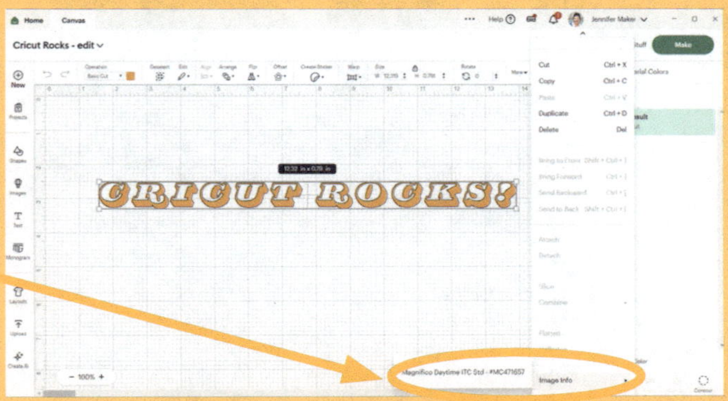

CHANGE FONT

HOW TO CHANGE COLORS AND PATTERN FILLS

Step 1: Select the layer you want to change, like the center of this flower. When selected, it turns blue in the Layers Panel.

Step 2: Click the square to the right of the Operation menu and click a new color. Click Advanced to choose a custom color.

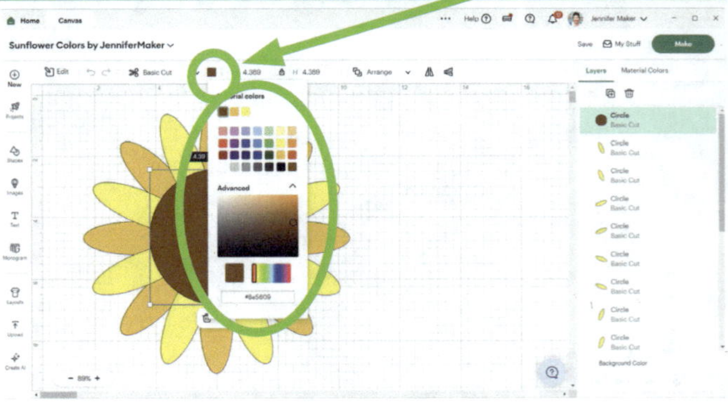

You can also give objects a pattern fill. Be aware that changing an object to pattern fill will also change it to a Print Then Cut image. Here's how you set pattern fills:

Step 1: Select the layer you want to change, then click Operation and change it to Print Then Cut.

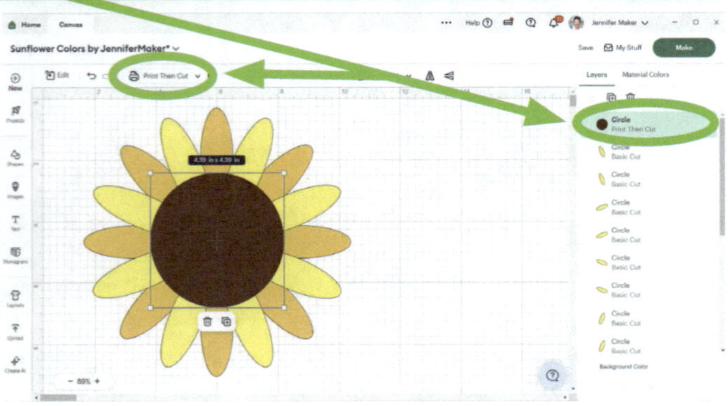

Step 2: Click the Fill menu and change the Print Type to Pattern.

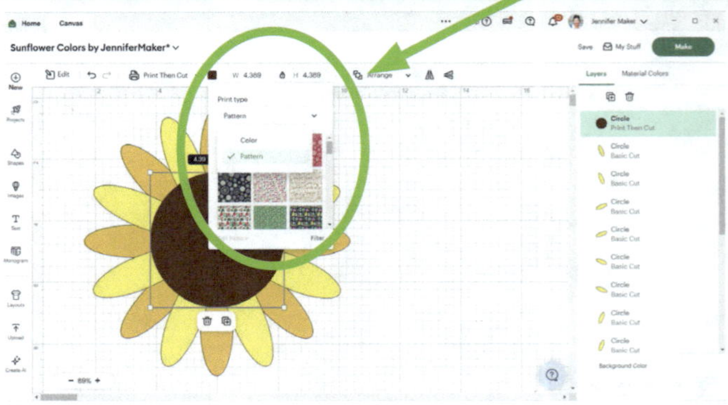

Step 3: Select a pattern from the list.

Tip: You can edit the scale, rotation, and orientation of the pattern by clicking Edit Pattern and making changes!

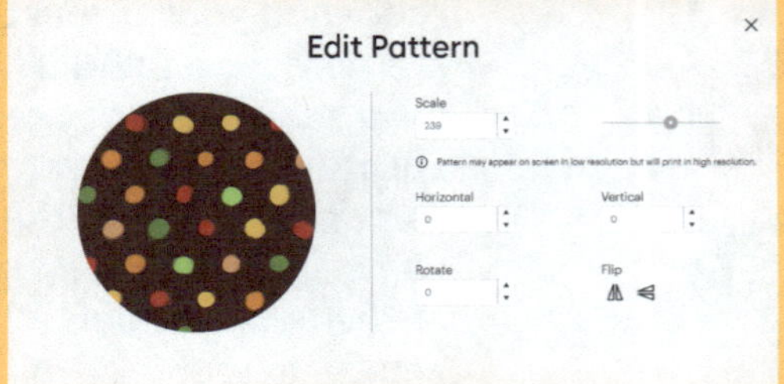

Practice this at jennifermaker.com/sunflower-colors

HOW TO CHANGE OPERATION AND TOOLS

The Operation menu lets you change a layer's type. Choices for the Cricut Joy and Cricut Joy Xtra are Basic Cut (default), Pen, Foil, and Guide. The Explores add Score and Print Then Cut. And the Cricut Makers add several more choices: Wavy, Perforate, Deboss, and Engrave. You will only see the Makers' operation choices if you've set your machine to Maker or Maker 4. The Venture adds a large format cutting capability of 25 inches! Here's how to set your machine and change the operation.

Step 1: Choose your machine, then select a layer and click the Operation menu at the top.

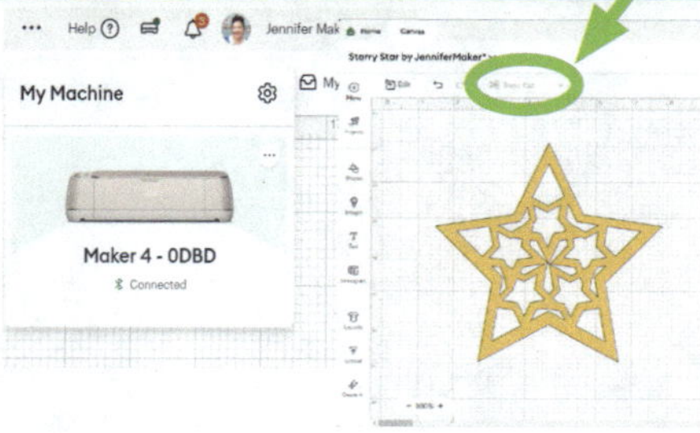

Use Basic for fine point, deep cut, fabric, knife (Makers only), or rotary (Makers only) blades.

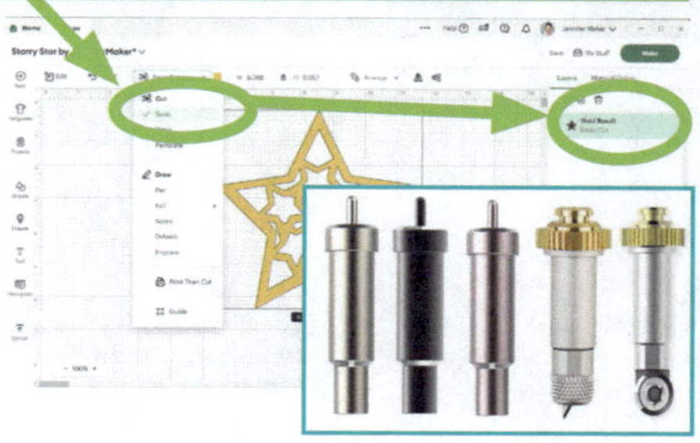

Use Wavy to use the Wavy Edge Tool or Perforate to use the Perforation Tool (Makers only).

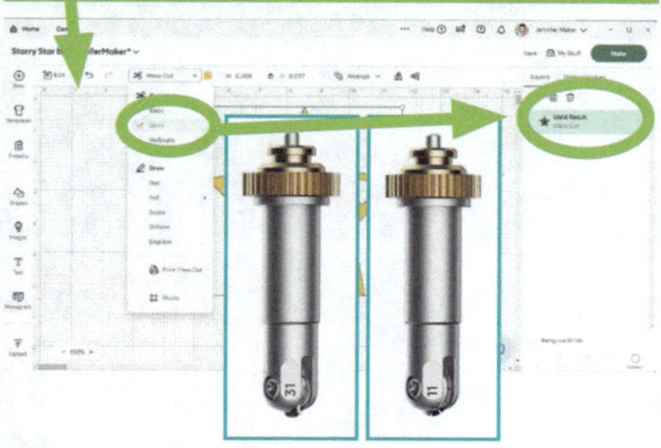

Change your operation to Pen to write with pens and markers. Click the box to the right to choose the color and thickness.

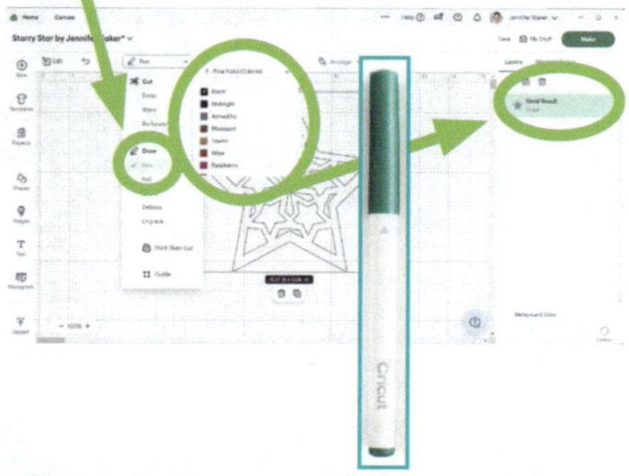

Change your operation to Foil to use the Foil Transfer Tool, then choose the tip size (all Cricuts).

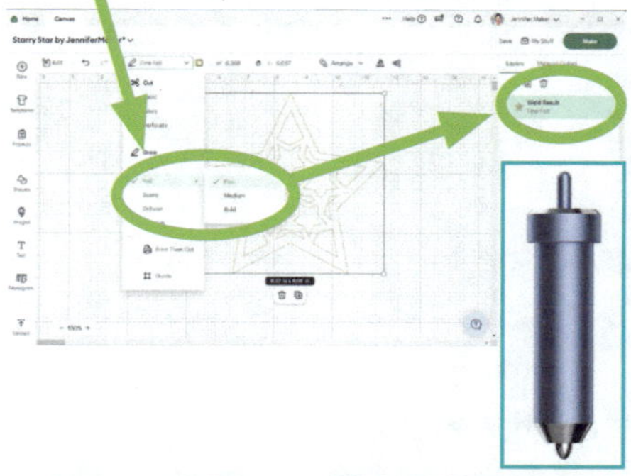

Change your operation to Score to score with the Stylus (Makers, Venture or Explores) or Scoring Wheel Tools (Makers only).

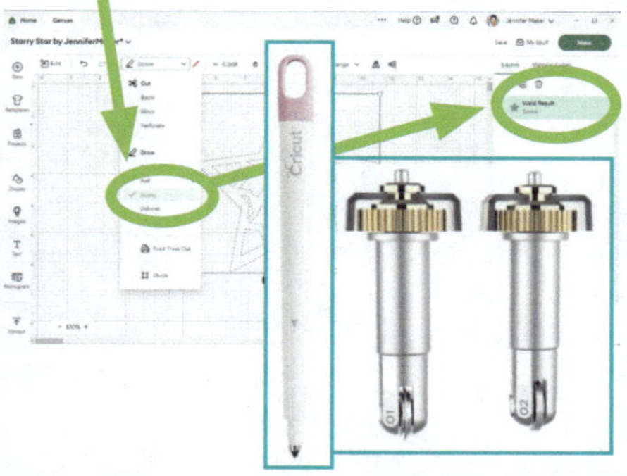

Change your operation to Deboss to use the Debossing Tool, or to Engrave to use the Engraving Tool (Makers only).

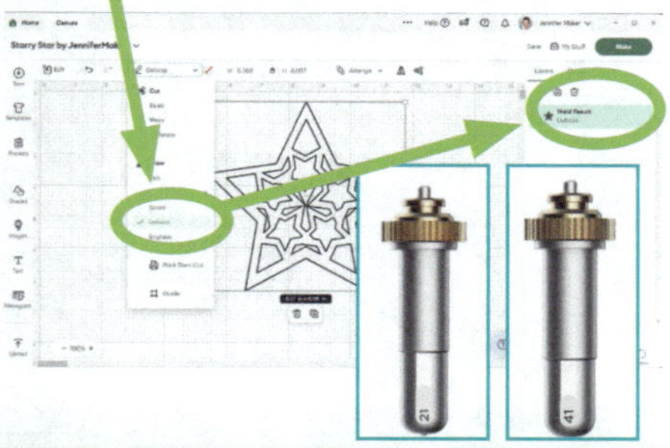

Change your operation to Print Then Cut to use the Print Then Cut feature.

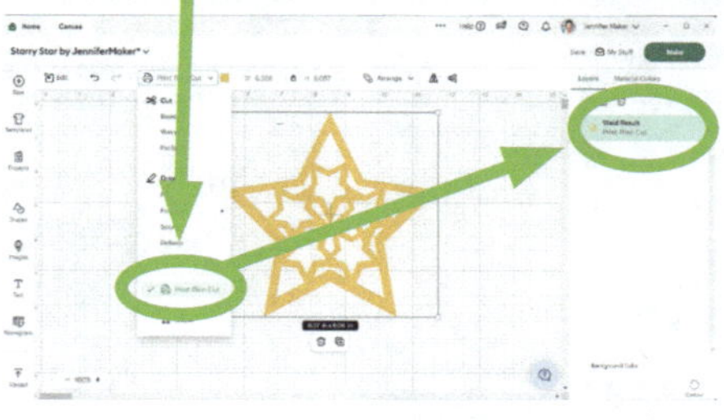

Change your operation to Guide to create Guides, which will not show up when you cut and are useful for designing projects.

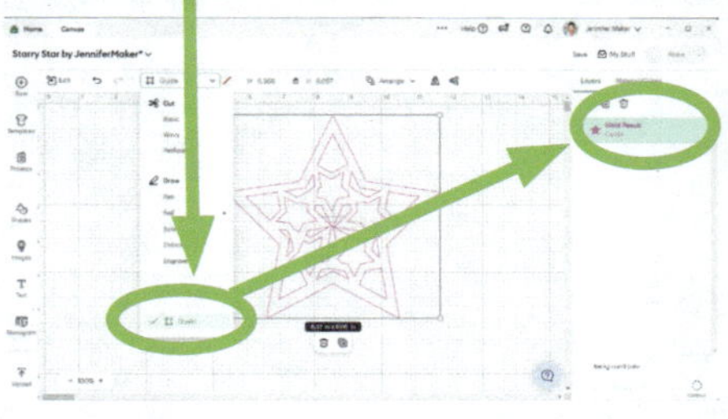

Practice this at jennifermaker.com/starry-star

Desktop

HOW TO SET TEXT TO WRITE WITH A PEN

You can insert a Cricut pen or marker into any Cricut machine and have it draw with it, and many crafters like to use this feature with a writing font to mimic handwriting. Be sure to check your pen to make sure it is compatible, as pens are designed for specific machines. Here's how to choose a good font that looks like handwriting and set it to Draw in Cricut Design Space:

Step 1: Click Text, click the Font menu, click Filters, and select Writing to see writing fonts. Note that some may have a fee, like this: $6.99

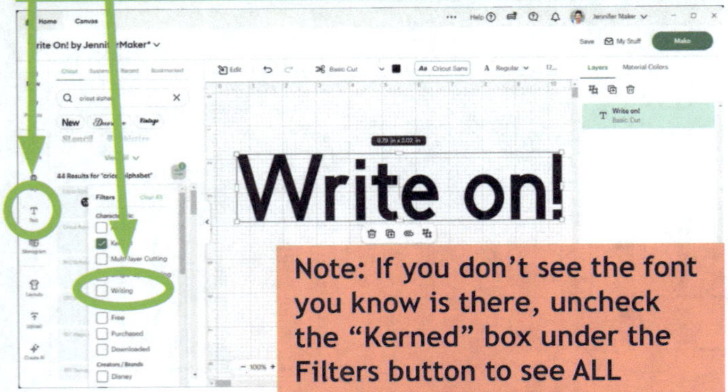

Note: If you don't see the font you know is there, uncheck the "Kerned" box under the Filters button to see ALL Cricut fonts available.

Step 2: Select a writing font (such as the free Cricut Sans or Cricut Alphabet font), click the Style menu, choose Writing, and type some text.

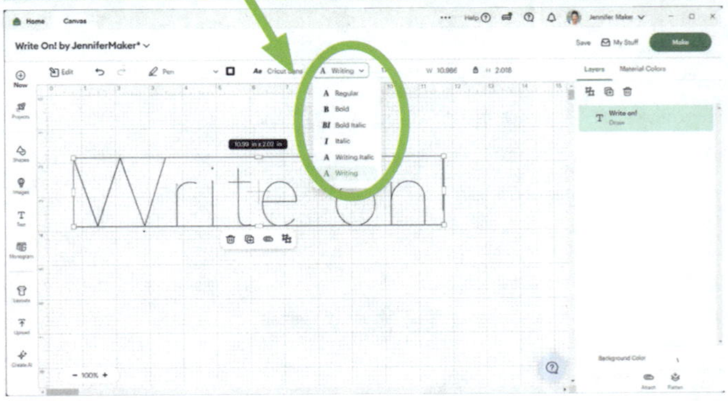

Step 3: Click Operation, select Pen under Draw, then click the square to the right of Operation, and select a pen type and color.

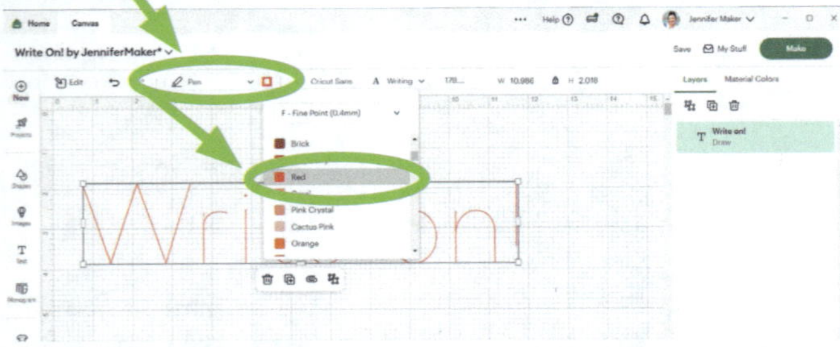

Step 4: Adjust the Font Size and Letter Space as necessary so it looks the way you want it to look, then click Make.

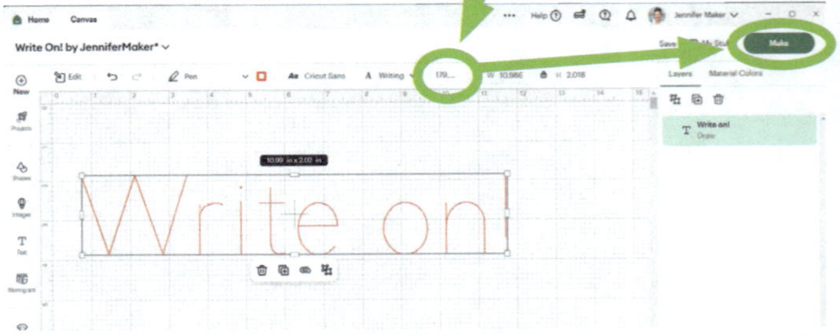

Step 5: Click and drag the text to the exact spot you want it to be written on your material on the machine mat (see page 27), then click Continue.

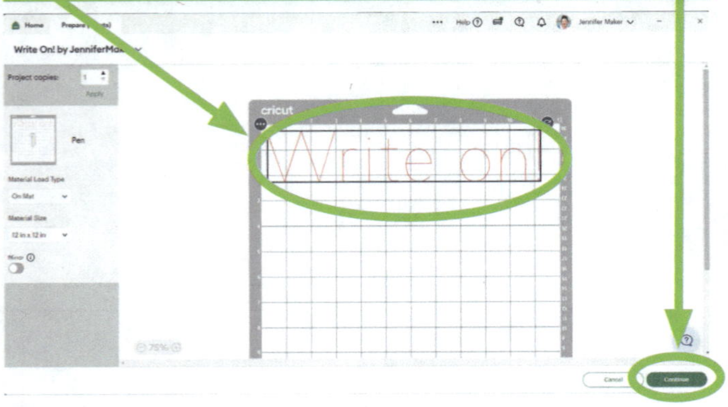

Step 6: Insert the pen in your Cricut's accessory clamp, position your material on the cutting mat, load your mat, and press the flashing button.

See my blog post at jennifermaker.com/cricut-writing for more tips on writing on your Cricut! I also have a free writing font you can use at jennifermaker.com/writing-font

Practice this at jennifermaker.com/write-on

Desktop

HOW TO SCORE WITH A STYLUS OR WHEEL

Step 1: Open or create a project with score lines. You can add a score line to any project by clicking Shapes, then selecting Score Line.

Step 2: Make sure any lines you want to be scored are identified as "Score" (click the Operation menu to change) and are also attached to the cut layer you want to score. Click Make.

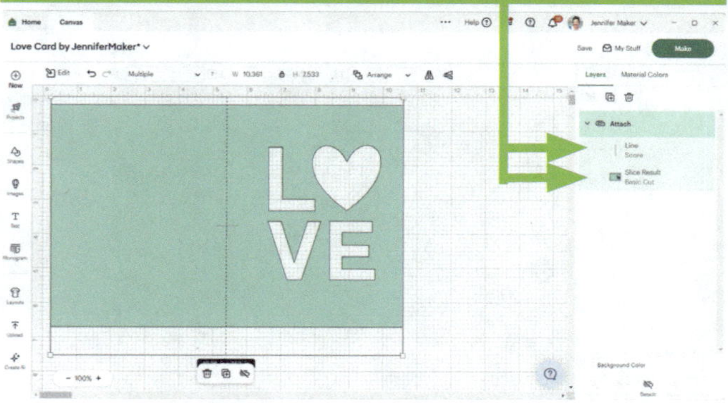

Step 3: Make sure the score line is on the same mat as the cut, then click Continue.

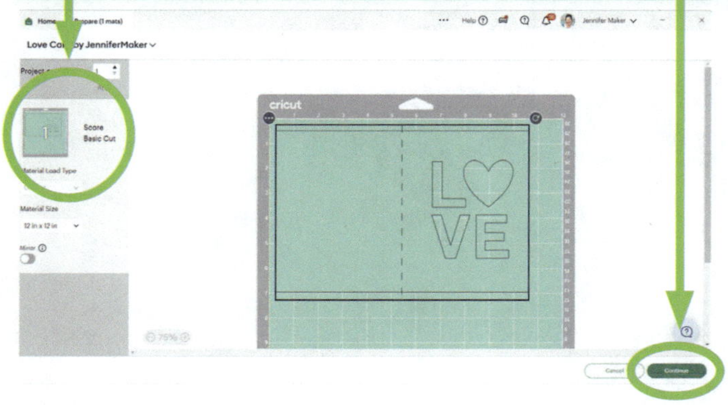

Step 4: Check the necessary tools. If the screen says to use a scoring wheel but you do not have one, click Edit Tools.

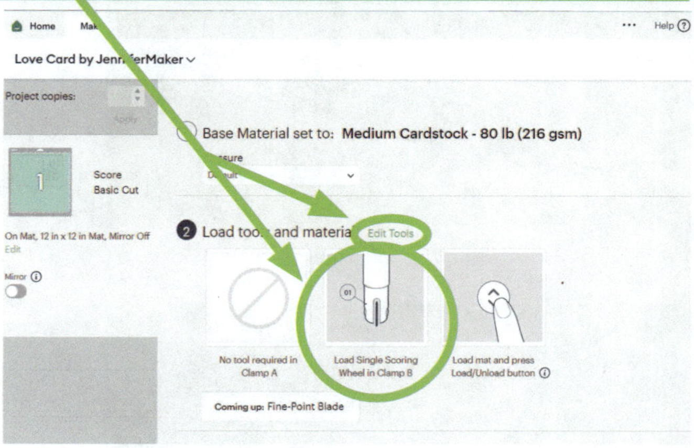

Step 5: Click on the preferred scoring tool, then click Apply.

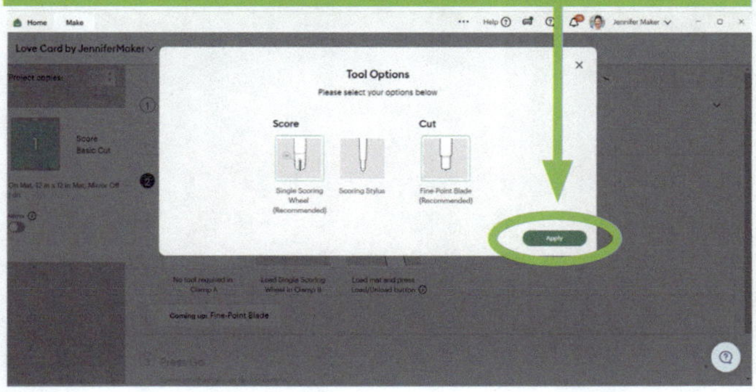

Step 6: Insert the scoring tool that matches Step 5, either a scoring stylus or a scoring wheel, then click the flashing icon on your Cricut. Note: The graphic shows both tools but you only need your specific tool in place.

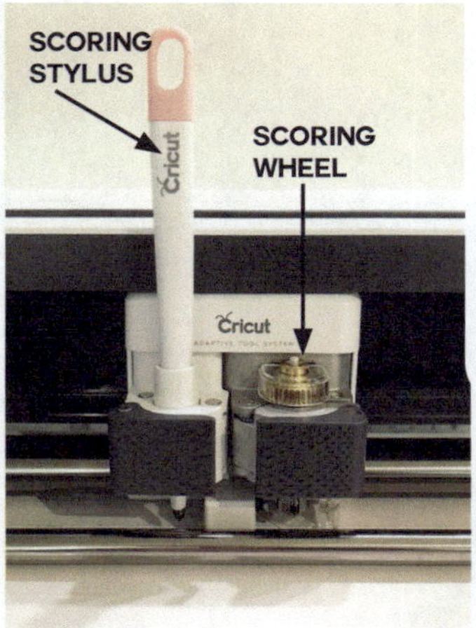

Practice this at jennifermaker.com/love-card

SCORE (STYLUS / WHEEL)

HOW TO USE THE CREATE STICKER TOOL

The Create Sticker tool is an easy way to turn any image into a sticker. It isn't absolutely required for sticker-making, but it does make it easier by telling your Cricut how much of a border to cut and whether to cut the sticker using the Die Cut method or the Kiss Cut method.

Step 1: Upload or create a design that you'd like to turn into a sticker.

Select the entire design, click the Edit icon, scroll down, and click Sticker.

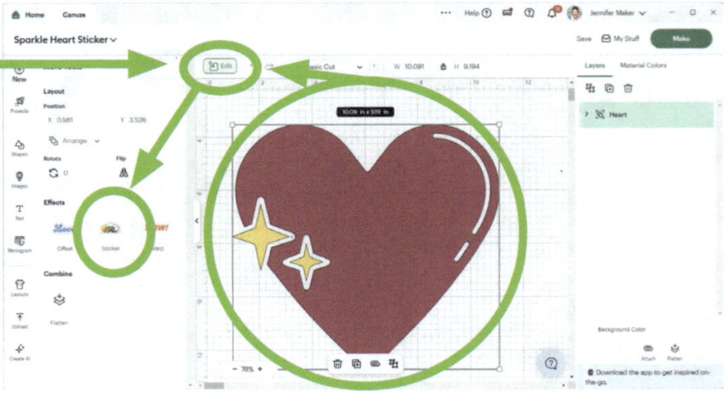

Step 2: Choose whether you'd like your sticker to be Die Cut or Kiss Cut (die cut means the sticker and its backing will be cut out, and kiss cut means that just the sticker is cut out, not the backing).

Select your Border Width and Border Fill Color. Click Apply.

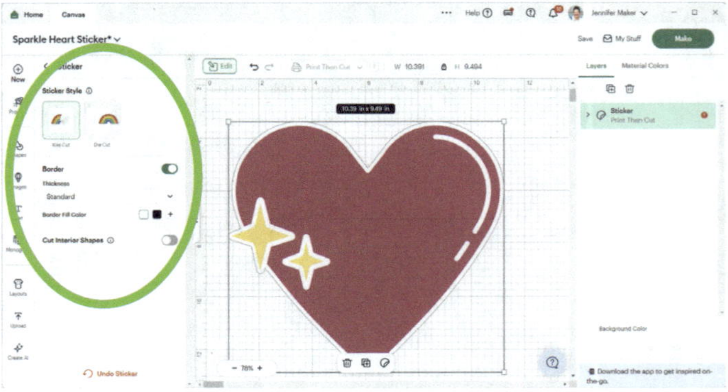

Your design will now be a single-layer Print Then Cut sticker! You will see a border around your design, and it will now be a Print Then Cut operation in the Layers Panel.

Print the sticker out on sticker paper using your color inkjet printer, then allow your Cricut to cut it out.

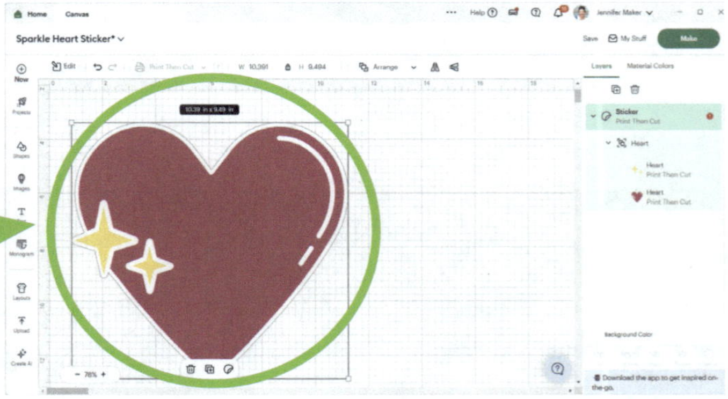

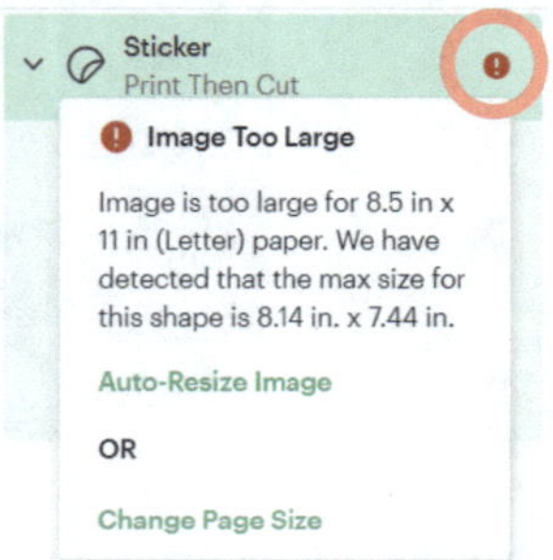

Note: If you see this icon, your design is too big for Print Then Cut based on your paper size. Click on the icon and choose "Auto-Resize Image" or "Change Page Size" to resolve the error.

Practice this at jennifermaker.com/heart-sticker

HOW TO REPOSITION ITEMS ON MAT PREVIEW

Need exact control over where items on your mat are cut? Want to cut one mat with multiple pieces of paper or vinyl in different colors? You can do this if you reposition items on your mat before you cut! Here's how to do it on a computer:

Step 1: Open or create a project. Make anything you want to appear on the same mat the same color. Click Make.

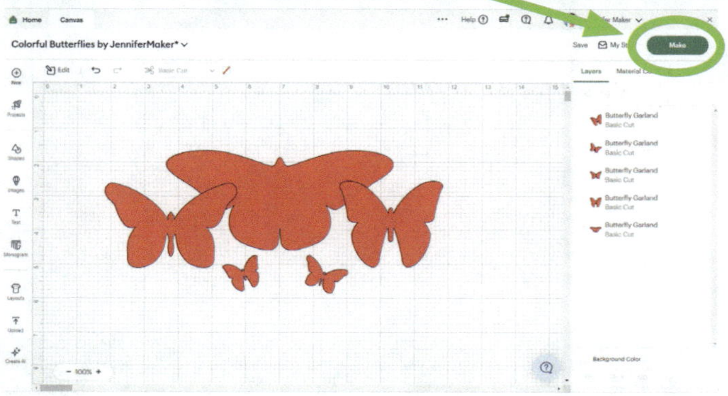

Step 2: Make sure the items you want to reposition are all on the same mat.

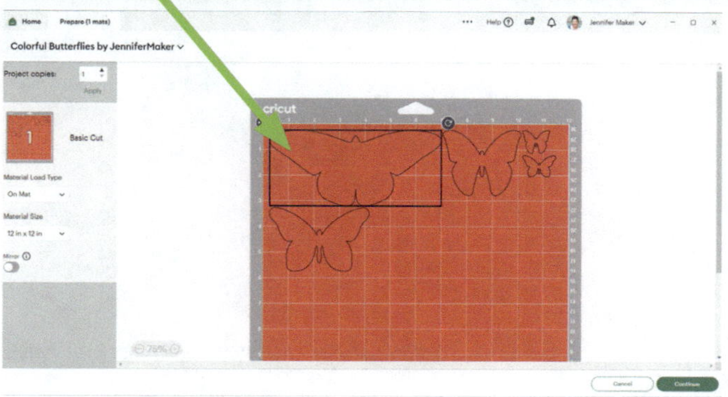

Step 3: Move each object on the mat by clicking and holding down the mouse, and dragging to a new position. You can also move to a new mat and hide by tapping the three dots icon on an element.

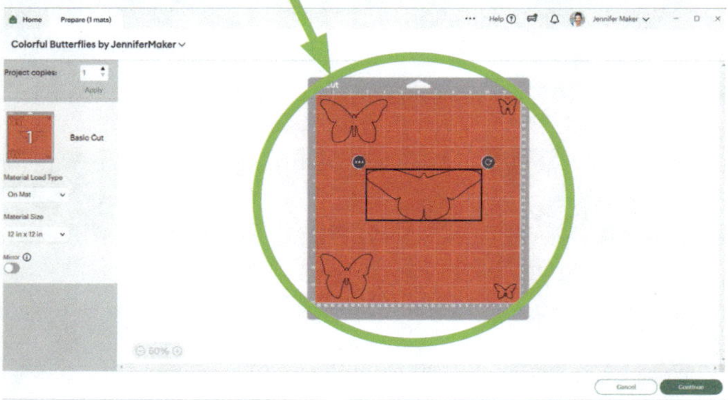

Step 4: Make sure the material on your actual mat matches the placement on this mat preview, then click Continue.

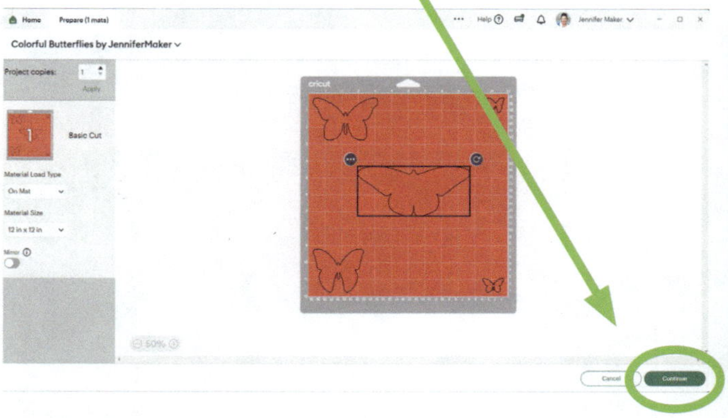

Practice this at jennifermaker.com/butterflies

HOW TO MIRROR AND CUT IRON-ON VINYL

Want to make a T-shirt or bag with iron-on vinyl? Here's how to mirror your image and position the vinyl on your mat for iron-on (heat transfer) vinyl!

Step 1: Select all the objects you want to iron-on and click Attach.

Attach

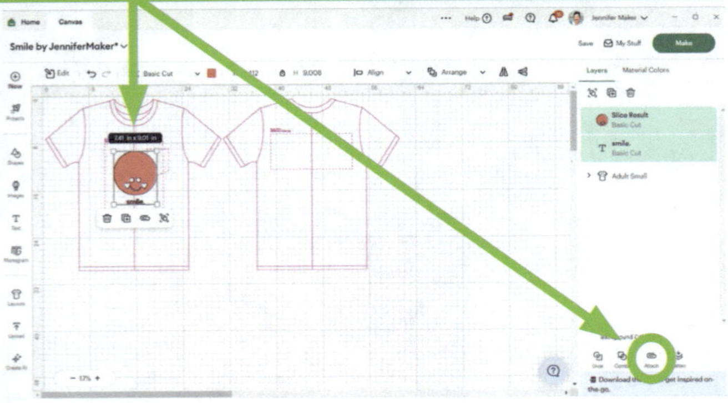

Step 2: Click Make.

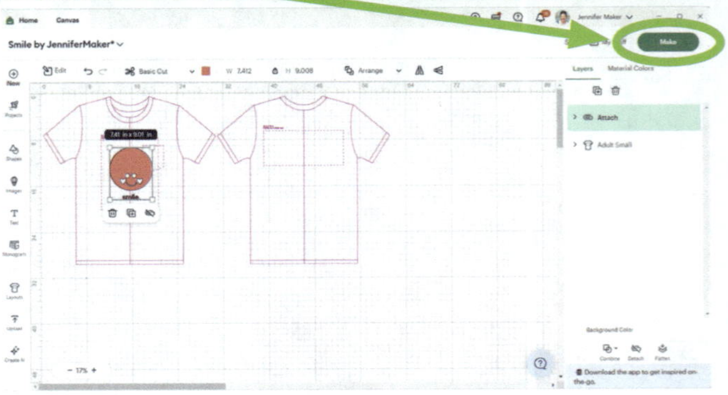

Step 3: Toggle Mirror to the on position, verify your image is now mirrored, and click Continue.

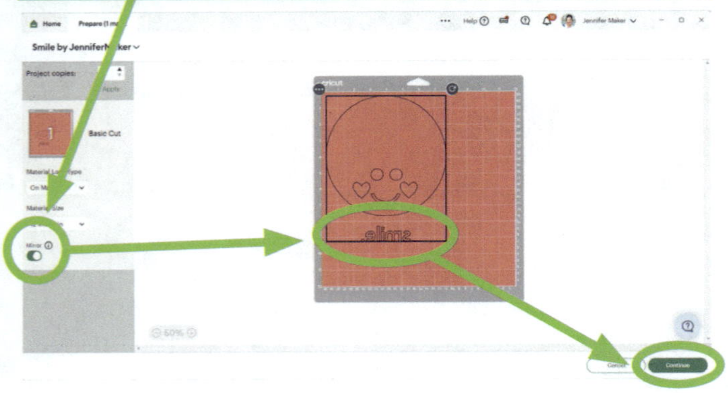

Step 4: Connect to your Cricut and click on Browse All Materials.

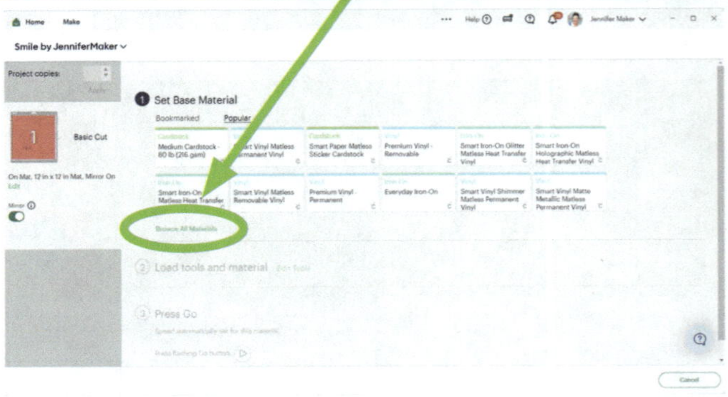

Step 5: Search for "iron" and select the type of iron-on vinyl you plan to use, then click Done.

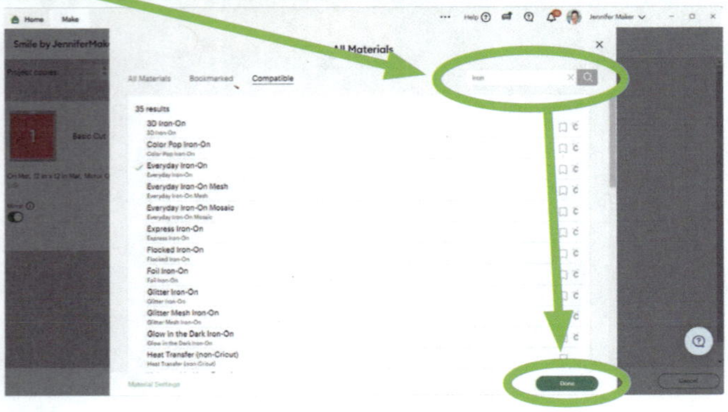

Step 6: Place your iron-on vinyl on your cutting mat shiny side down, insert the mat, and press Go.

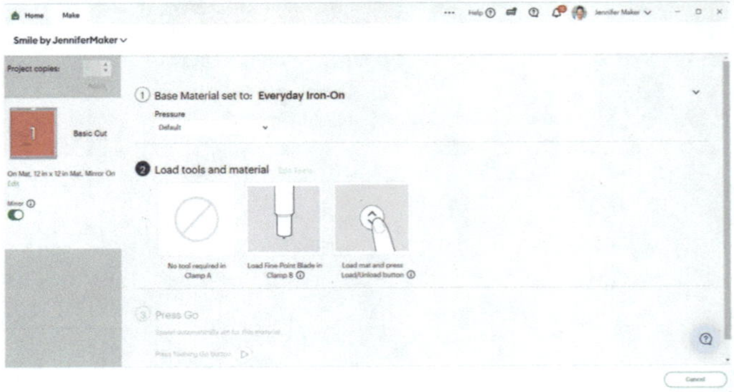

Practice this at jennifermaker.com/simple-smile

HOW TO USE A LAYOUT

Step 1: Open a new project and click the Layouts button on the left side.

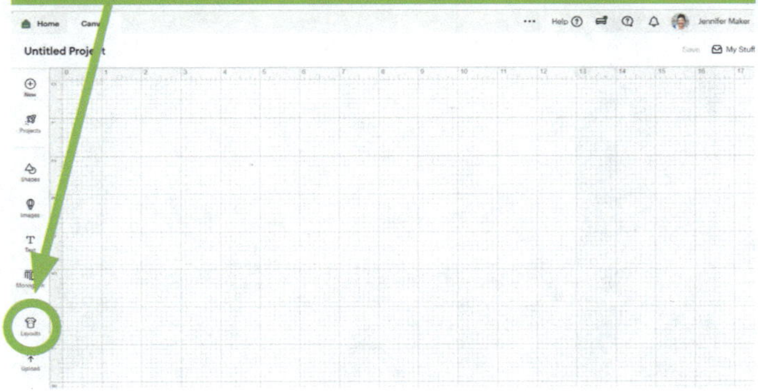

Step 2: Choose a layout category that best fits your project. I will click "T-Shirt."

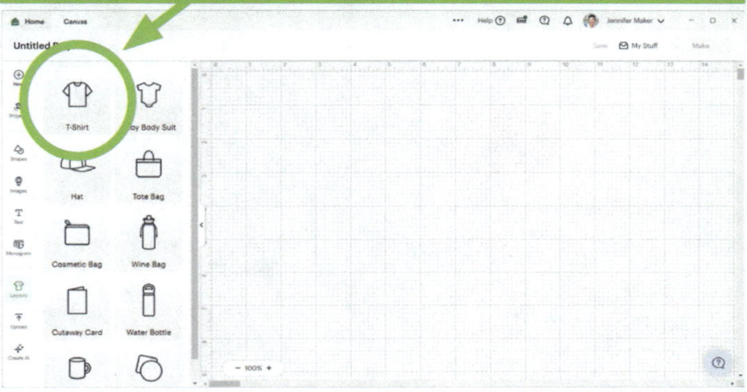

Step 3: Choose the size of the layout (template) you'd like to choose. I'm going to click "Adult Small."

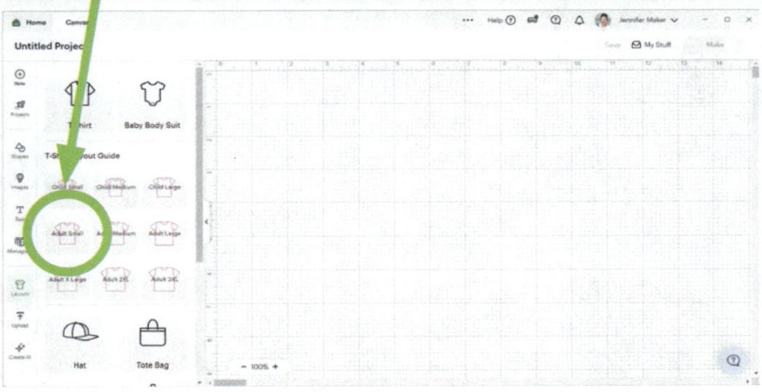

Step 4: The layout will appear on the Canvas. The Operation for the template is Guide.

Step 5: Add your design to your layout. The T-Shirt has two suggested areas for the front and one for the back of the shirt.

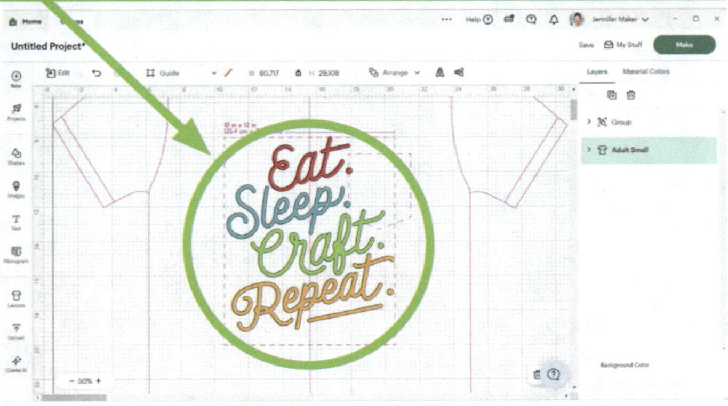

NOTE: The layout will not cut out, so you don't have to worry about hiding or deleting it before clicking Make.

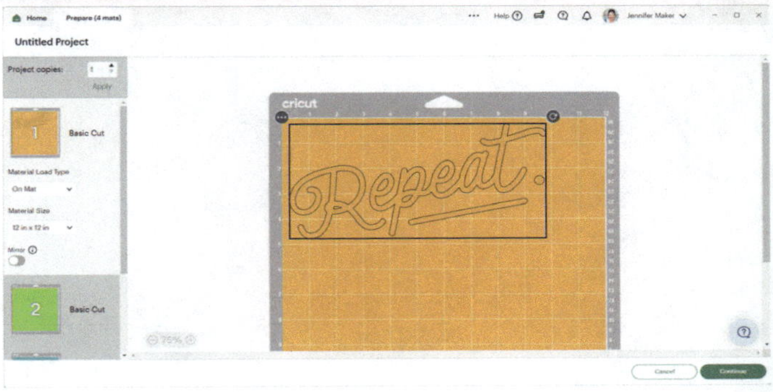

HOW TO SAVE WORK AND VIEW SAVED PROJECTS

Step 1: Create something and click Save. You can tell if something is unsaved if an asterisk * appears next to the project name at the top of the window.

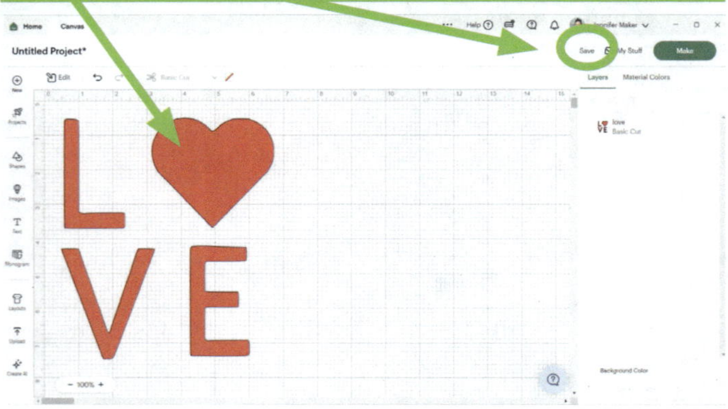

Step 2: Type a name for your project, check any collections you'd like to add it to (optional), and click Save.

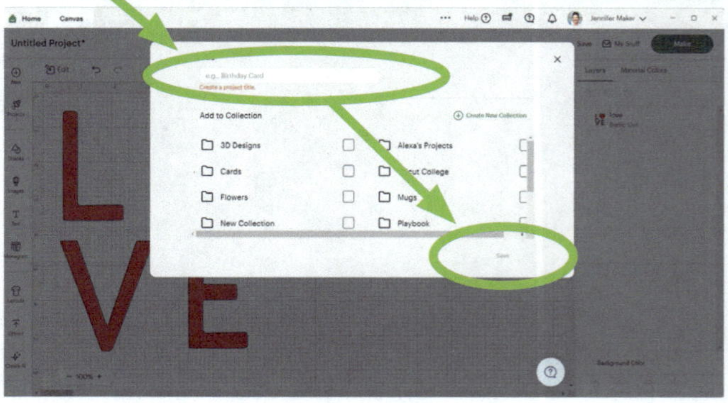

Step 3: Wait while Cricut saves your project—when saved, a blue confirmation box will flash near the top of your screen and the new name will appear at the top of the window.

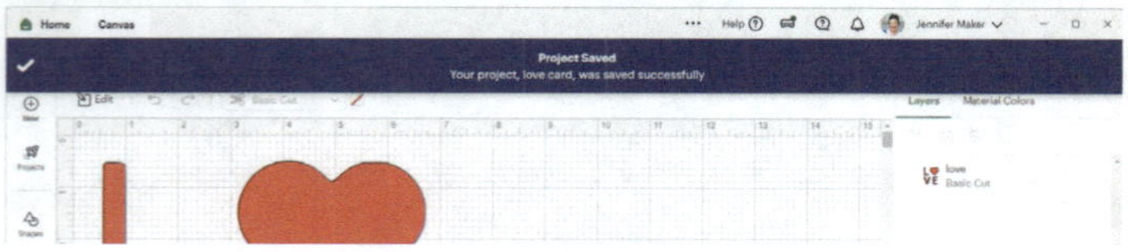

Collections allow you to organize projects you create for ease in finding them later. Click New Collection to create a new category. All Cricut members can create up to five free Collections. Cricut Access subscribers can create unlimited Collections.

To view your Saved Projects, click the My Stuff link in the top right corner of your window, or click the Projects icon on the left side of the window and select "My Projects" from the Projects drop-down menu.

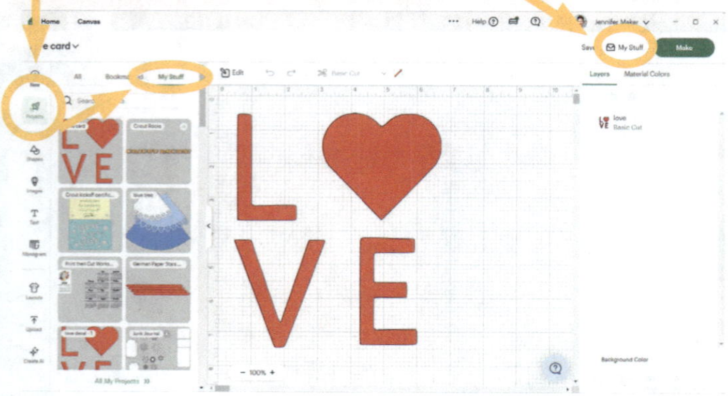

To share a project, click on the Share button on the bottom of its box. Then click Copy Private Link to copy the URL and then share it with someone as a link or in an email.

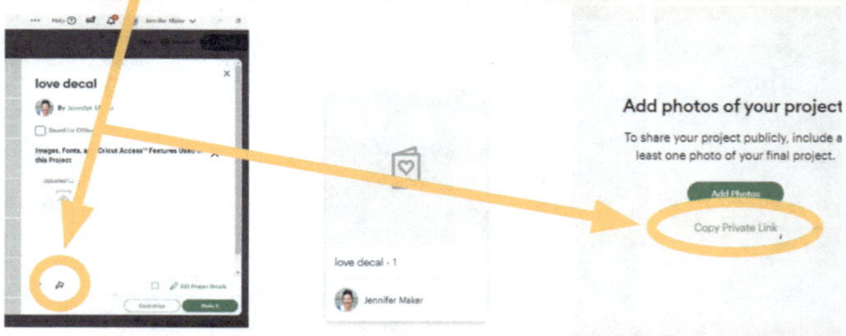

Note: Projects with uploaded images can be saved and shared, but they can only be customized and made by you — others will not be able to open and make them.

Practice this at jennifermaker.com/love-decal

HOW TO
SAVE FOR OFFLINE WORK

Design Space for Desktop (see pages 3 and 4) lets you save projects for offline and access them even when you aren't connected to the Internet. Here's how to do it:

Step 1: Click your name in the upper right, choose Settings, and select Cloud & Computer under the General tab.

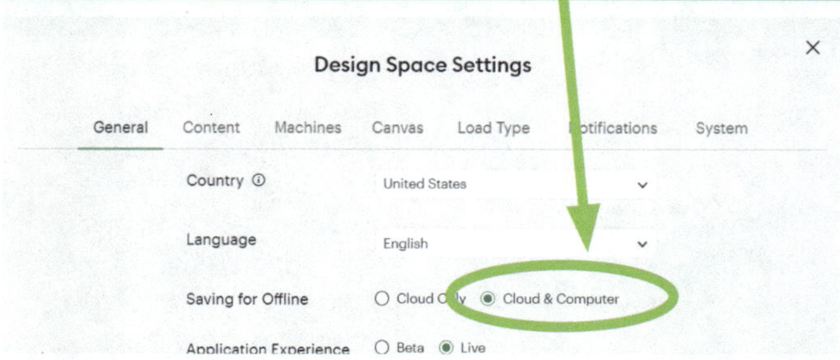

Step 2: Click on My Projects, find a project, and double-click on it to view its options.

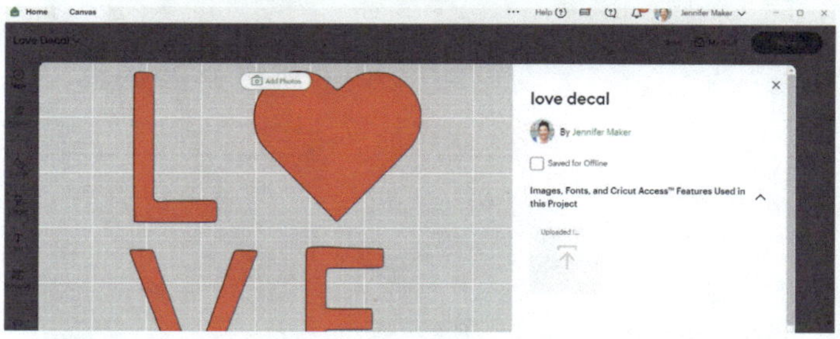

Step 3: If you see the "Save for Offline" option toggled on then you know it's saved for offline.

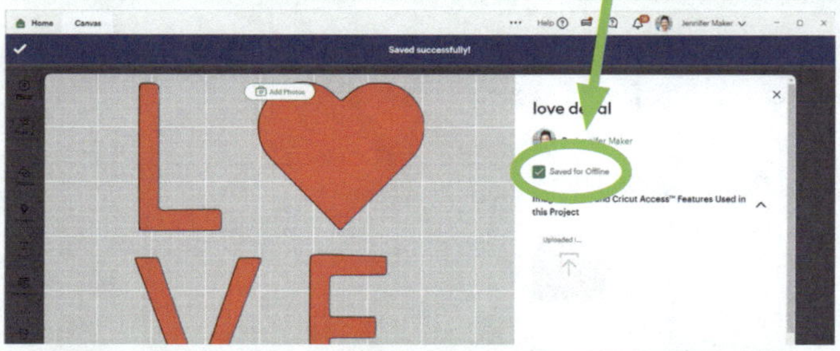

If you change it, confirmation that your project saved successfully appears at the top of the screen.

If you lose Internet access, you are notified and any projects you've saved for offline are listed.

Open the project and continue working! The "Offline" indicator stays lit when offline.

- You can batch save all of your projects for offline with step 1. You no longer need to click each one and select "Save for Offline" individually.
- If you are working offline and the online version is not synced up to the offline version, the next time you go online a pop-up will appear asking you to select a version to keep.
- Any images you have in a project from Cricut Access will expire after 30 days if you do not go online at all during those 30 days (even if you have monthly access). So be sure to set a reminder to go online at least once every 30 days.
- You cannot upload anything new while offline (this means even from your desktop or images within Design Space). So be sure to save all images you want in a project/Canvas before heading offline.

Practice this at jennifermaker.com/love-decal

HOW TO
SHARE LINKS TO PROJECTS

Have you made an awesome design and now want to share it? You can share projects, but in order for someone else to open and make them, there must be no uploaded images in your project. (Others cannot open and make projects with images you uploaded.)

Step 1: Open a project you saved and click **Share**.

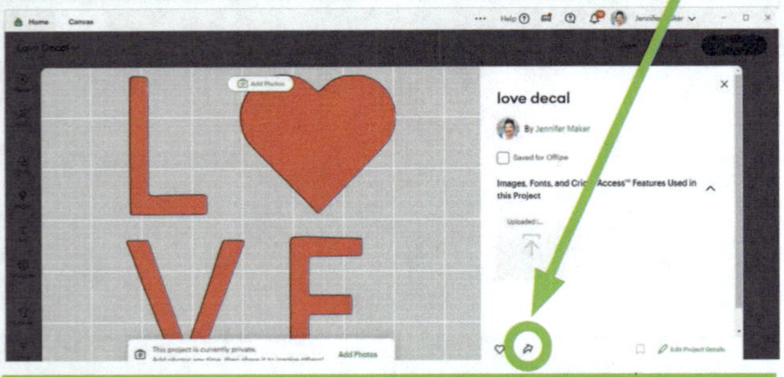

Step 2: To share a project, you must first add photos of your design. Click **Add Photos**.

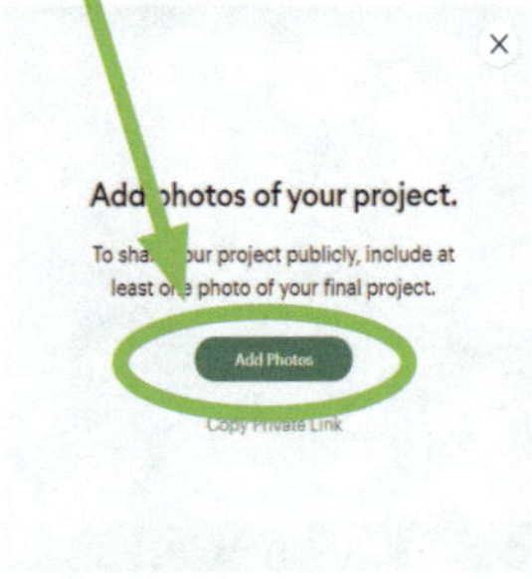

Note: If your design has any purchased elements from Cricut Access or cartridges, anyone attempting to use your design must also have them or they will be prompted to pay for them.

Step 3: Select **Browse** or drag photos of your project to add them. Once you have uploaded images, select **Save**.

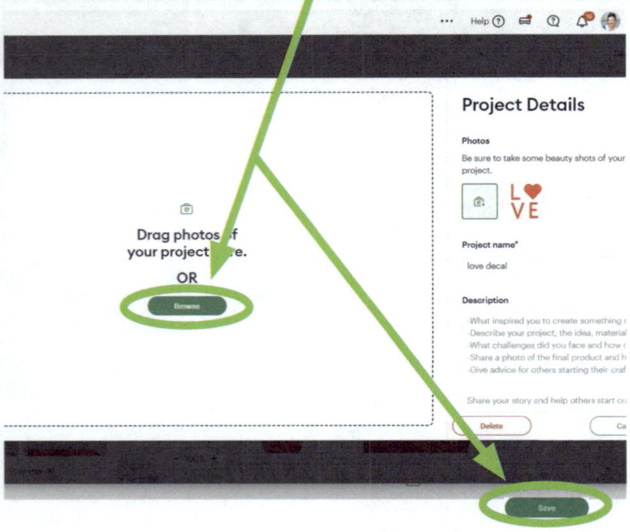

Step 4: Add a project name, description, and/or tags. When done editing, click **Save**

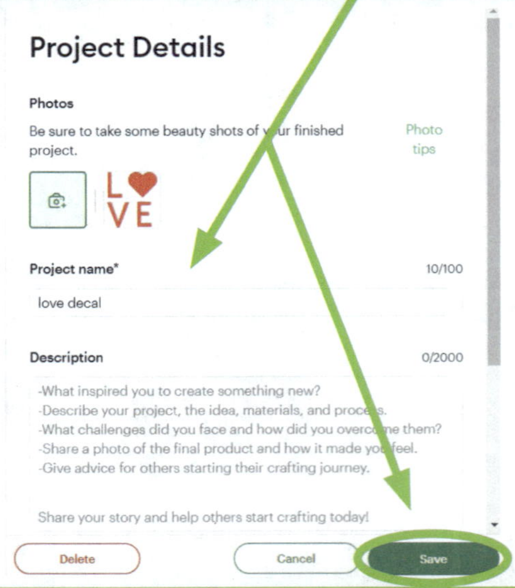

Step 5: Once you have saved your project click the **Share** icon.

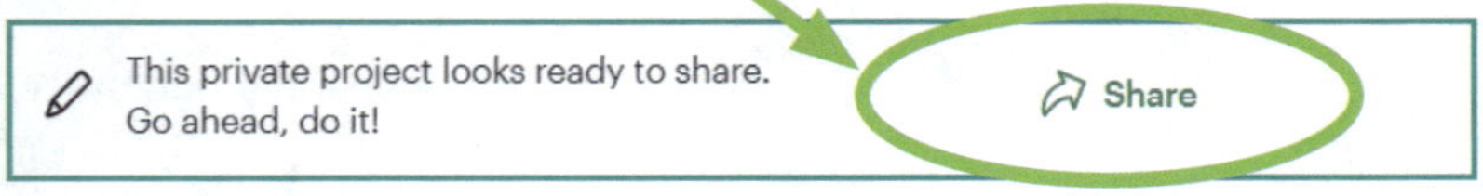

Select **Share to Design Space** to make your project public or **Copy Private Link** to send a link.

Here is an example of a project link: design.cricut.com/landing/project-detail/609ed93969c5040d507810c5

SHARE PROJECT LINKS

Desktop

HOW TO LINK CARTRIDGES

LINK CARTRIDGES

Step 1: Open Cricut Design Space, click your name in the upper right corner, choose Settings, Machines, then Start beside Link Cartridges. *(If you're using a Cartridge Adapter, it will need to be inserted into a USB port on your computer first.)*

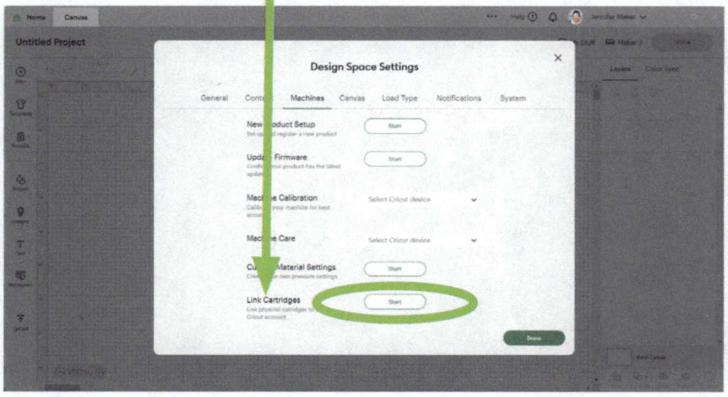

Step 2: Choose your Cricut from the drop-down menu. If you do not see it, make sure it is turned on and connected. For best results, connect your Cricut to your computer via the USB cable.

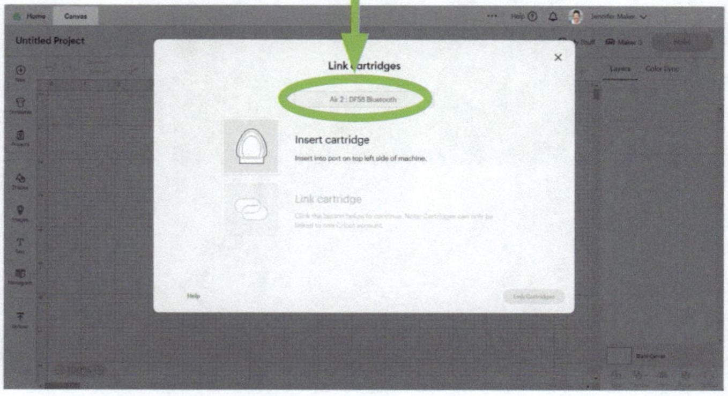

Step 3: Once the cartridge is detected, the Link Cartridge button will become available. Click the Link Cartridge button to continue.

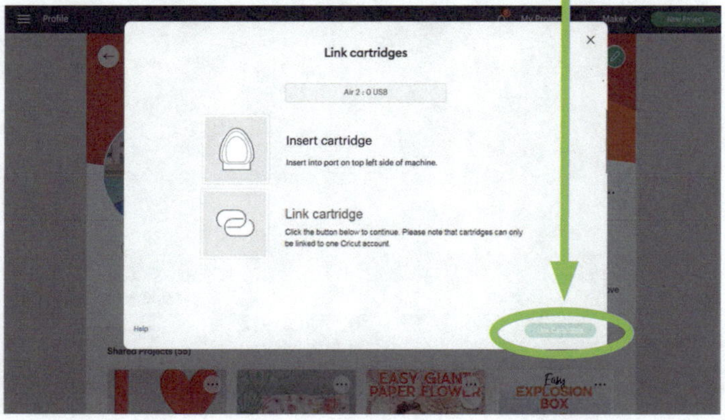

Step 4: Once the link is complete, remove the cartridge from the adapter and choose what to do next. You can continue to link other cartridges, view your cartridges, or close the window.

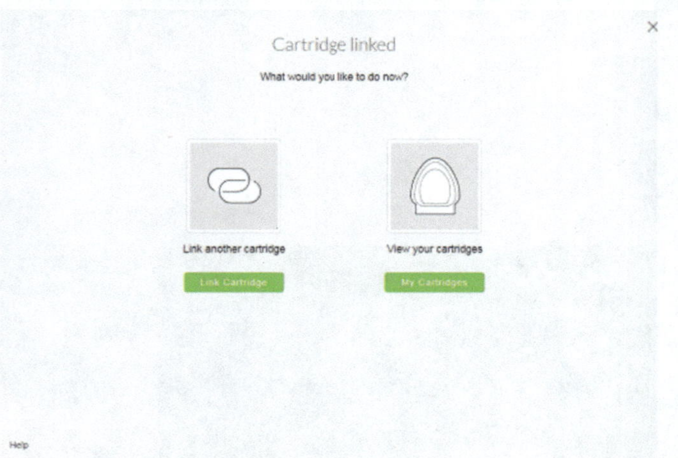

When a physical cartridge has been linked to your account, the digital versions of those images are activated on your account and the physical cartridge is no longer needed in order to use those images with Cricut Design Space.

Get more help at cricut.pxf.io/dogDKM

Tip: If you have issues linking your cartridges, contact Cricut Member Care for assistance getting them uploaded to your Design Space account. Note that they may ask for photos of the cartridges to do this.

Note: You cannot link physical cartridges on iOS or Android devices at this time.

HOW TO FLATTEN AN IMAGE

Need to make a Print Then Cut project? Flatten is your friend! The Flatten tool allows you to turn any image into a single, printable layer for the Print Then Cut feature.

Step 1: Add two or more items to your Canvas that you want to flatten.

Note: Flatten is used only for Print Then Cut.

Step 2: Click and drag a bounding box around all objects you want to flatten to select all of them.

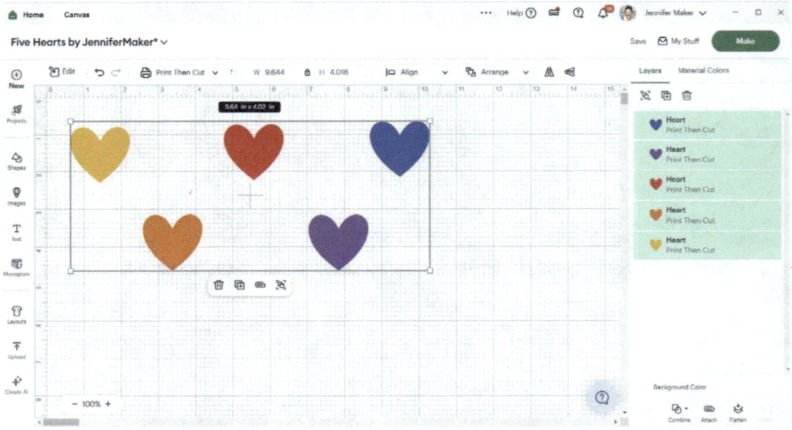

Step 3: Click the Flatten icon in the bottom right corner. Flatten

Note that all items are now on one layer and now work only for Print Then Cut.

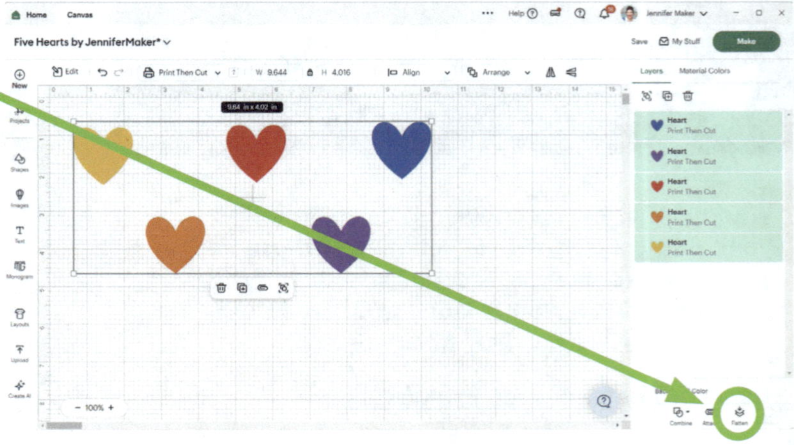

If you decide this isn't what you wanted to do, click the Unflatten button right away. Unflatten

Practice this at jennifermaker.com/five-hearts

HOW TO PRINT THEN CUT

Step 1: Find or upload up to a 10.64" x 15.43" printable image with one of these two methods:

Method A: Search for printable images in Design Space by clicking on Images > Filters. Check the box next to "Print Then Cut."

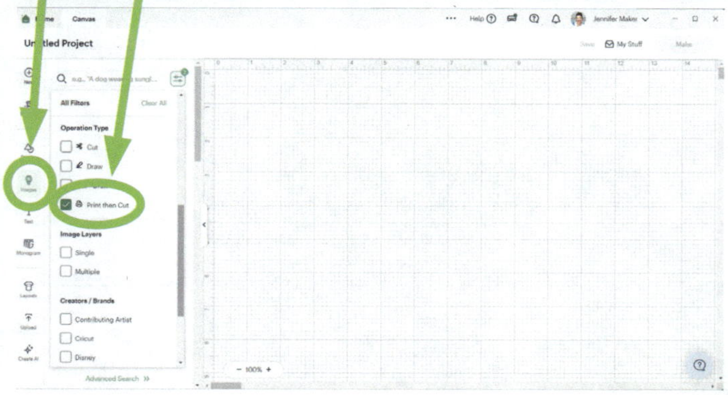

Method B: Click Upload, choose an image, and then make sure the correct image loaded. Then click Continue.

Tip: Click "Free" on the search page to see all images that are free for use.

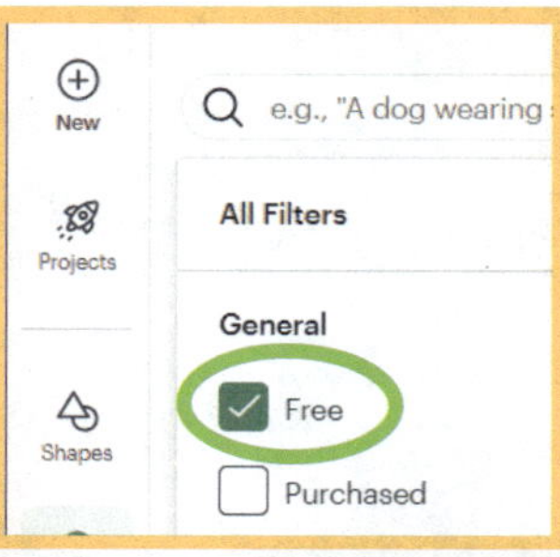

Erase anything you do not want to print and click Apply & Continue.

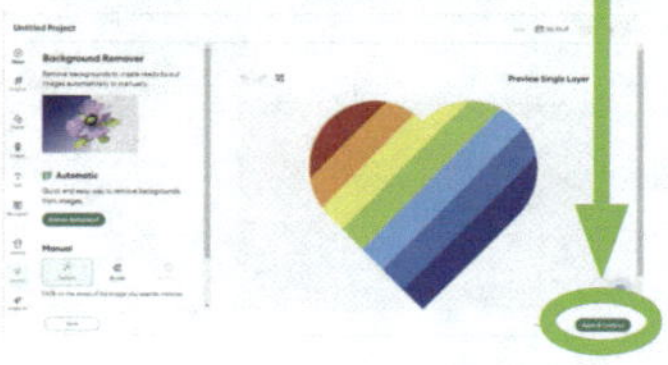

Select Flat Graphic, then click Continue.

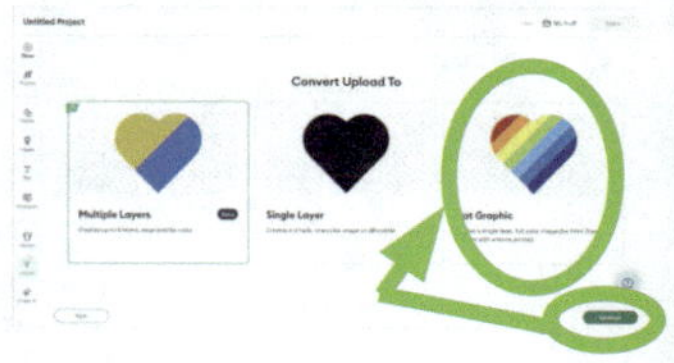

Step 2: Select and insert the image onto your Canvas, then click Make.

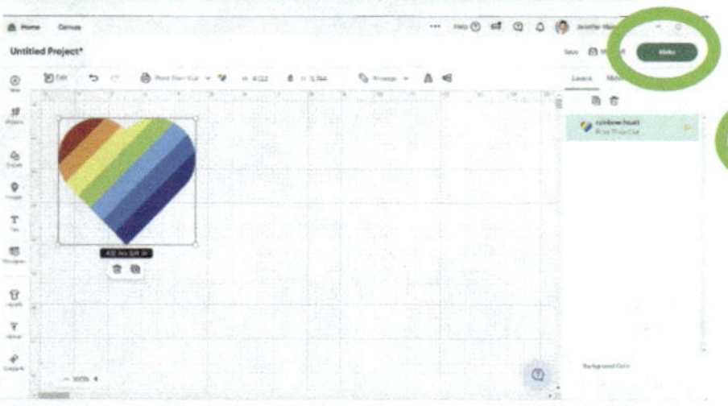

Step 3: Make sure the mat details say "Print Then Cut" here, then click Continue.

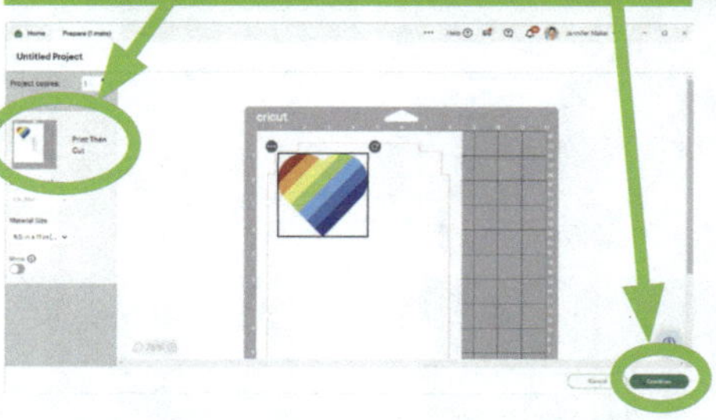

Step 4: On the Make screen, click Send to Printer.

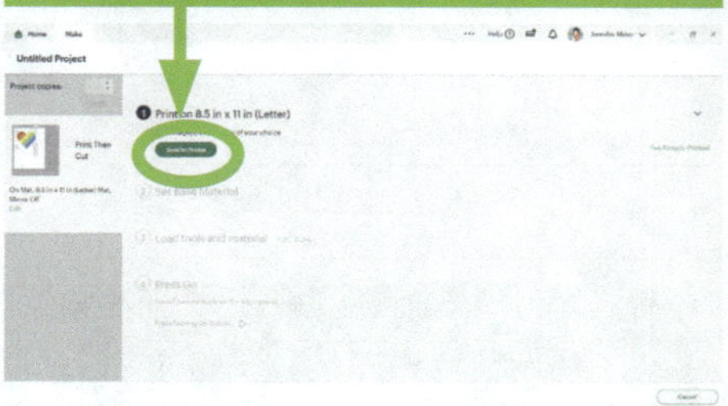

Step 5: Select your printer, turn on Bleed, and click Print. I also recommend Use System Dialog.

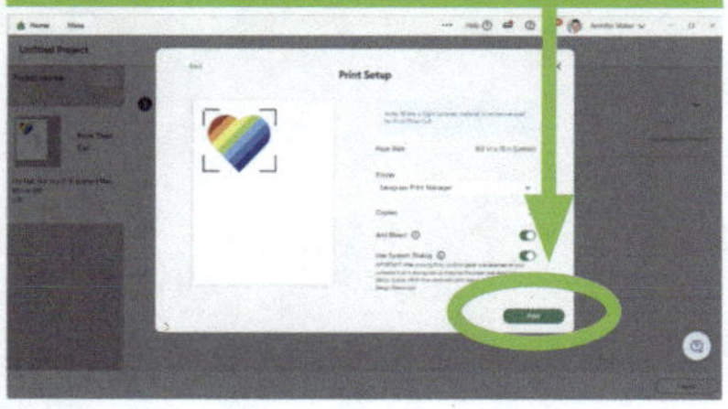

Step 6: After printing, check the print quality, then click Done.

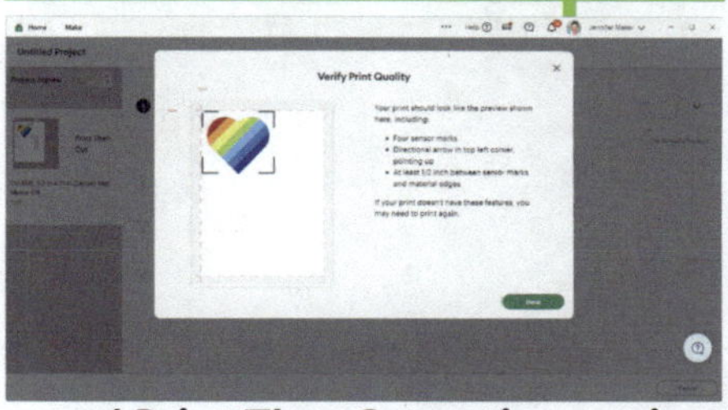

Step 7: Select your Material (i.e., Printable Vinyl) by clicking Browse All Materials.

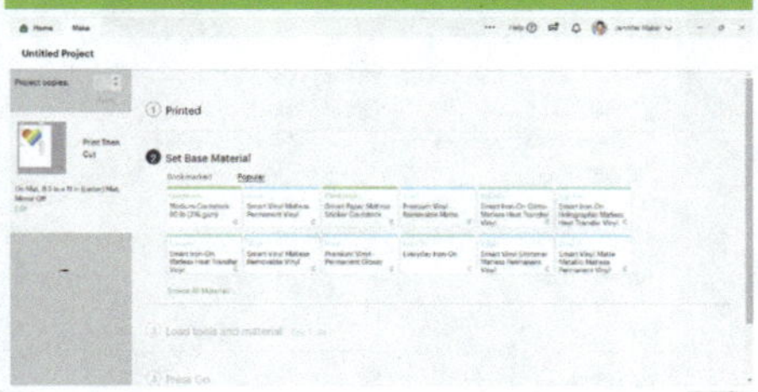

View more information on sizing and Print Then Cut options at jennifermaker.com/cricut-print-and-cut-size

Desktop

HOW TO
UPLOAD IMAGES ON A MAC

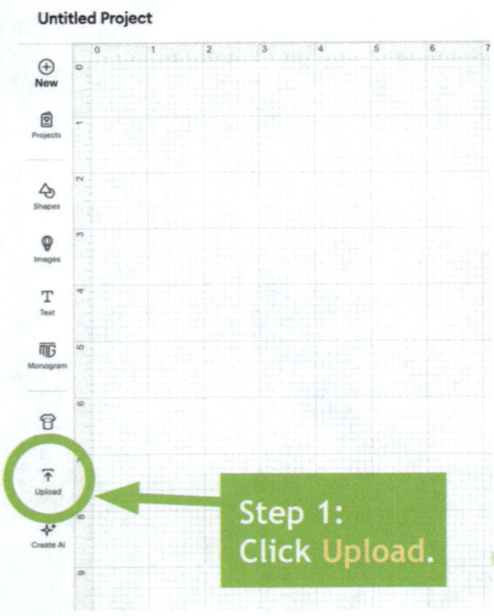

Step 1: Click Upload.

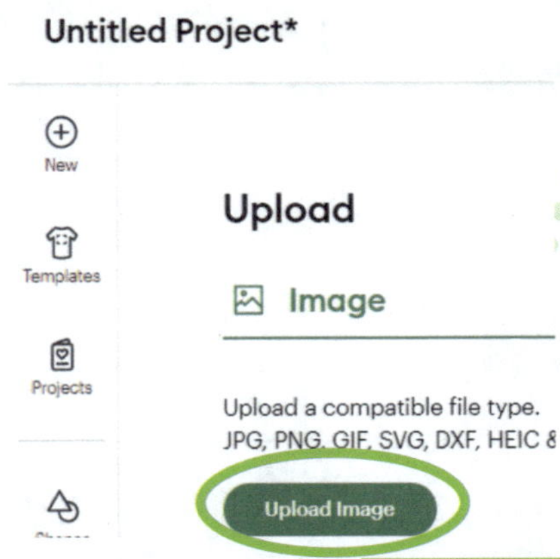

Step 2: Click Upload Image.

Step 3: Click Browse.

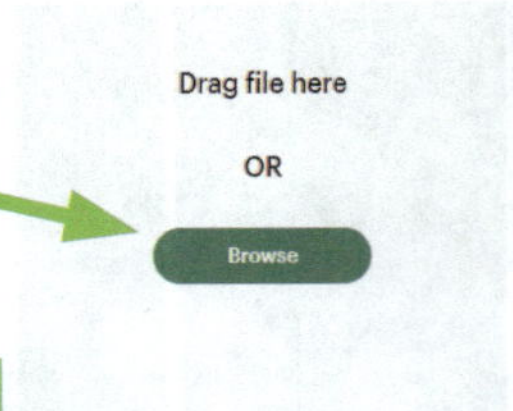

Step 4: Select a PNG, JPG, GIF, HEIC, or BMP File and click Open.

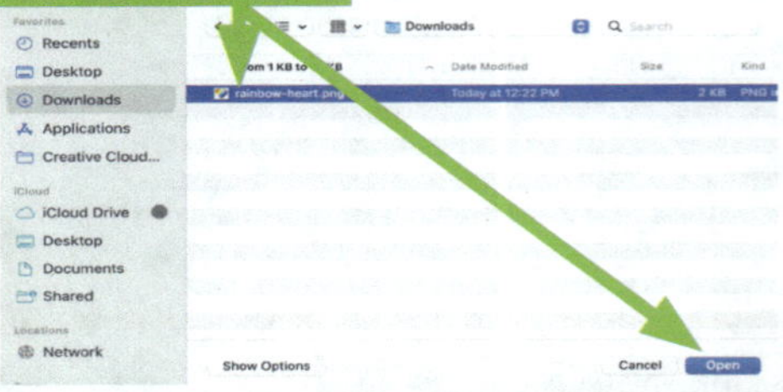

Step 5: Make sure your image looks right, then click Continue.

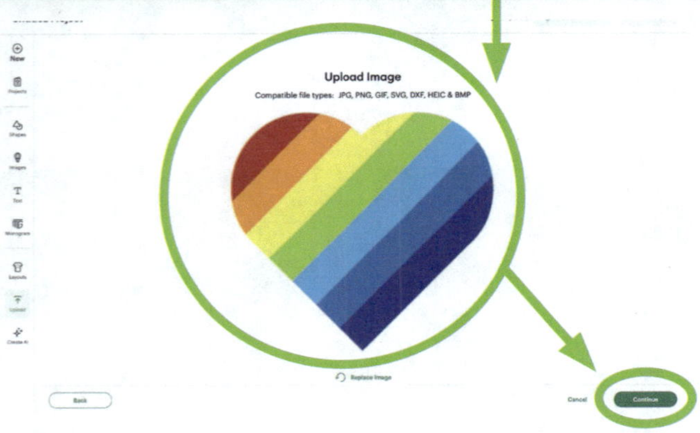

Step 6: Clean up and refine your image using the tools, if you wish, then click Apply & Continue.

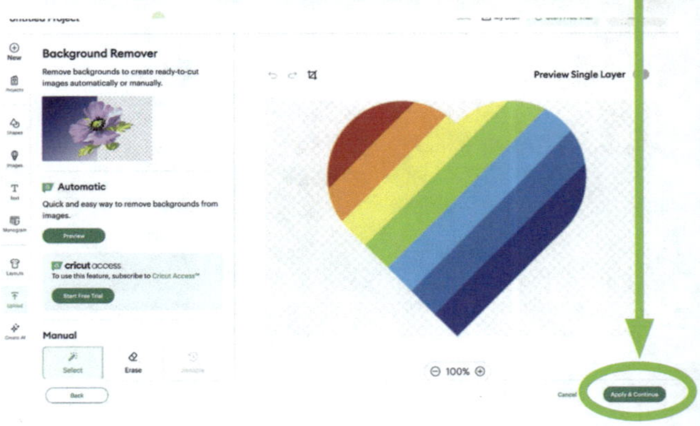

Step 7: Choose your upload type and Continue. On the next screen, name your image and go on.

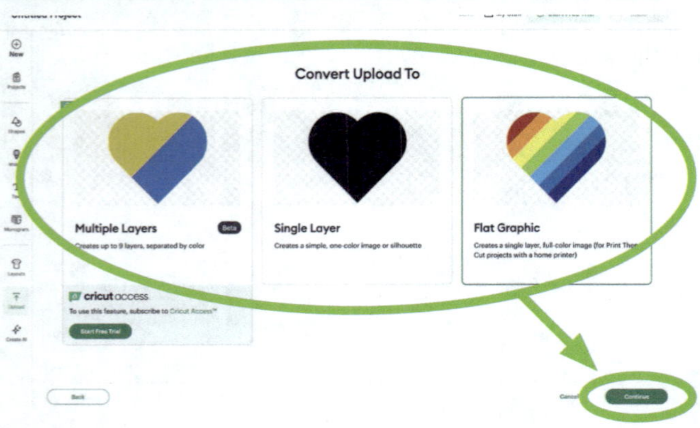

Your image appears on your Canvas in Cricut Design Space.

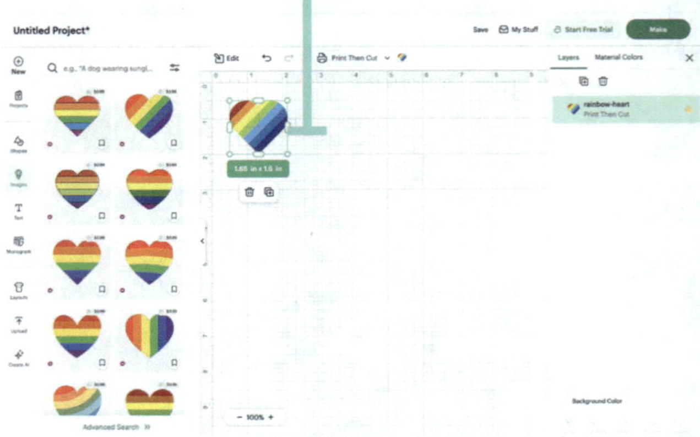

Practice this at jennifermaker.com/rainbow-heart

UPLOAD IMAGES (MAC)

HOW TO
UPLOAD IMAGES ON A PC

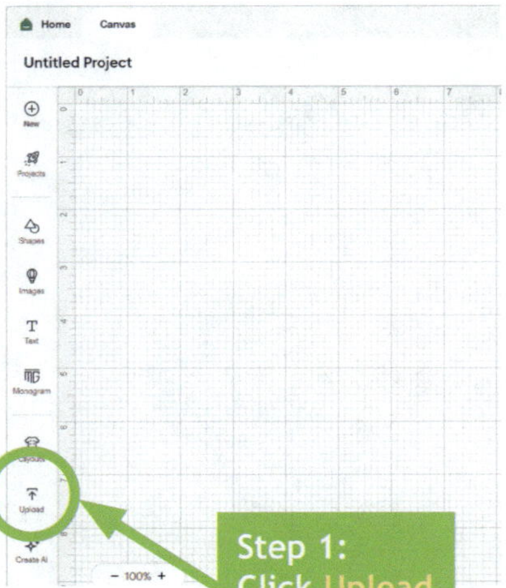

Step 1: Click Upload.

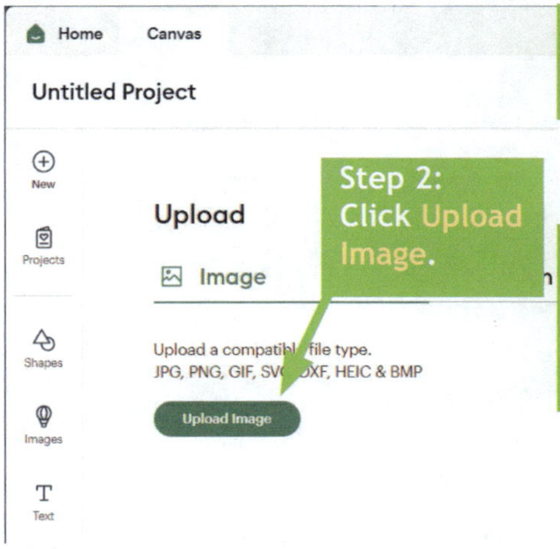

Step 2: Click Upload Image.

Step 3: Click Browse.

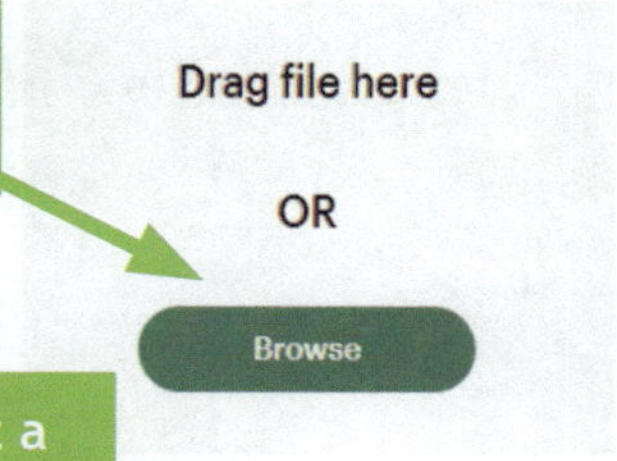

Step 4: Select a PNG, JPG, GIF, HEIC, or BMP File and click Open.

Step 5: On the next page, make sure your image looks right, then click Continue.

Step 6: Clean up and refine your image using the tools, if you wish, then click Apply & Continue.

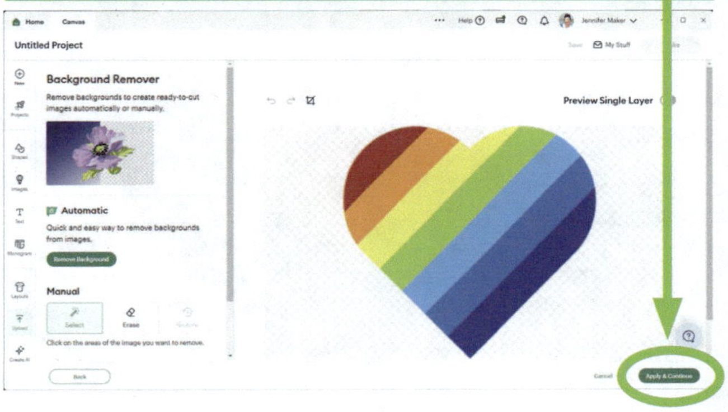

Step 7: Choose your upload type and Continue. On the next screen, name your image and click Upload.

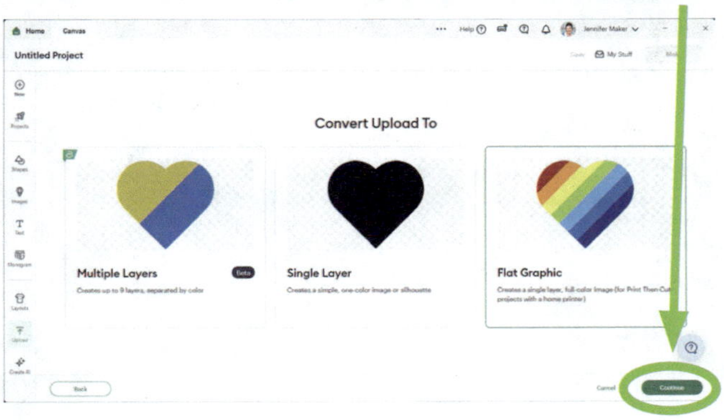

Your image appears on your Canvas in Cricut Design Space.

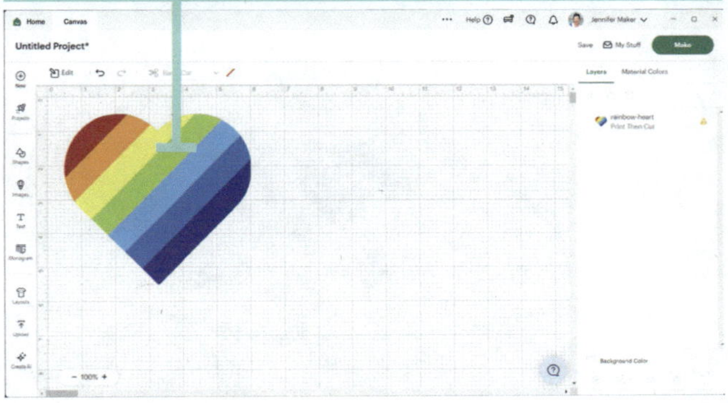

Practice this at jennifermaker.com/rainbow-heart

Desktop

HOW TO ERASE A BACKGROUND FROM AN IMAGE

Step 1: Find or upload a JPG, PNG, GIF, HEIC, or BMP file that you want to use. Click Upload, then Browse. Select your image.

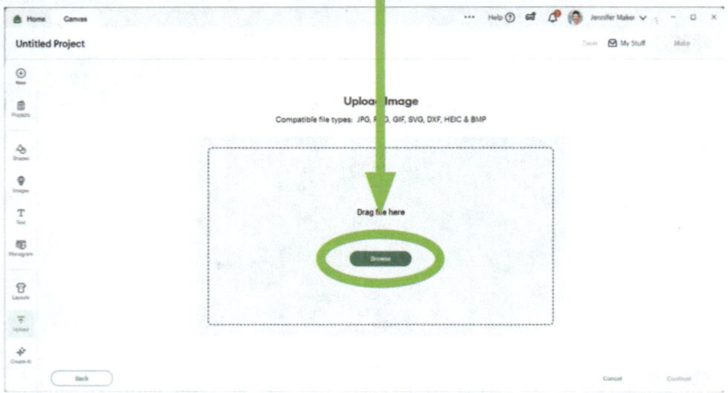

Step 2: If you have Cricut Access, click Remove Background. Otherwise, click the Select tool.

Select

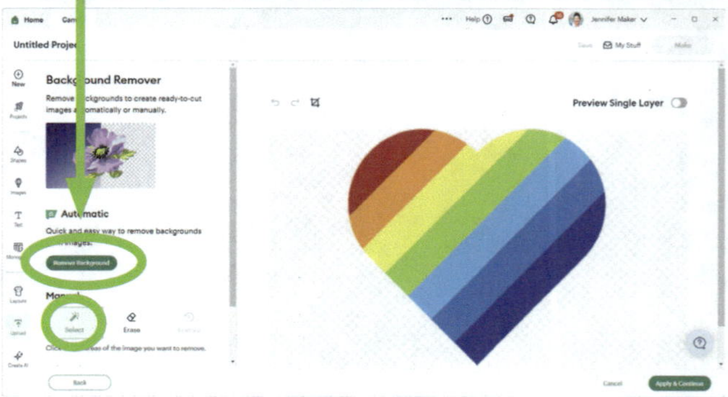

Step 3: If using the Select tool, click on the background around your image to erase it. You may need to click several areas to get it all.

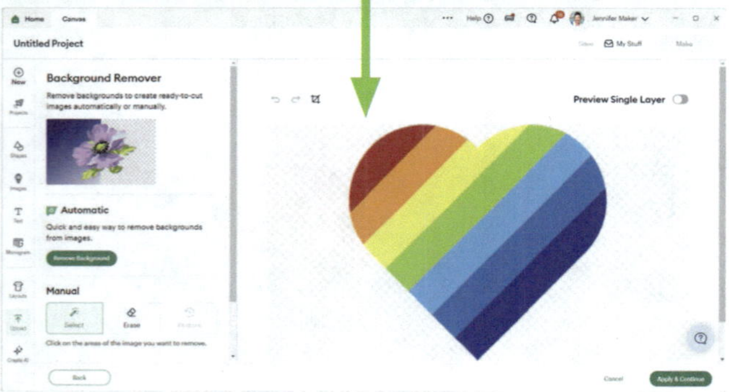

Step 4: Click Preview Single Layer to see the cut lines of the object remaining. If it looks good, click Apply & Continue.

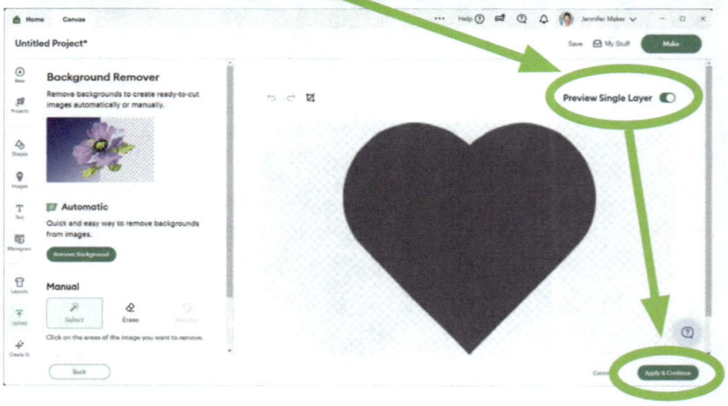

Step 5: Click an upload method, then click Continue.

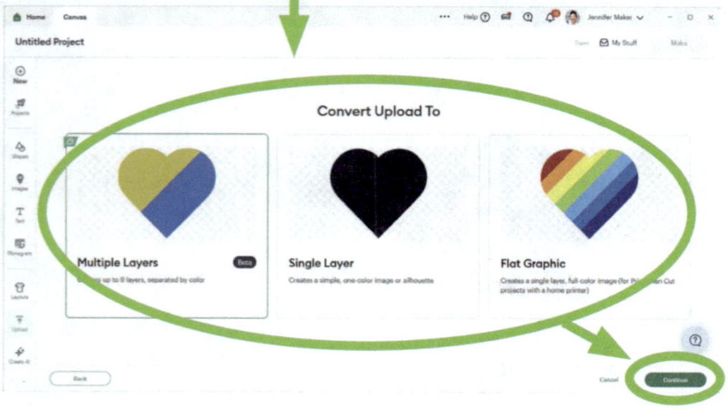

Step 6: Give your image a name, then click Upload. Your image will appear on your Canvas!

Practice this at jennifermaker.com/rainbow-heart

HOW TO USE FILE/PHOTO TO LAYERS

The File/Photo to Layers function allows you to upload an image and lets Design Space convert it into up to nine layers. It doesn't always work perfectly, but it can be a really cool tool to use.

Step 1: Click the Upload button in the menu on the left side of the screen.

Step 2: Upload an image that you'd like to convert to layers. Remove the background. Then click Apply & Continue.

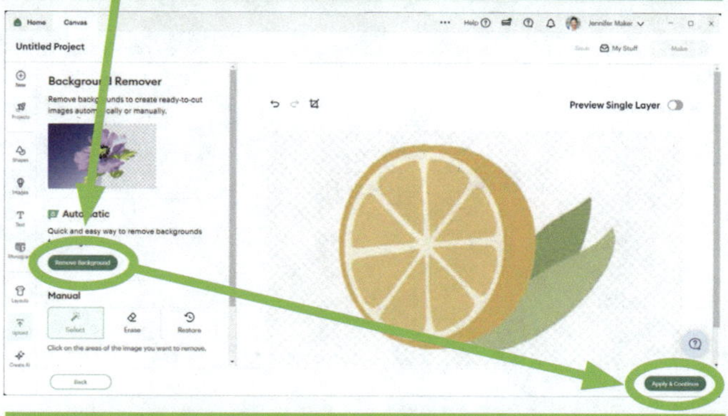

Step 3: Select Multiple Layers and then click Continue.

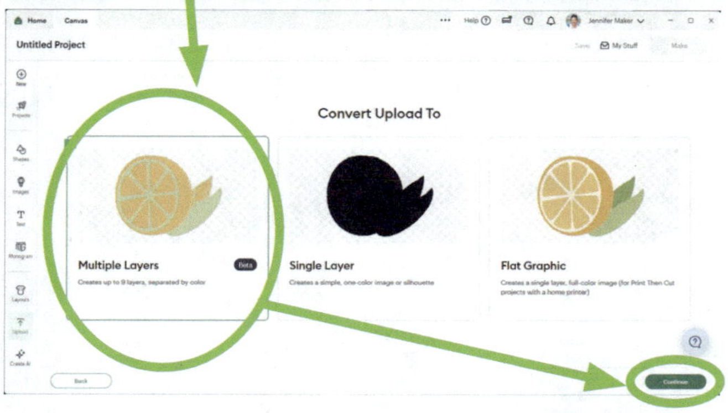

Step 4: Choose options from the menu on the left side of the screen. Then click Continue. On the next screen, name your image and click Upload.

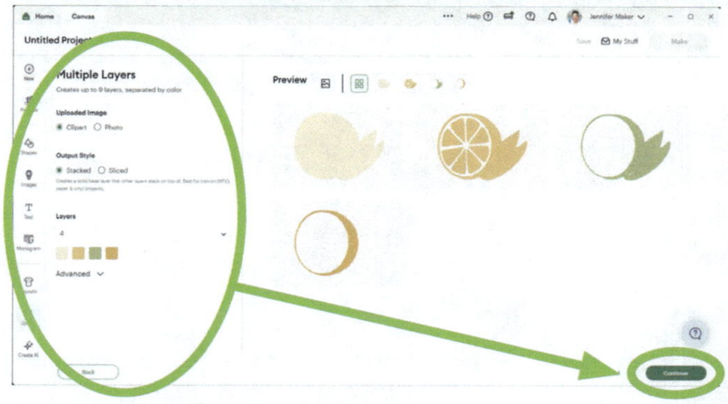

Step 5: Your image will appear as layers on your Canvas!

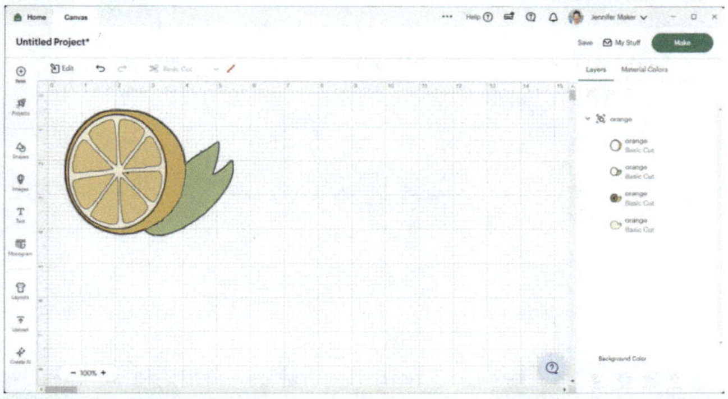

Step 6: Ungroup your image layers and spread them apart to see all the layers.

HOW TO COMBINE MULTIPLE PROJECTS

While there is no built-in function in Design Space that allows you to combine projects, there is a simple workaround. Here's how you do it:

Step 1: Open the project you want to add to another, select all layers, right-click,- and select Copy.

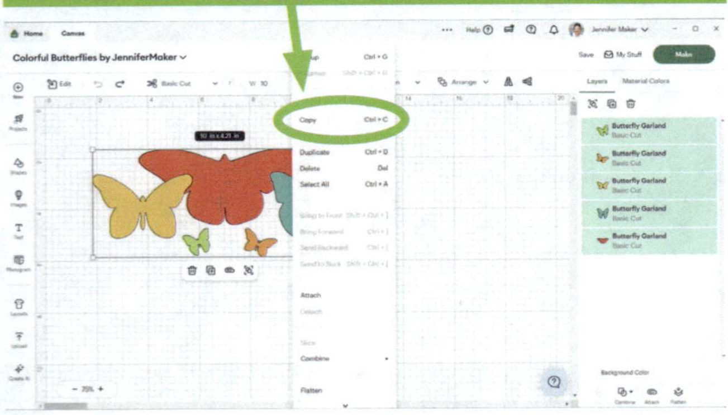

Step 2: Select the three dots in the top right and click File. Select New Window. If you are using a Mac, select File, then New Window.

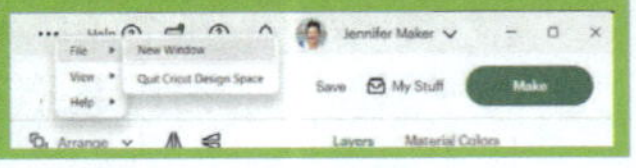

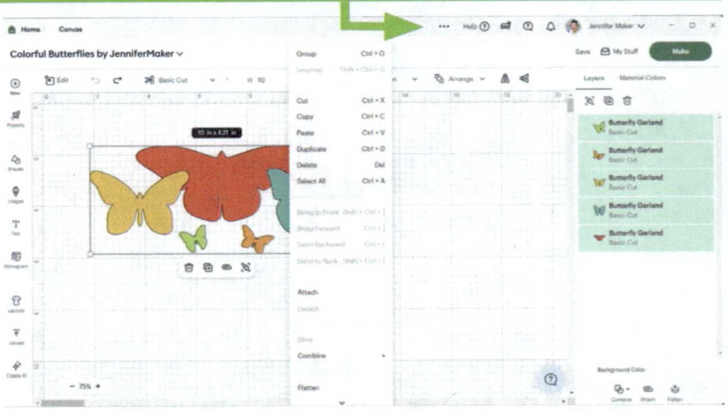

Step 3: Locate and open the project you want to combine with your first project.

Step 4: Right-cick and choose Paste.

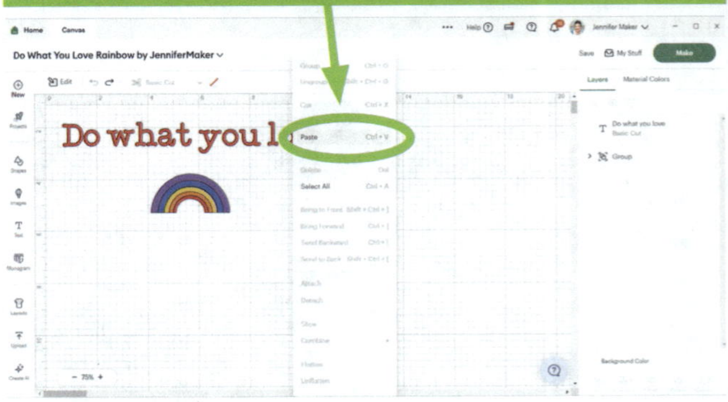

Your layers from the first project appear on the Canvas with the second project!

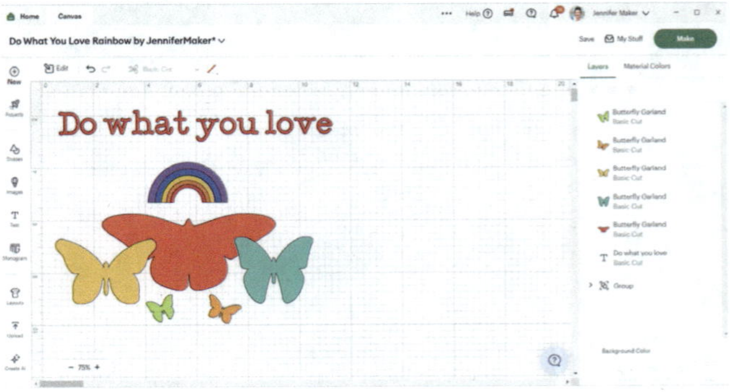

Practice this at jennifermaker.com/butterflies and jennifermaker.com/rainbow-love

HOW TO UPLOAD SVG FILES ON A MAC

Step 1: Click Upload.

Step 2: Click Upload Image.

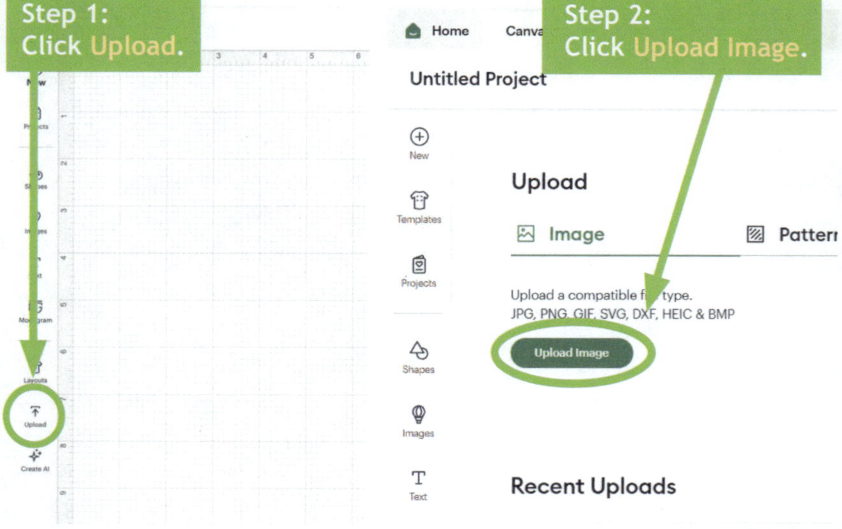

Step 3: Click Browse.

Step 4: Select the SVG File and click Open.

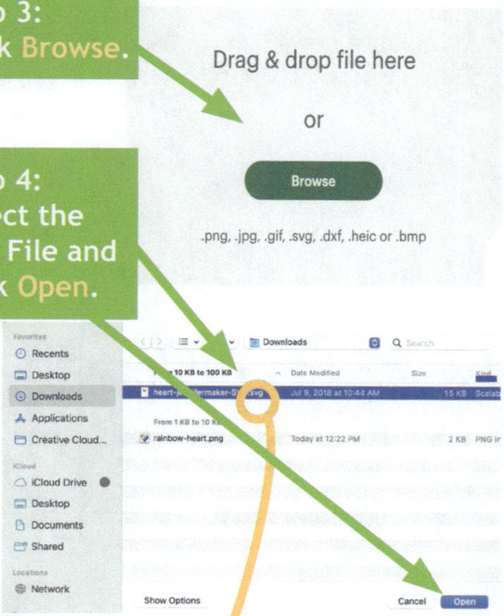

Step 5: Click Continue.

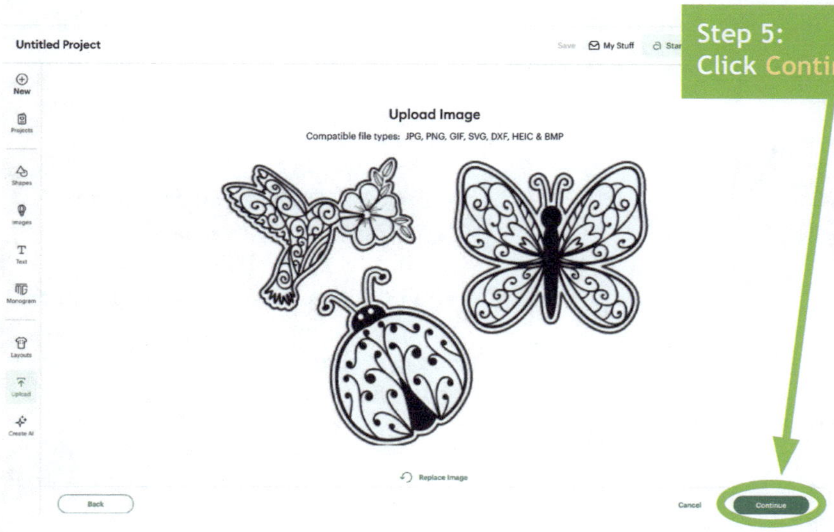

Notes: Be sure you select the SVG file, not the ZIP file. You can tell it is the SVG file because its "Kind" is listed as "Scalable Vector Graphics Image" in your file browser. If you only see the ZIP file, you'll need to first decompress the ZIP file (open it) by double-clicking it in your Finder. If you do not, you'll see this message:

> You have selected an unsupported file type.

Step 6: Give your SVG file a name, add it to a collection if needed, then click Upload.

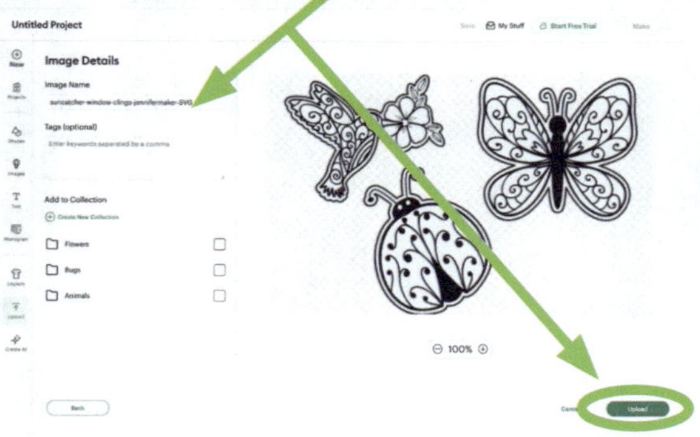

Once inserted, your image appears on your Canvas, ready to be modified or made!

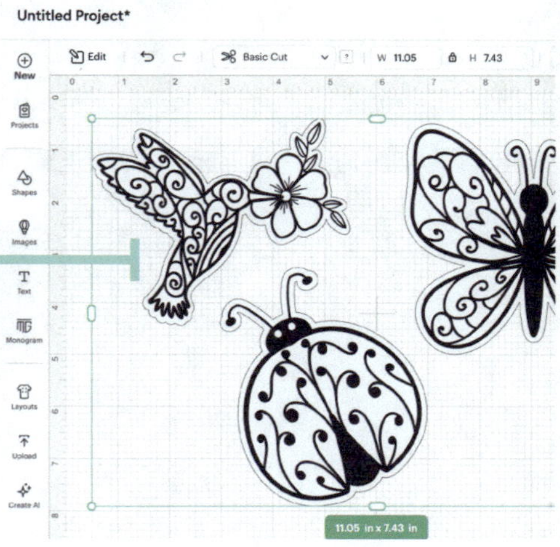

Practice this at jennifermaker.com/suncatcher-window-clings

Desktop

HOW TO UPLOAD SVG FILES ON A PC

Step 1:
Click Upload.

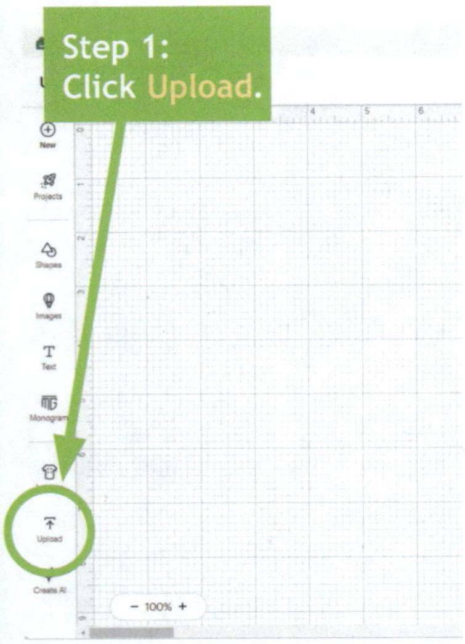

Step 2:
Click Upload Image.

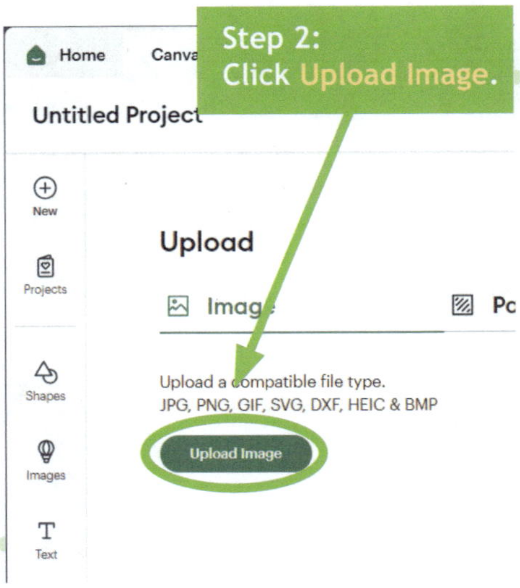

Step 3:
Click Browse.

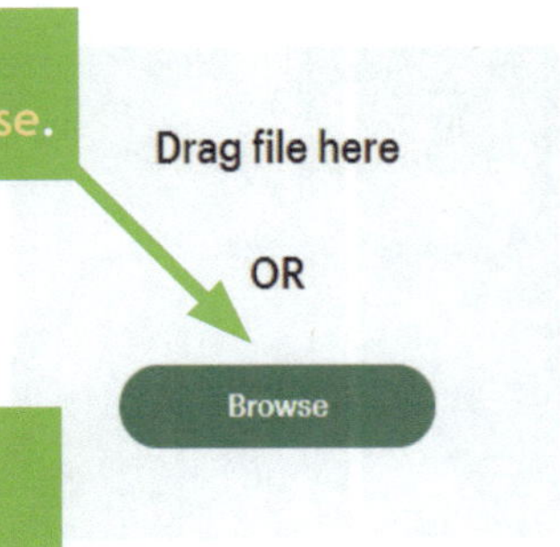

Step 4:
Select the SVG File and double-click to open.

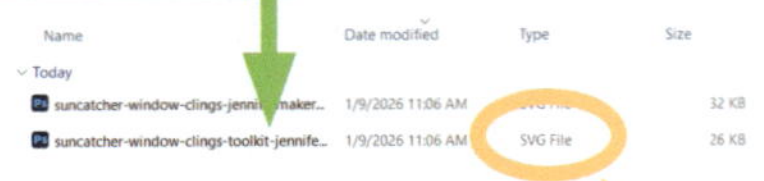

Step 5:
Click Continue.

Notes: Be sure you select the SVG file, not the ZIP file. You can tell it is the SVG file because its "Type" is listed as "SVG Document" in your file browser (it may say "Chrome HTML" or "Edge HTML" instead). If you only see the ZIP file, you'll need to first decompress the ZIP file (open it) by double-clicking it in Windows Explorer.

You have selected an unsupported file type.

Step 6: Give your SVG file a name, add it to a collection if needed, then click Upload.

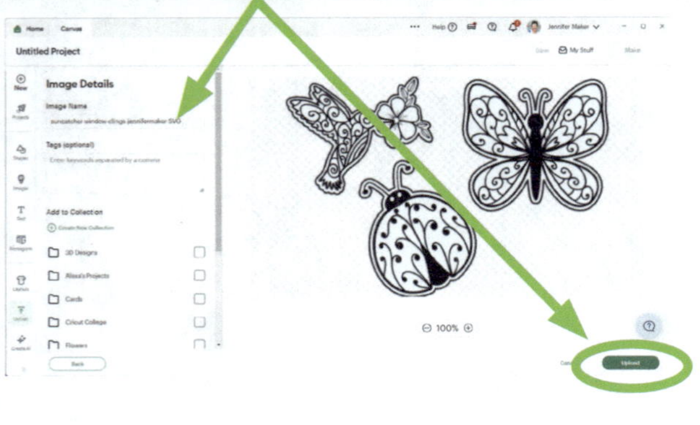

Once inserted, your image appears on your Canvas, ready to be modified or made!

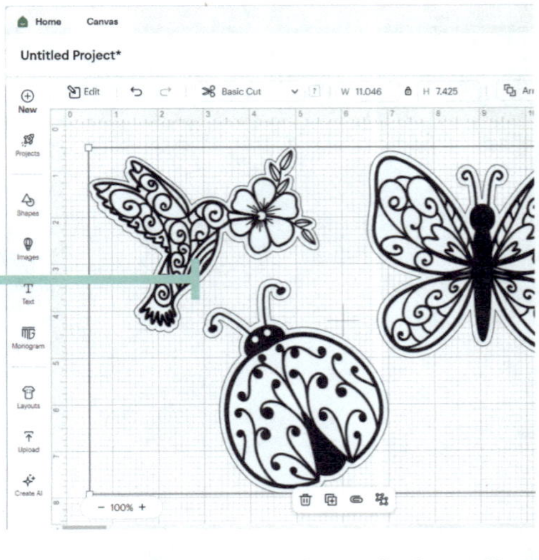

Practice this at jennifermaker.com/suncatcher-window-clings

HOW TO RESIZE A PROJECT

Have you ever uploaded an SVG design, cut it out, and realized it was too small or too big? Here's how to check the size before you cut, and how to resize an entire project:

Step 1: Insert, upload, or create an image on your Canvas, right-click, then click Select All.

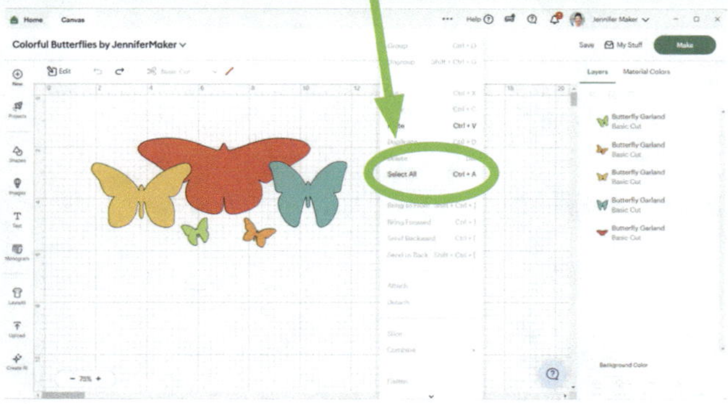

Step 2: Note the size at the top of the window (it also appears above or below the selection itself).

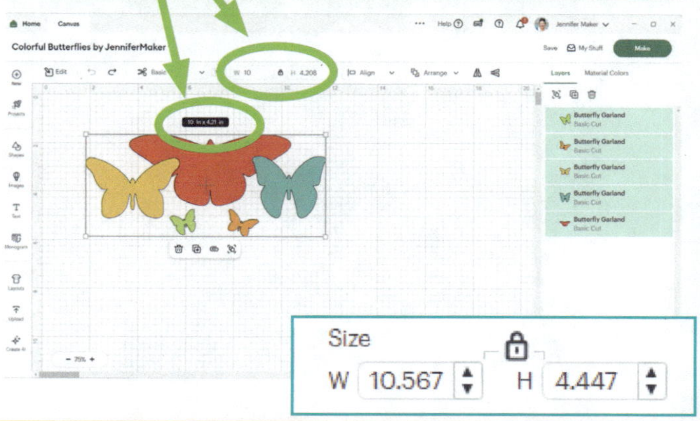

To determine if the sizing is right, compare it to the sizing in the original instructions or tutorial. If no sizing is provided, you'll have to use your best judgment.

Step 3: Be sure the lock icon indicates it is locked, then type the proper size in either the W or H field at the top of the screen.

LOCKED
UNLOCKED

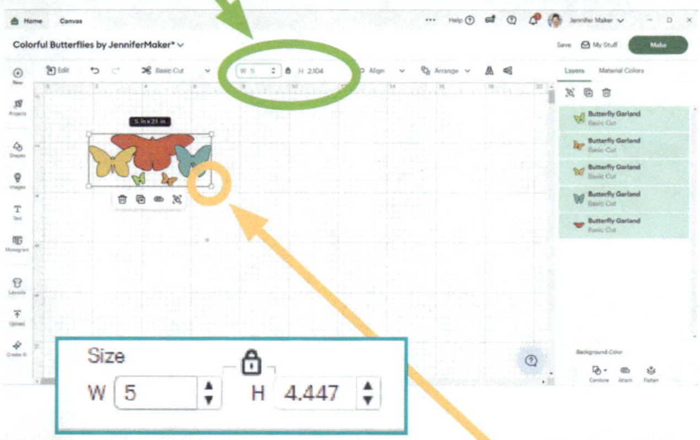

The entire selection is resized and retains its proportions.

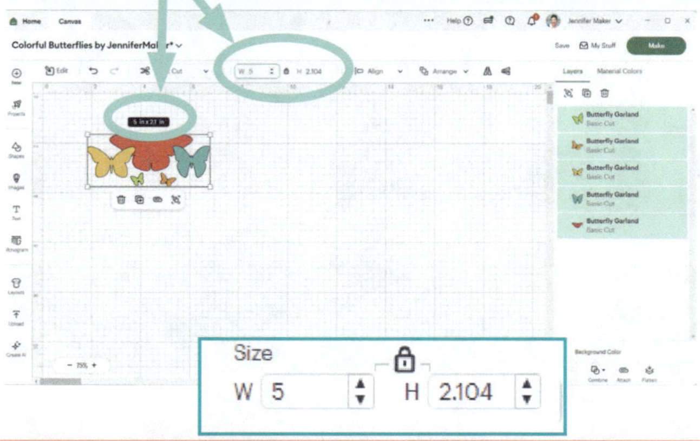

You can also resize images with any corner of the bounding box. Just click, hold, and drag to resize.

Note that Cricut Design Space has been known to automatically resize some SVG files that measure over 12″ (either wide or high) down to 12″ on their longest side, without notification. So if you place an image on your Canvas and notice that one side measures exactly 12," that is a strong indicator that your image has been resized. To learn how to fix this, visit jennifermaker.com/resize-svg.

Practice this at jennifermaker.com/butterflies

HOW TO USE CREATE AI

Create AI is a feature in Design Space that lets you describe what you want, and Cricut will generate original art for you. Here's how to use it:

Step 1: Open a Blank Canvas and click Create AI in the menu on the left side of the screen.

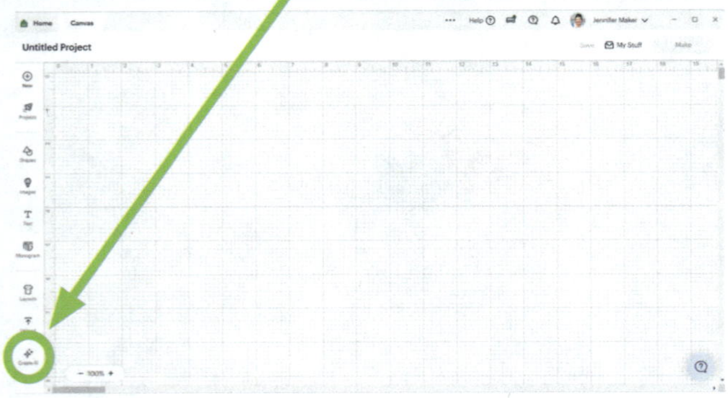

Step 2: In the panel, describe the image you want to create. Be clear and specific!

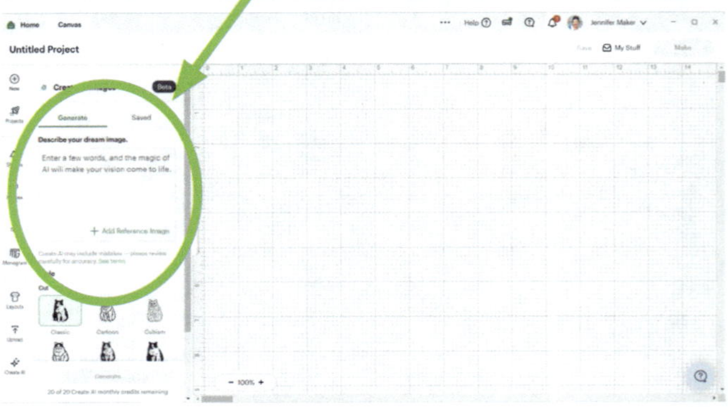

Step 3: Choose the style of image you want and click Generate.

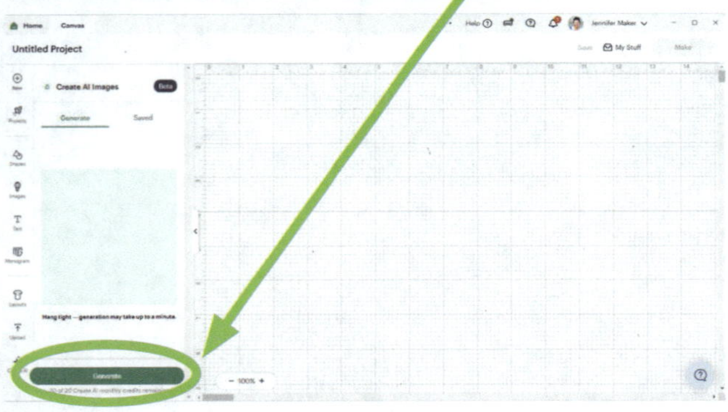

Step 4: Wait for your image to generate. When the image is ready, it will appear in the panel.

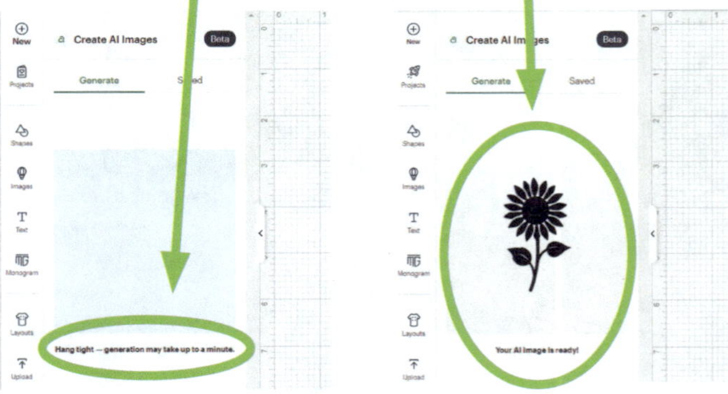

Step 5: Click on the new AI image to add it to your canvas and edit your image.

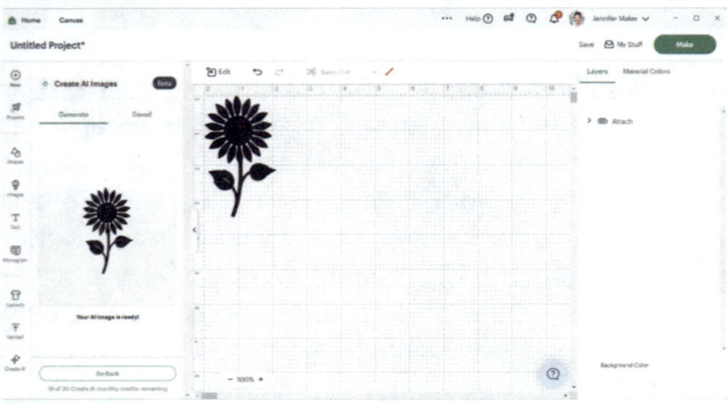

All images generated by Create AI, can be found under Saved in the Create AI Images panel.

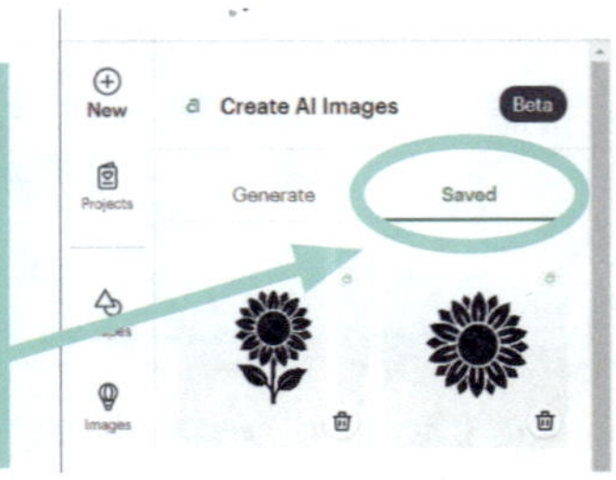

Note: The Create AI tool is currently only a feature for Cricut Access members, who receive 20 AI credits each month to generate new designs.

CREATE AI

HOW TO FOLLOW SOMEONE IN DESIGN SPACE

You can follow your friends and other Cricut crafters in Design Space, and even get notifications on their new projects! Here's how to follow someone and how to set your notification settings:

Step 1: Open Cricut Design Space and type their name into the search bar, and press Enter.

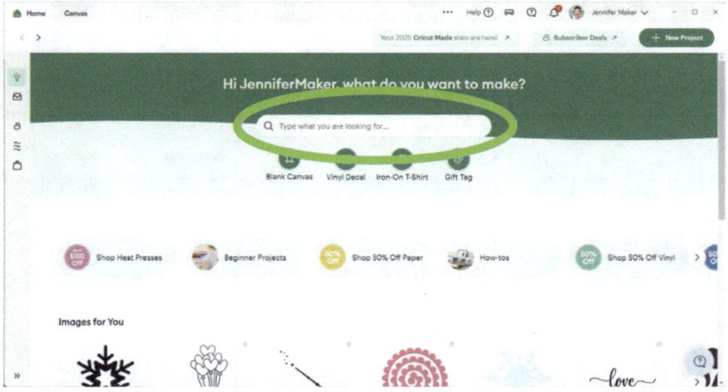

Step 2: On the page that appears, scroll down to the bottom and find their profile. Click on it.

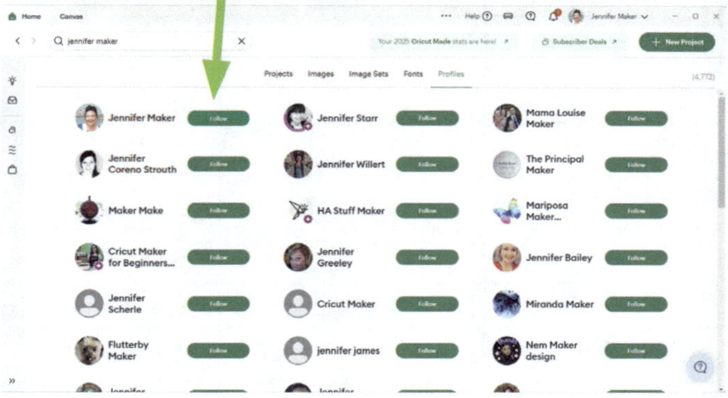

Step 3: Click the green Follow button. This is also where you'll see any projects they are sharing!

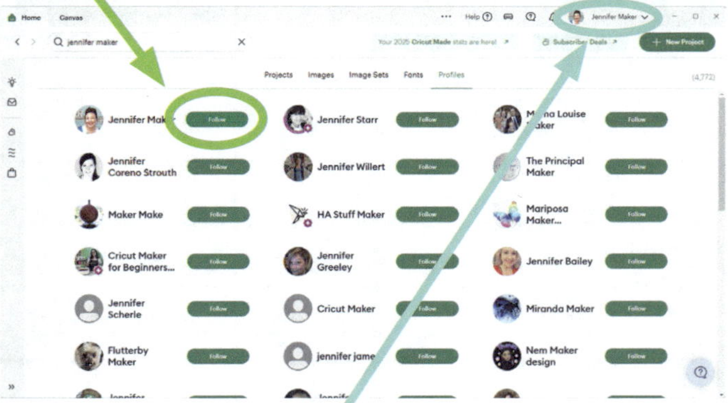

When the person(s) you're following shares a project, you're notified here! Click the notification to view the project.

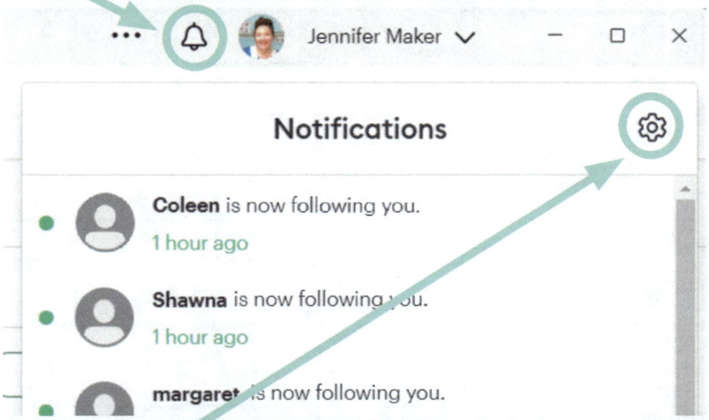

To choose what others see about you and your projects, click on your name in the upper right corner, click Profile, and click Edit Profile.

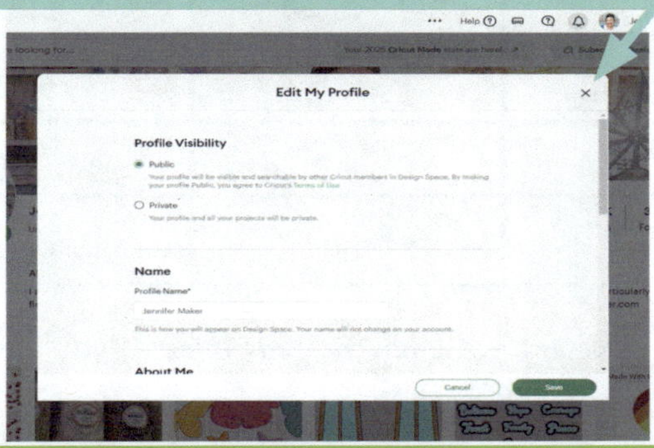

Click the ⚙ icon here to change your notification settings.

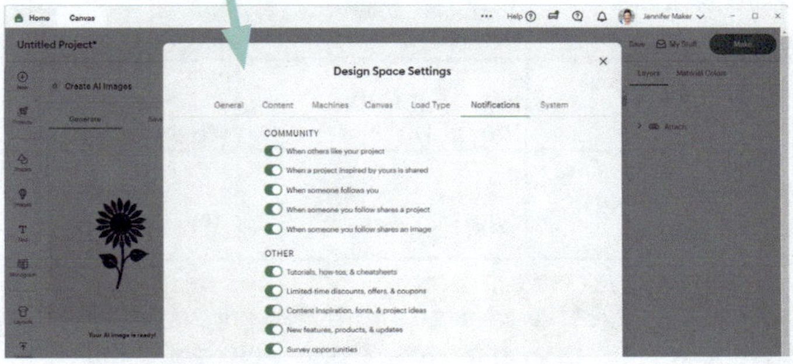

Follow me at jennifermaker.com/follow-me-on-cricut

CRICUT® COACH PLAYBOOK

HOW TO USE KEYBOARD SHORTCUTS

You can do many tasks in Cricut Design Space easier and faster using keyboard and mouse shortcuts. Here is a list of the all of the keyboard and mouse shortcuts on both Mac and Windows:

Function	Mac	Windows
Copy	Command + C	Ctrl + C
Cut	Command + X	Ctrl + X
Delete	Delete	Backspace
Paste	Command + V	Ctrl + V
Select All	Command + A	Ctrl + A
Undo Last Action	Command + Z	Ctrl + Z
Redo Last Action	Command + Shift + Z	Ctrl + Shift + Z
Nudge Right 1/8"	→	→
Nudge Right 1"	Shift + →	Shift + →
Nudge Left 1/8"	←	←
Nudge Left 1"	Shift + ←	Shift + ←
Nudge Up 1/8"	↑	↑
Nudge Up 1"	Shift + ↑	Shift + ↑
Nudge Down 1/8"	↓	↓
Nudge Down 1"	Shift + ↓	Shift + ↓
Move Backward	Command + [	Ctrl + [
Move to Back	Shift + Command + [	Shift + Ctrl + [
Move Forward	Command +]	Ctrl +]
Move to Front	Shift + Command +]	Shift + Ctrl +]
Scroll Screen Up	Mouse Scroll Up	Mouse Wheel Up
Scroll Screen Down	Mouse Scroll Down	Mouse Wheel Down
Scroll Screen Right	Shift + Mouse Scroll Up	Shift + Mouse Scroll Up
Scroll Screen Left	Shift + Mouse Scroll Down	Shift + Mouse Scroll Down
Zoom Canvas In	Command + Mouse Wheel Up	Ctrl + Mouse Wheel Up
Zoom Canvas Out	Command + Mouse Wheel Down	Ctrl + Mouse Wheel Down

Function	Mac	Windows
"Secret" contextual menu	Ctrl + left- click (or just right-click)	Shift + F10 (or right-click)
Move to Next Field	Tab	Tab
Move Back to Previous Field	Shift + Tab	Shift + Tab
Delete	Delete	Backspace
Save Project	Command + S	Ctrl + S
Save As Project	Shift + Command + S	Shift + Ctrl + S
Quit Design Space	Command + Q	Alt + F4
Hide Design Space	Command + H	n/a
Toggle Full Screen	Ctrl + Command + T	Alt + Space + X
Toggle Grid	Shift + G	Shift + G
Duplicate	Command + D	Ctrl + D
Select None	Esc	Esc
Group	Command + G	Ctrl + G
Ungroup	Shift + Command + G	Shift + Ctrl + G
Zoom In	Command + +	Ctrl + +
Zoom Out	Command + -	Ctrl + -
Zoom to 100%	Command + 0	Ctrl + 0
Zoom to Fit	Command + 1	Ctrl + 1
Zoom to Selected Item	Command + 2	Ctrl + 2
Pan Canvas	Space + Drag	Space + Drag
Duplicate + Move	Option + Drag	Alt + Drag

If you're unsure where to find these keys on your keyboard or how to right click on your mouse, you can get a handy guide over at jennifermaker.com/cricut-tricks-keyboard-shortcuts.

HOW TO USE AND MODIFY CUSTOM MATERIAL SETTINGS

You can use and modify settings for MANY materials using the Custom Materials settings in Design Space. Here's how you access and change them:

Step 1: Click your name in the upper right corner and select Settings, then Machines, and finally Start beside Custom Material Settings.

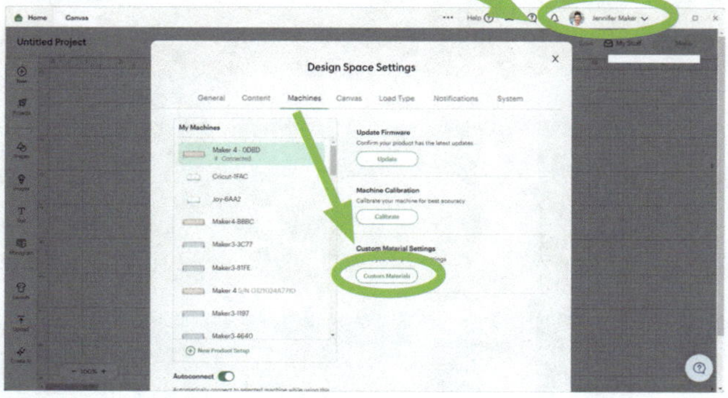

Step 2: If prompted, select your Cricut and click Done. Give it some time to load your settings.

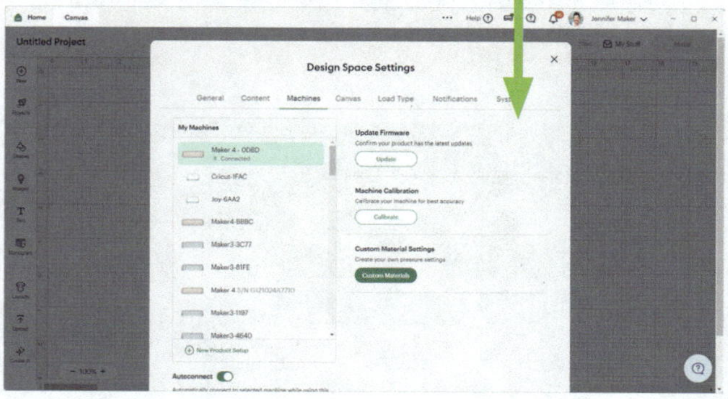

Step 3: Scroll through the list of materials, find one you want to edit, and click the Edit button next to it.

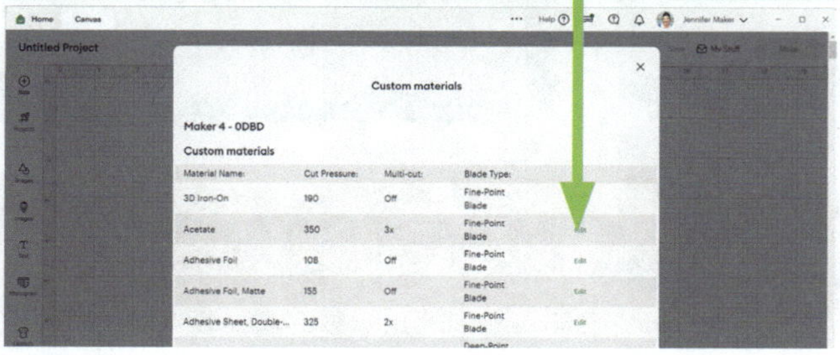

Step 4: Change your settings as needed. Usually, I just increase the pressure with the slider. When done, click Save.

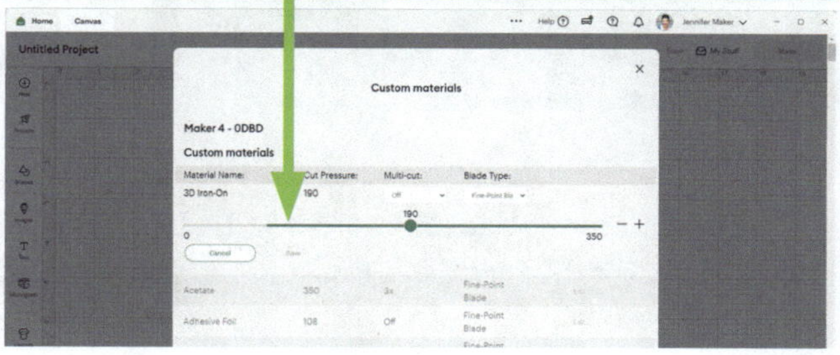

Step 5: If you want to create an entirely new custom material, click Add New Material, enter settings, and click Save. Then click Done. You may need to experiment to get it just right.

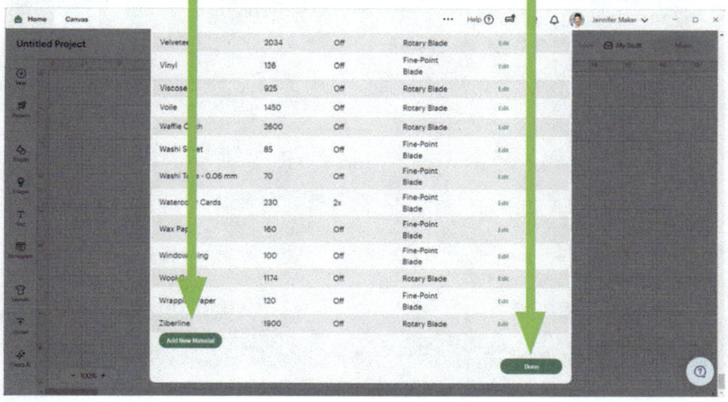

Step 6: Explore One, Air, and Air 2 machine owners must set their dial to Custom (Joy, Explore 3, and Makers are on Custom by default), and then you can choose your custom material before you cut out your project.

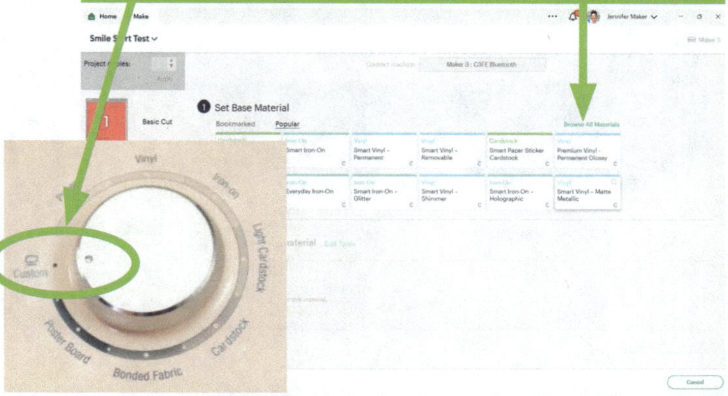

Desktop

UPDATE APP (MAC)

HOW TO GET NEW UPDATES ON MAC

Cricut Design Space updates often and changes are rolled out to groups of users in phases rather than all at once to make sure the updates go smoothly. Updates may happen automatically upon launching the app, or if the app is open when the update is detected, you will be prompted to update your application—if this happens, save your work and accept the update.

If you are ever unsure if you have the latest version of the app, go to the Release Notes at jennifermaker.com/cricut-release-notes, check the latest version, and compare it to yours. Here's how you can download the latest version of the Cricut app:

Step 1: Download the installer at design.cricut.com

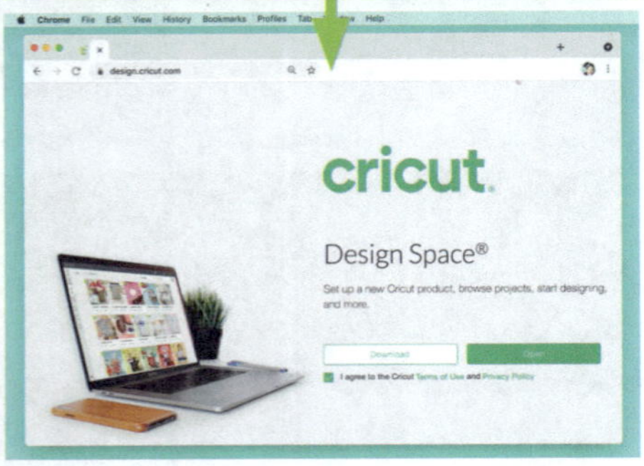

Step 2: Open the downloaded file and drag (click, hold, & move) the Cricut icon over the folder, then let go of the mouse.

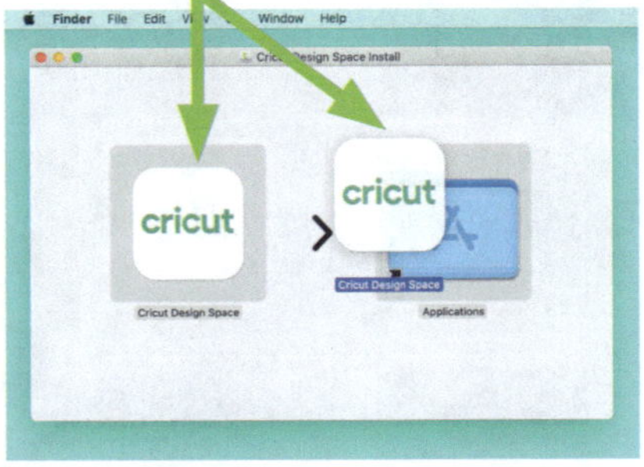

Step 3: Click Replace when you are asked if you want to replace it with the one you are moving.

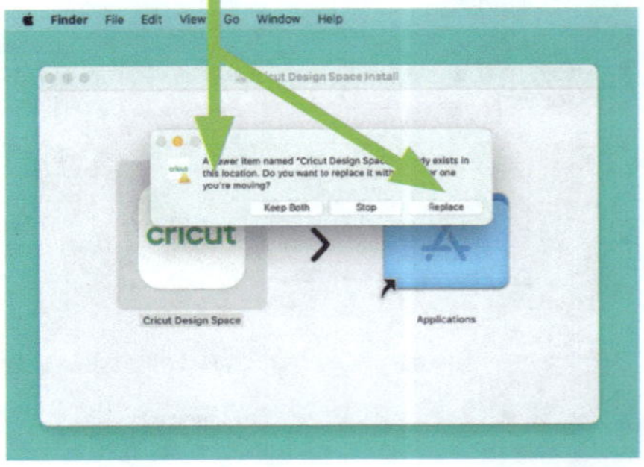

To see what new features are available to you, click the notification bell in the upper right and choose Settings, then General or go to jennifermaker.com/cricut-release-notes.

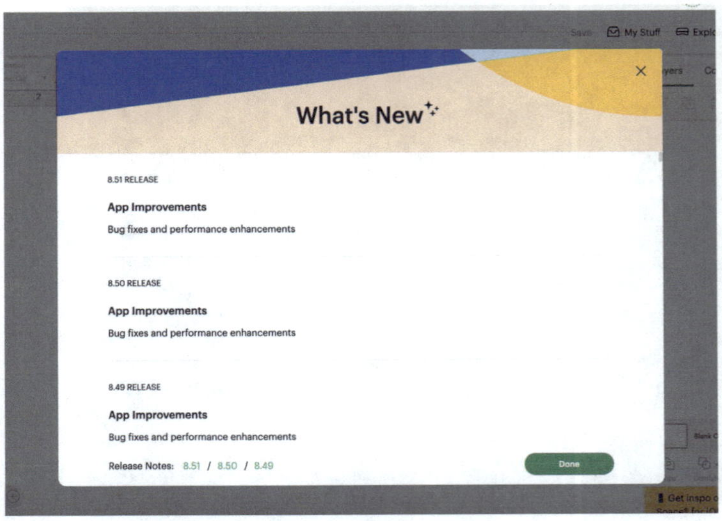

HOW TO GET NEW UPDATES ON PC

Cricut Design Space updates often and changes are rolled out to groups of users in phases rather than all at once to make sure the updates go smoothly. Updates may happen automatically upon launching the app, or if the app is open when the update is detected, you will be prompted to update your application—if this happens, save your work and accept the update.

If you are ever unsure if you have the latest version of the app, go to the Release Notes at jennifermaker.com/cricut-release-notes, check the latest version, and compare it to yours. Here's how you can download the latest version of the Cricut app:

Tip: To check the version, hover over the Design Space icon in the Taskbar when it's running.

Version 9.11.69

Step 1: Download the installer at design.cricut.com

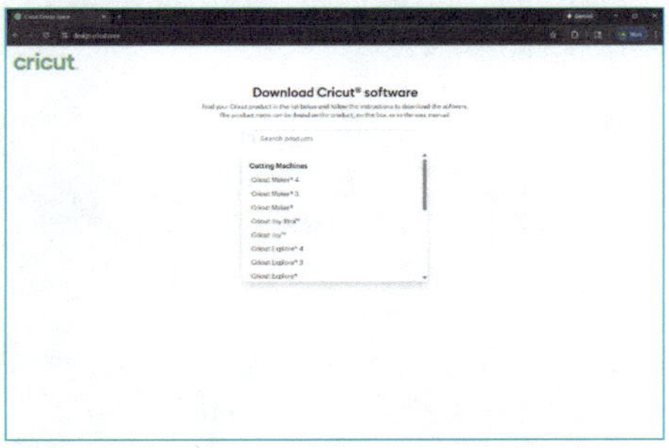

Step 2: Open the downloaded file to install it and give it time to install. It is fine to replace it if you are asked.

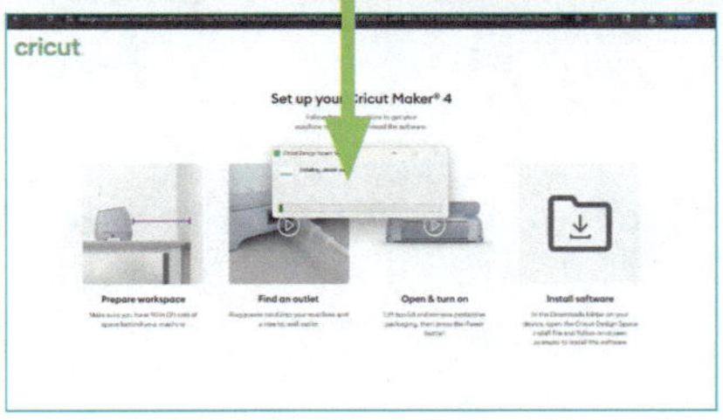

Step 3: Open the updated Design Space. You will not lose access to any of your images or fonts.

To see what new features are available to you, click your name in the upper right and choose Settings. Under About Design Space, click What's New or go to jennifermaker.com/cricut-release-notes.

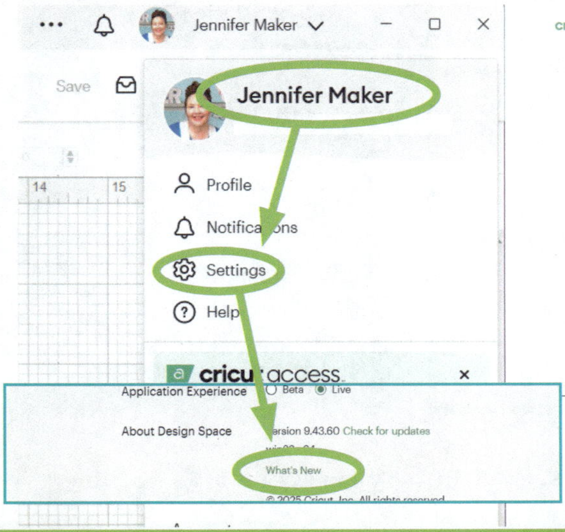

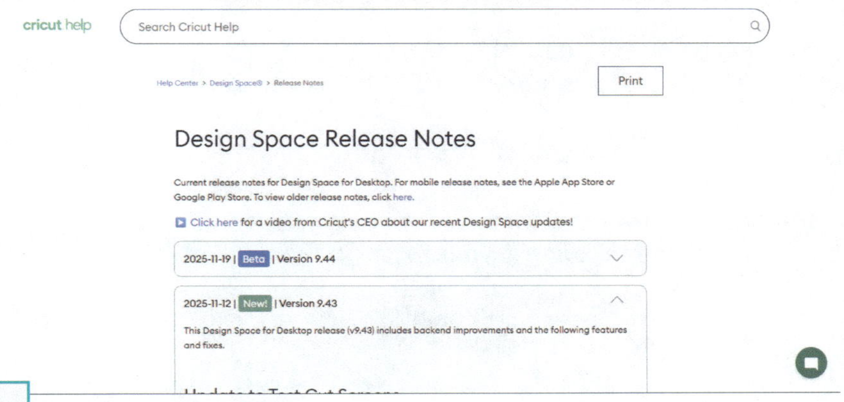

HOW TO TROUBLESHOOT DESIGN SPACE PROBLEMS

Your ability and willingness to troubleshoot problems is a high factor in your success with your Cricut (and really, most things in life). Problems happen, but you CAN solve them. Here are the steps I take when I encounter problems with Cricut Design Space:

Cricut Design Space is acting weird or not working at all.

Is it down?
- Yes → Watch for it to come back.
  - **Still having problems?**
    - Yes → Do you have a strong Internet connection?
    - No → Have fun and make something awesome!
- No → Have fun and make something awesome!

Is it installed and up-to-date?
- Yes → Restart your computer.
- No → Have fun and make something awesome!

Are you still having problems?
- Yes → Do you have a strong Internet connection?
- No → Have fun and make something awesome!

Do you have a strong Internet connection?
- Yes → Keep the Design Space app active and don't move away while cutting.
  - **Are you still having problems?** → Close any other applications running on your computer.
- No → Connect to Internet & move your Cricut and computer closer to router.
  - **Still having problems?**
    - Yes → Close any other applications running on your computer.
    - No → Have fun and make something awesome!

Close any other applications running on your computer.

Are you still having problems?
- Yes → Make sure your Cricut is actually connected via USB or Bluetooth.
- No → Have fun and make something awesome!

Are you still having problems?
- Yes → Disconnect your Cricut, restart your computer, and reconnect your Cricut.
- No → Have fun and make something awesome!

Are you still having problems?
- Yes → Contact Cricut Member Care at help.cricut.com. Cricut Member Care is very helpful!
- No → Have fun and make something awesome!

Have fun and make something awesome!

Contact Cricut Member Care at help.cricut.com. Cricut Member Care is very helpful!

Having different problems? Here are more solutions:

Machine problems:
Check the Cricut site at help.cricut.com

Cutting problems:
Check my ideas at jennifermaker.com/cricut-cutting-problems-tips-cleaner-cuts

Mat problems:
Check my mat tips at jennifermaker.com/cricut-cutting-mats-sticky

Blade problems:
Check my blade tips at jennifermaker.com/cricut-blades-cutting-tips

HOW TO INSTALL CRICUT DESIGN SPACE

Step 1: Connect your iPhone or iPad to the Internet through WiFi or Cellular Data and tap the App Store icon on your iPhone or iPad.

Step 2: Tap the Search icon and type in Cricut, then tap Cricut Design Space.

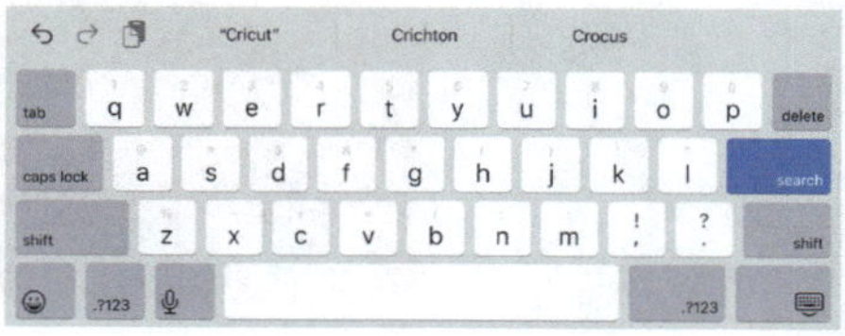

Step 3: Tap Get to download and install Cricut Design Space. It will start installing.

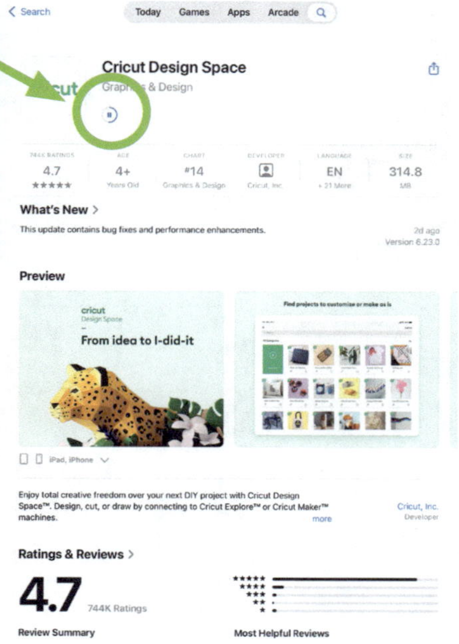

If you already have Cricut Design Space installed, you'll see a blue Open button to tap.

Step 4: When prompted, sign in with your Cricut account email and password.

HOW TO OPEN AND START A NEW PROJECT

Step 1: Tap the Design Space icon on your device.

Step 2: Sign in and tap the + button. Then tap Blank Canvas.

Step 3: If you see this message, it means you left something on your Canvas the last time you used the app. So either tap Keep Previous (if you want to see what you left there) or tap Replace for a new, blank Canvas.

You will get a new Canvas, ready for you to add images, shapes, text, and projects!

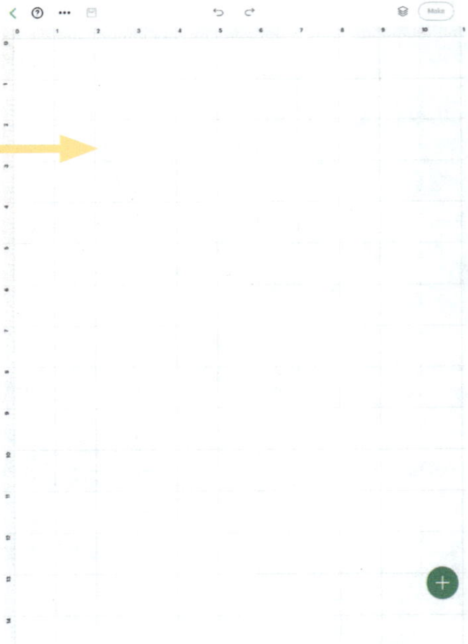

Note: If you don't see any of your saved projects, it may be because you're not signed in. You can get signed out when you update your app, too!

HOW TO CONNECT IOS TO CRICUT VIA BLUETOOTH

Step 1: Tap the Settings app.

Step 2: Tap Bluetooth.

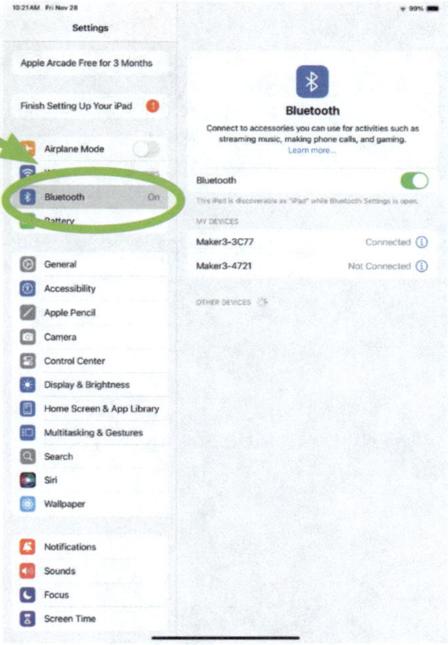

Note: Your Cricut must be within 10-15 feet of your device. If you need to use a Wireless Bluetooth Adapter, make sure it is inserted.

Step 3: Turn on Bluetooth if it is off. Look for your Cricut device in this list and tap on it. If you do not see it listed, make sure your Cricut is turned on and no other Bluetooth device is connected to it.

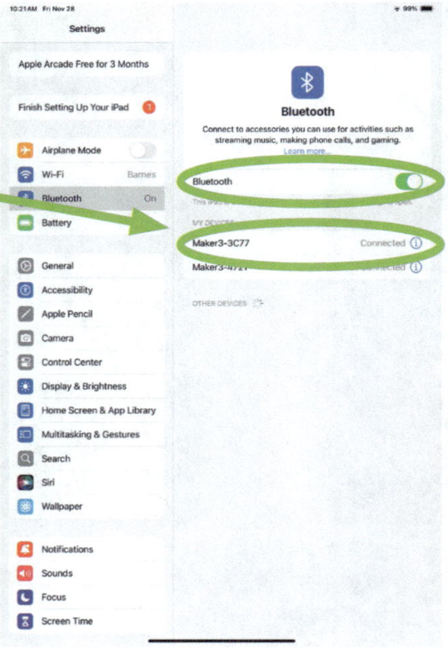

Step 4: If you get a pairing request, type 0000 (that's four zeros) as the passcode and tap Pair.

Once connected, you can go to the Cricut Design Space app and send projects to your Cricut machine.

HOW TO REINSTALL THE IOS APP

Does something just not seem right? If so, you may need to delete and reinstall the app to get things back to working order. Here's how to do it:

Step 1: Make sure all of your projects are saved to the Cloud.

Step 2: Go to your Home screen, tap Settings, then tap General.

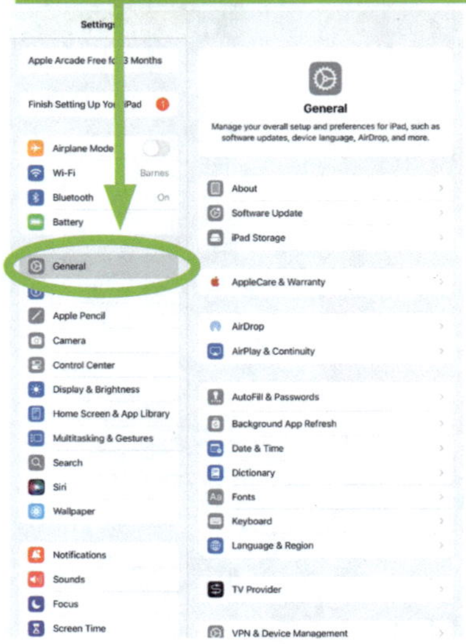

Step 3: Tap iPhone Storage or iPad Storage, based on which device you have.

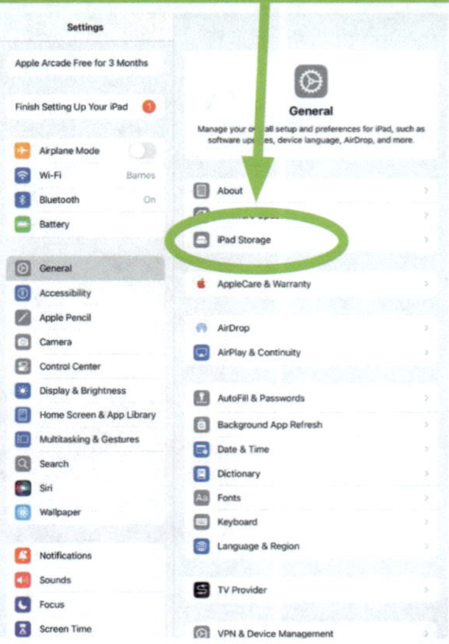

Step 4: Locate the Design Space app and tap it.

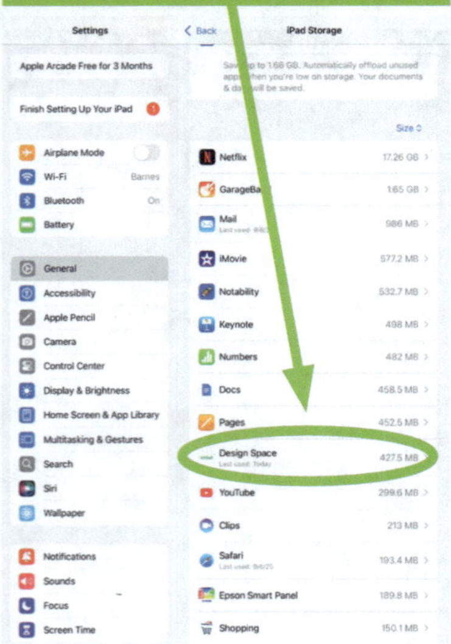

Step 5: Tap Delete App.

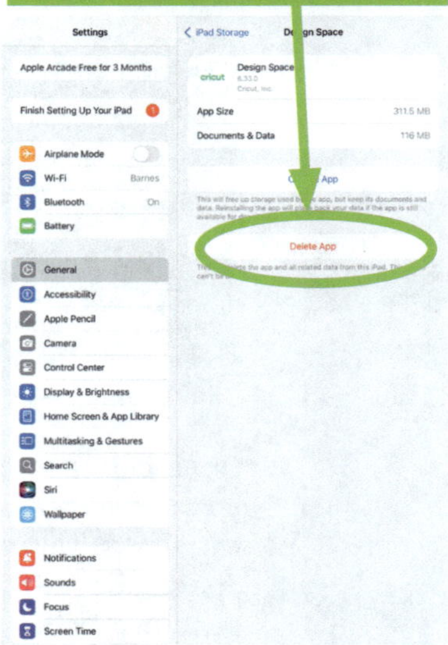

Step 6:
Do a hard reset (force restart) of your iPad or iPhone. This is NOT the same as turning your device on and off. How you do a hard reset depends on your iPhone or iPad model. Get directions on Google or at jennifermaker.com/hardresetiphone or jennifermaker.com/hardresetipad

Step 7:
Tap the App Store icon, search for Cricut Design Space, and tap this icon to download the most recent version.

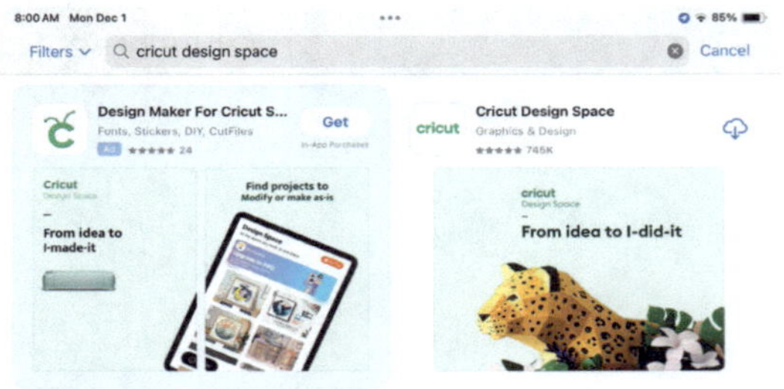

HOW TO ATTACH TO KEEP THINGS TOGETHER

Did you tap Make and find all of your elements re-ordered and out of place? Fix this and keep everything exactly where you want with the ATTACH button. Use Attach to hold your cuts in the same position relative to each other on the cutting mat. The Attach feature also helps you affix a write or score layer to a cut layer.

Step 1: Add all of your elements to the Cricut Design Space app on your iOS device, including text, SVG designs, score lines, write lines, etc.

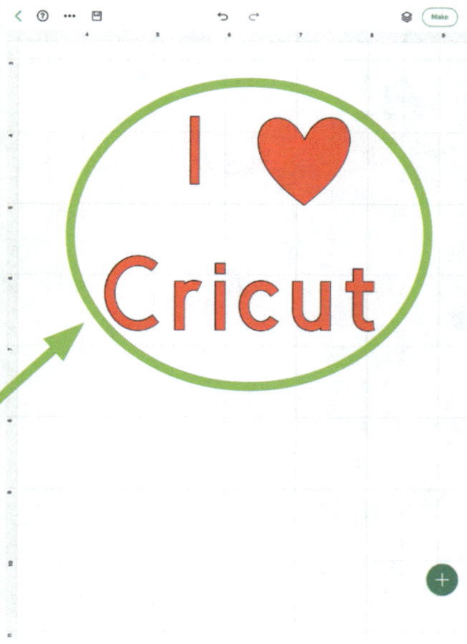

Step 2: Tap and drag a selection box around all of the images you want to attach together, tap on Actions at the bottom of the screen, then tap Attach.

Note that attached layers will take on the same color. So only attach layers that you really want to be the same color!

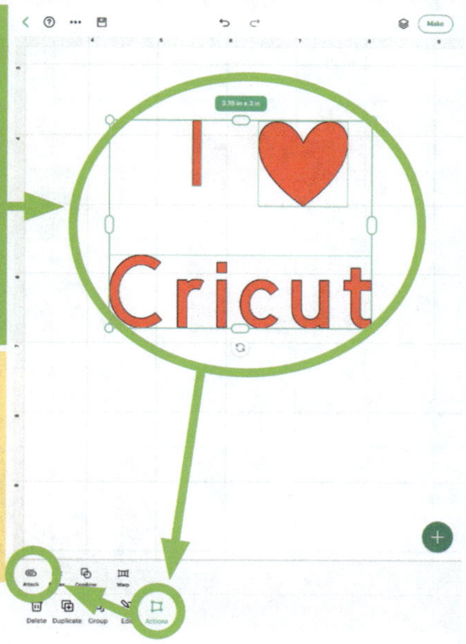

You can verify that your images are attached by tapping "Layers" and noting that they are now labeled "Attach."

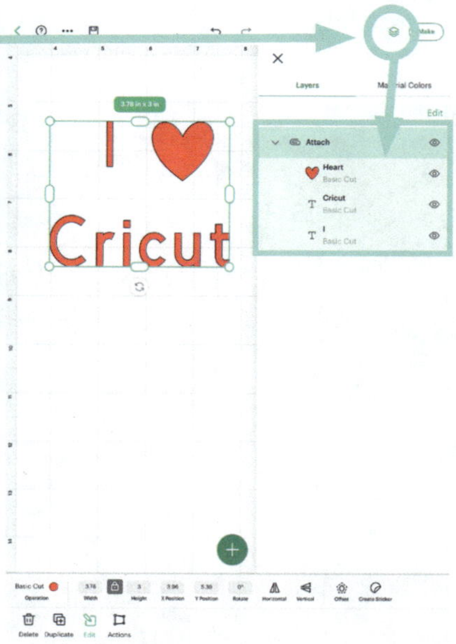

Score lines must be attached with the appropriate "Basic Cut" layer in order for them to score on the right layer, as shown to the right.

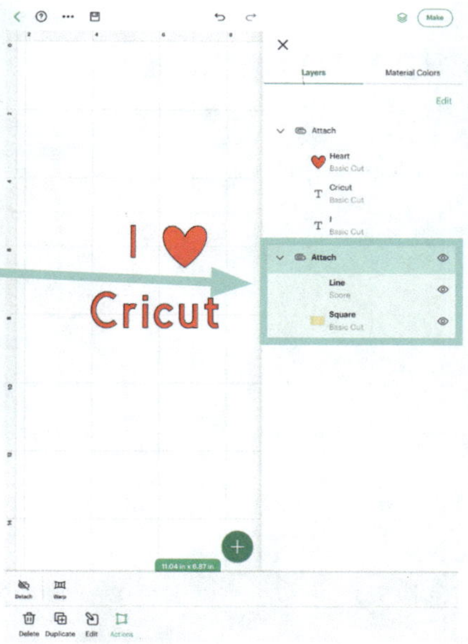

Note: If you are having a problem attaching layers, try ungrouping layers first.

Practice this at jennifermaker.com/i-love-cricut

HOW TO GROUP AND UNGROUP

Grouping lets you keep objects together in your design but not necessarily on your mat (you still need to use the Attach function to keep things together on the mat). Sometimes projects and uploaded images will be grouped when you open/insert them, and you'll need to ungroup them so you can make changes.

HOW TO GROUP:

Step 1: Tap Layers and select each layer you want to group together. You can also tap and drag a box to select objects.

Step 2: With all objects you want to be in a group selected (layers are highlighted when selected), tap the Group button.

Group

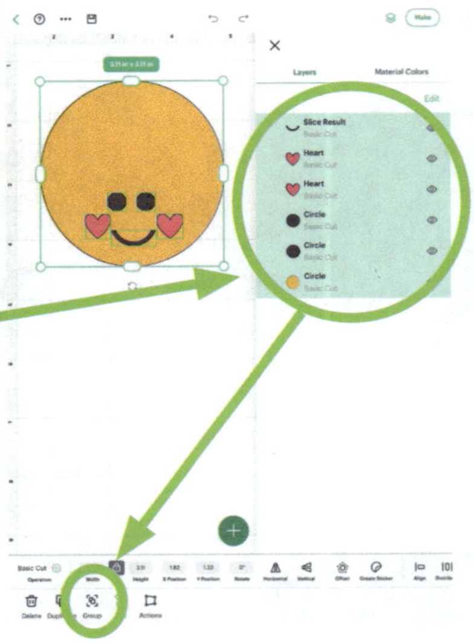

Tip: Once your objects group, they will be nested under a new line item in your Layers Panel called "Group." Group

HOW TO UNGROUP:

Option 1: To ungroup, tap the grouped item and tap Ungroup. Double check that you have the right layers selected and click Ungroup.

Ungroup

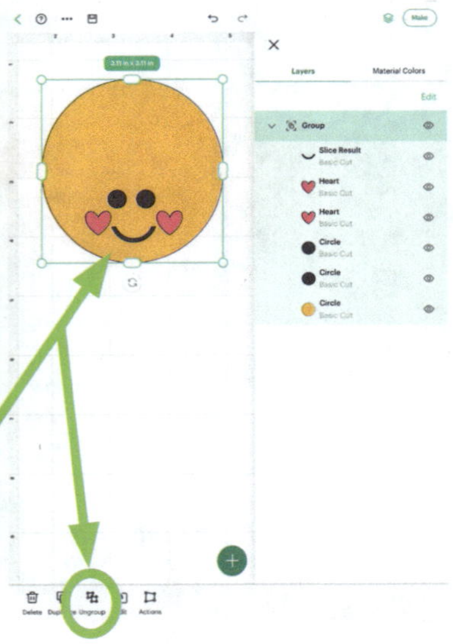

Option 2: Tap the layer titled Group in the Layers Panel to select it, then tap the Ungroup button.

Ungroup

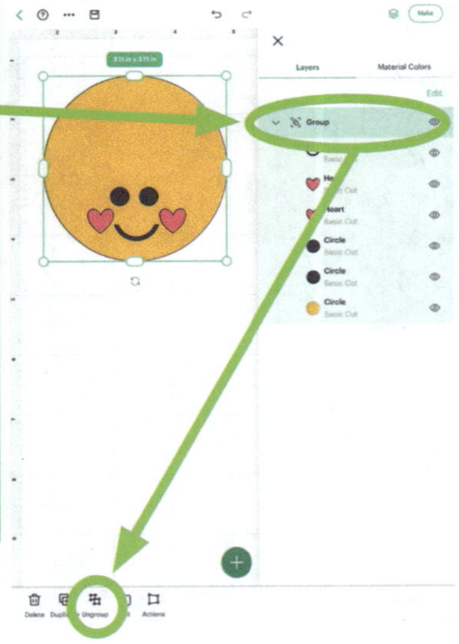

You often need to ungroup before you can attach objects. Sometimes, a project or image set has multiple groups. So if you want to attach and have an issue, look for ALL groups and ungroup them first.

Practice this at jennifermaker.com/smiley-face

iOS

HOW TO WELD (MAKE NEW SHAPES)

Need to join elements to create a new image? Do it with the Weld tool! The Weld tool can simplify a design, keep the letters of a word connected, and combine shapes to create new designs.

Step 1: Upload any images you want to weld onto your Canvas.

Note: If you are trying to create a single image with Weld, make sure all elements are overlapping.

Step 2: Tap and drag a selection box around all of the images you want to weld together, tap on Actions at the bottom of the screen, then tap Combine.

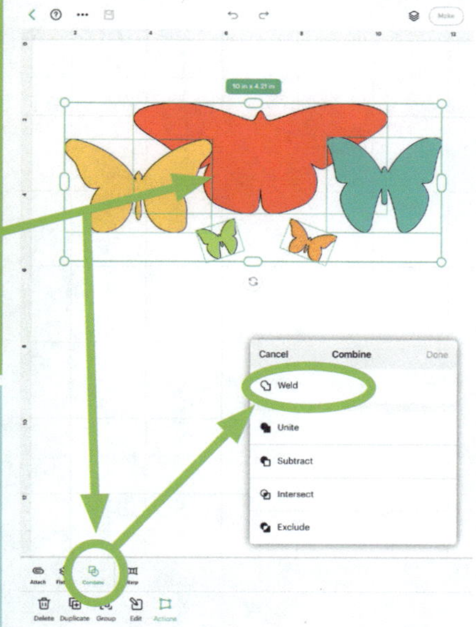

Tip: You can select items within groups to weld by tapping on their names in the Layers Panel.

Step 3: Once you are in the Combine window, select the Weld option. This will now show as one layer in the Layers Panel.

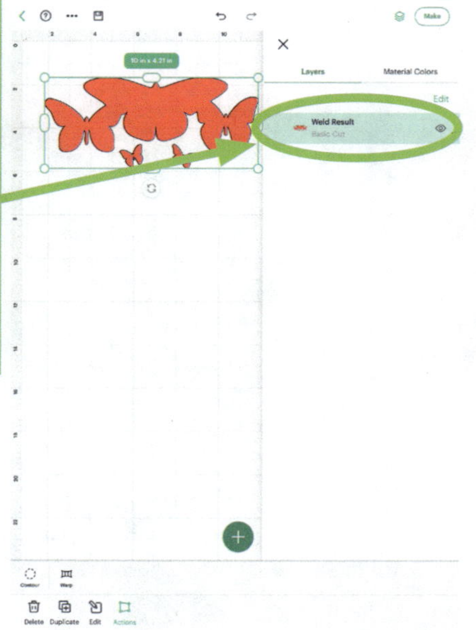

Note: You can unweld ONLY if it is the current project on your Canvas and you recently welded it. If so, tap Undo until you unweld the image(s).

WELD

Practice this at jennifermaker.com/butterflies

HOW TO UNION, SUBTRACT, INTERSECT & EXCLUDE

Need to join elements to create an image? These tools are similar to what can be found when you select Combine. The Union tool is similar to Weld (previous page) but it is not permanent. Your layers will still be accessible individually. Subtract is similar to Slice (next page) but it does not leave you with remaining pieces; it subtracts the bottom layer and top layer. Intersect takes two overlapping layers and combines them, leaving only the parts that intersect. Exclude is the opposite of intersect; it takes two overlapping layers and cuts what overlapped, leaving behind what did not overlap.

Step 1: Upload your images onto your Canvas and reposition so they are overlapping.

UNION: Select your images and tap Actions > Combine > Unite. This action combines the items together.

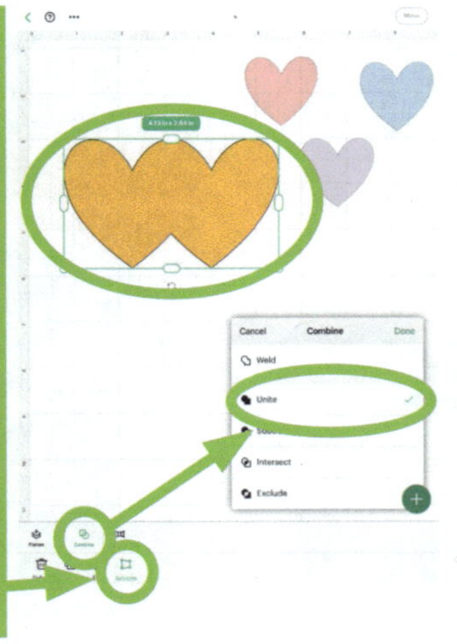

SUBTRACT: Select your images and tap Actions > Combine > Subtract. This action subtracts the two layers from each other.

INTERSECT: Select your images and tap Actions > Combine > Intersect. This action leaves only the pieces that overlap.

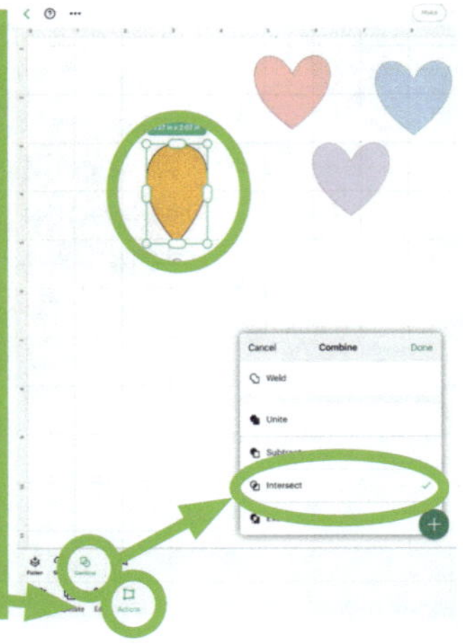

EXCLUDE: Select your images and tap Actions > Combine > Exclude. This action removes the parts that intersected between the two images.

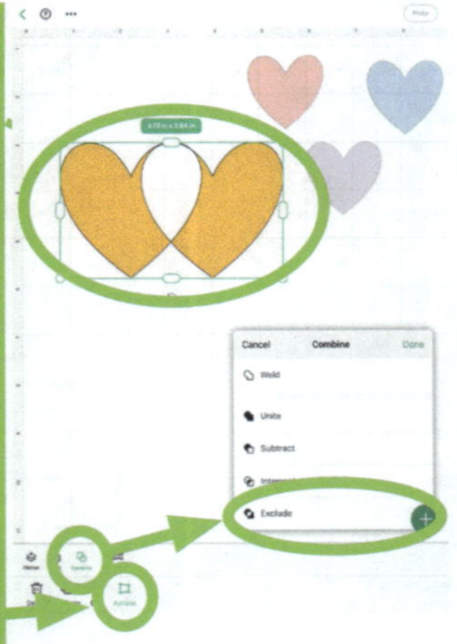

Tip: If you don't like how the action operated on your images, press the undo button and try a different one!

Practice this at jennifermaker.com/five-hearts

iOS

HOW TO SLICE (CUT AN IMAGE OUT OF ANOTHER)

SLICE

Want to cut out parts or even make your own custom designs? If so, Slice is the tool for you! Slice lets you cut out parts of another object. If you keep slicing, you can make some pretty amazing designs!

Step 1: Upload your images onto your Canvas and reposition so they are overlapping.

Step 2: Tap the Layers icon to open the Layers Panel.

Step 3: Select the layers you want to Slice (tap each layer to select both).

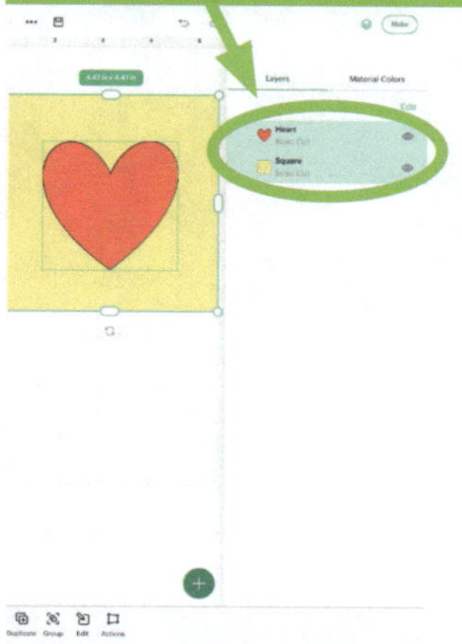

Step 4:
Exit the Layers Panel. Then tap Actions, then tap Slice.

Three layers called "Slice Result" will appear in your Layers Panel.

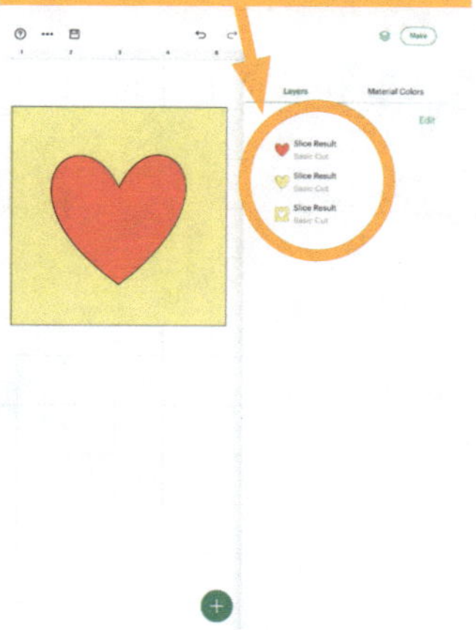

Step 5: Move, hide, or delete the layers you do not want, then you're good to go!

Things to Know about Slicing:

- You can Slice both images and text.
- You can only Slice with two layers. If you have multiple images you want to Slice out of another, use the Weld tool on the multiple images first.
- Layers in groups can be Sliced if you select just the individual layers, not the entire groups.
- If you use Slice with hidden layers, all hidden layers will be removed.
- If text is multi-layered and one layer is hidden, you can use the Slice tool. However, if you ungroup text from its shadow layer, it becomes an image and will no longer work with the Slice tool unless the text is ungrouped to individual letters.

Practice this at jennifermaker.com/heart-slice

HOW TO REMOVE PARTS WITH CONTOUR

Need to erase parts of an existing design? Don't want that word or that circle, but can't ungroup or hide a layer? Use Contour to remove existing parts from projects.

Step 1: Choose an image with elements that you'd like to remove, then tap Actions, then tap the Contour tool in the lower app window.

Step 2: Tap on the elements you want to remove. Elements that appear darker are those that you'll keep. If you hid everything and want to revert to the original, tap Show All.

The Contour tool is a great way to modify pre-existing designs to meet your personal needs!

Step 3: When your image looks the way you want it to, tap the Done icon again in the upper right hand corner to return to your Canvas.

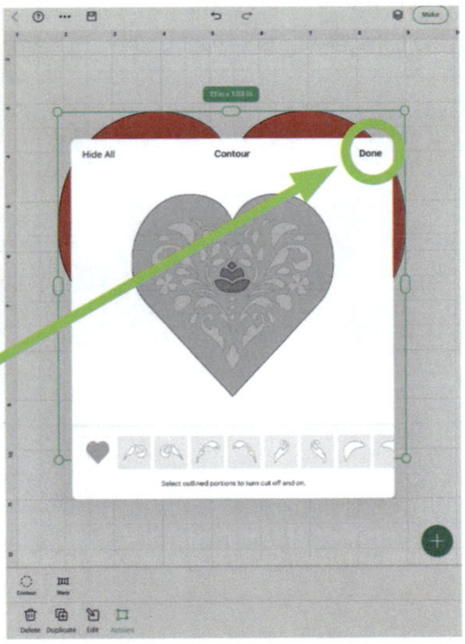

Step 4: Confirm that your image looks the way you want it to look. If you need to make more changes, just tap the Contour tool again.

Note: Contour isn't permanent so long as you don't Weld your images! If you decide later you want a Contoured image to go back the way it was, or to simply edit it further, all the hidden parts are retained!

Practice this at jennifermaker.com/svg-heart

iOS

HOW TO CURVE TEXT

Step 1: Tap the + (green circle), then tap Text. Add some text, or double-tap existing text on your Canvas.

Step 2: Tap on the text and tap Edit, and then tap Curve.

Step 3: Slide the slider to the right for a downward curve. The more you slide, the tighter the curve. To curve your text upward, slide the slider to the left. Tap Done to apply your changes.

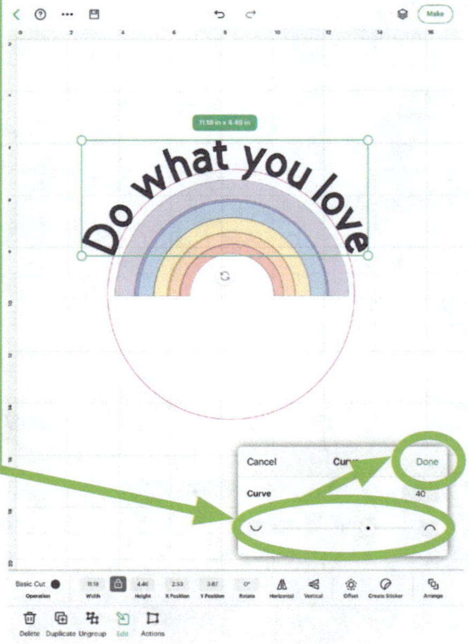

Tip: You can change the font, color, size, line spacing, etc. at any time (so long as you don't flatten or weld it) thanks to this curve text feature!

Practice this at jennifermaker.com/rainbow-love-ios

iOS

HOW TO WARP TEXT, SHAPES AND IMAGES

WARP TEXT

Step 1: Select the + (green circle), then tap Shape. Add a rectangle to the Canvas, drag a corner of its bounding box it to make it wider.

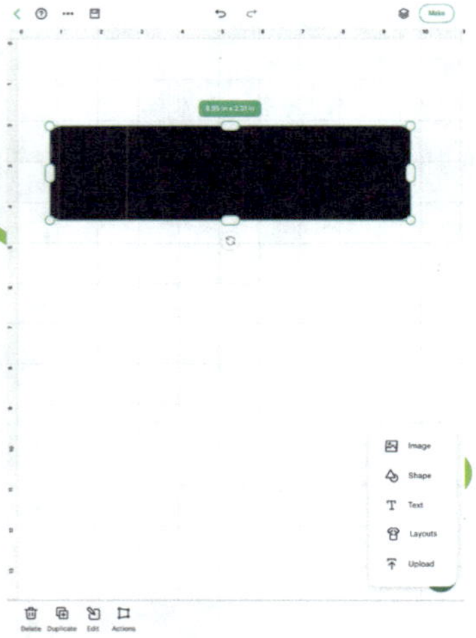

Step 2: Select the + (green circle), then tap Text. Type some text on the Canvas.

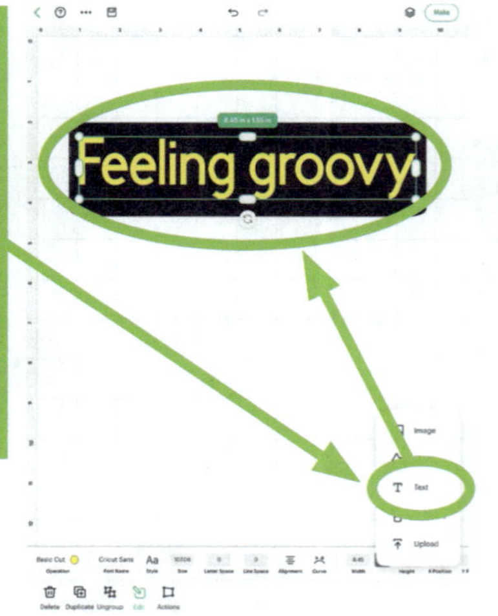

Step 3: With your shape and text selected, tap Actions then the Warp button.

Step 4: Choose a warp style. You can also choose how much you want the warp effect by sliding the bar or using the number box at the bottom of the screen.

Step 5: Your text and shape will change to the warp style you chose!

Tip: If you decide that you want to use a different warp style other than the one you originally selected, just select your text or shape, click the Warp button again, and choose a new style.

Warning: There are some fonts that cannot be warped, as well as Print Then Cut images. Design Space will notify you about it if you try to warp a font or image that cannot be warped.

Warning: Warp is currently only a feature for Cricut Access members.

iOS

HOW TO ALIGN AND DISTRIBUTE OBJECTS

Step 1: Add three or more items to your Canvas that you want to align or distribute evenly.

Step 2: Tap and drag a selection box around all items you want to align and/or distribute.

Step 3: Tap on the Edit tool in the bottom toolbar, tap Align, and tap Center Horizontally.

Edit Align

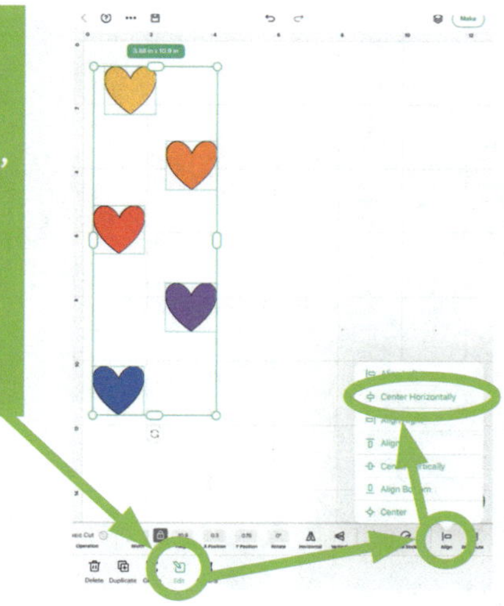

Step 4: All selected items are centered. Now let's space them out evenly.

Step 5: Tap on the Edit tool in the bottom toolbar, tap the Distribute tool, and choose Distribute Vertically.

Edit Distribute

Step 6: Note that all the hearts are now in a perfect row with the same spacing.

Practice this at jennifermaker.com/five-hearts

HOW TO CHANGE LETTER SPACE

Step 1: Tap the + (green circle), then tap Text. Choose a font and type something onto the Canvas. Note how the letters are spaced. Let's fix that.

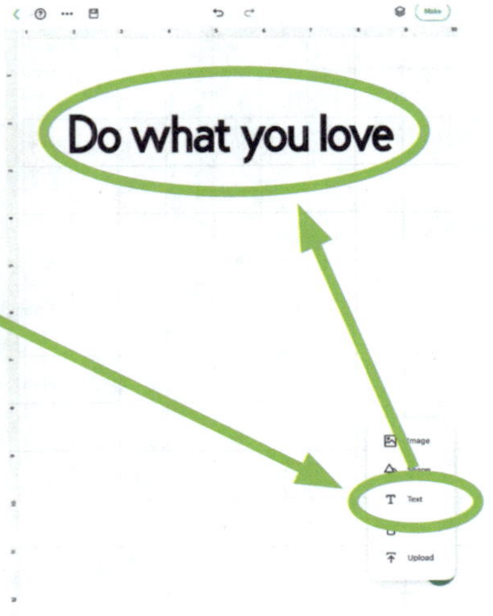

Step 2: Select the text, tap Edit, tap Letter Space, and tap the minus sign until the letters look better.

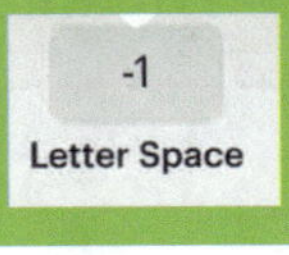

Step 3: The letter "D" is too close to the "o" in the example here. Select the text layer, tap Actions, tap Isolate, then tap Ungroup to Letters.

Step 4: Select just the letter "D" then tap Edit, then tap X Position, and tap the - (minus) symbol to move it to the left. Now these words are properly spaced.

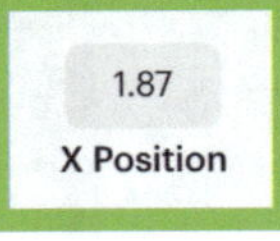

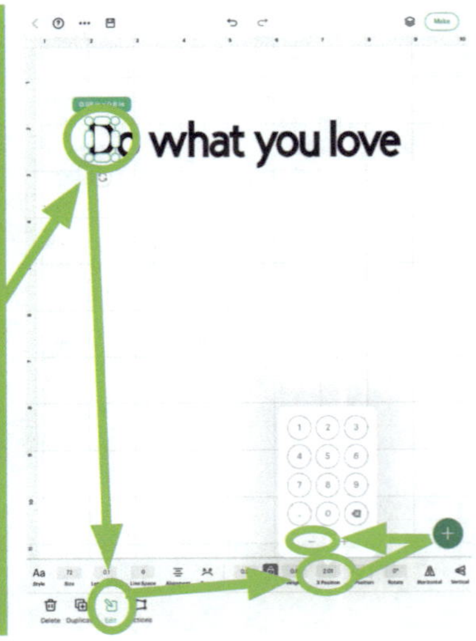

Tip: When you are done adjusting the letter space, select them all and tap Group to keep them together from now on. Tap Attach to cut or draw them together. Tap Weld to stick them together permanently.

Practice this at jennifermaker.com/rainbow-love-ios

iOS

HOW TO WELD TEXT AND KEEP LETTER CENTERS

Welding text can be a little tricky. Typically, you weld script fonts (which can have overlapping letters) so words cut out as single units. Sometimes when you weld, the centers fill in—here's how to fix that:

Step 1: Tap Text, type in script text, change your letter spacing so the letters overlap a bit (see previous page), select all, then tap Actions > Combine > Weld.

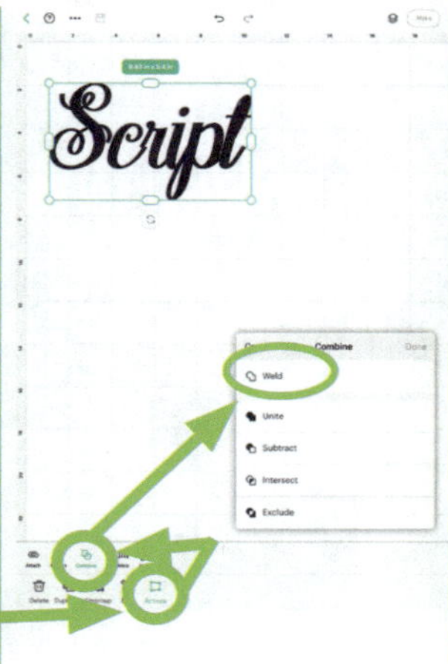

Step 2: If you get a center filling in (like the "p"), tap Undo, then use a corner handle to make your text MUCH larger, then tap Actions > Combine > Weld again.

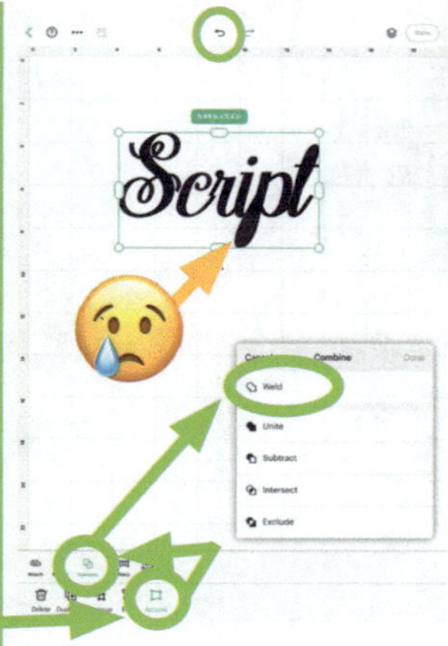

Step 3: Repeat Step 2 until you can weld and the letter center does not fill in, then resize back down to the right size.

Another thing that can happen with text is that letter centers (the interior white space) can disappear when you cut them out. But you can connect the spaces and keep the centers! Here's how to fix that:

Step 1: Tap + (green circle), then tap Text. Type text with letters & numbers with interior white space. Tap + (green circle), then tap Shape. Select a square, Unlock it, and Resize it so it forms a rectangle about the width of the letter's strokes.

Step 2: Drag it over a letter with interior white space so it's connecting the space inside to the space outside.

Step 4: Select the word and the rectangle, then tap Actions > Slice. Delete all layers except the layer with the word in it.

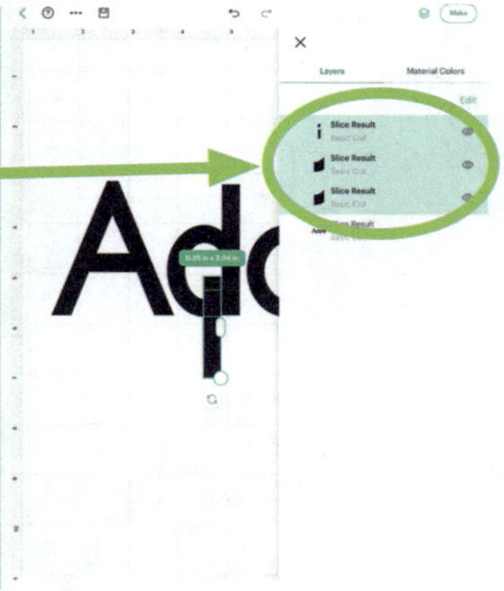

Repeat steps for all letters as needed.

Practice this at jennifermaker.com/script-text and jennifermaker.com/adore-text

iOS

HOW TO OFFSET & KNOCKOUT TEXT

Offsets and knockouts are a popular decorative effect. It's now possible to do them completely in Design Space for iOS. Here's how:

Step 1: Tap + (green circle), tap Text, and type your word in a bold chunky font like Cricut Sans Bold. Unlock, resize to make it taller, and tap Actions > Combine > Weld.

Step 2: Tap + (green circle) and Text again, type an accent word in script font (i.e., I Love Glitter). Adjust letters as needed, unlock, resize, and tap Actions > Combine > Weld.

Step 3: Tap on the accent word layer, tap on Edit, then tap Offset. Slide the distance bar to the right so it's a little larger than your accent word. Tap Done.

Step 4: Select and separate the new offset layer, which is thicker than the accent layer, and drag it on top of the bold word.

Step 5: Select both this bold text layer and the knockout layer (and only those two layers), and tap Actions, then tap Slice. Delete the extra layers.

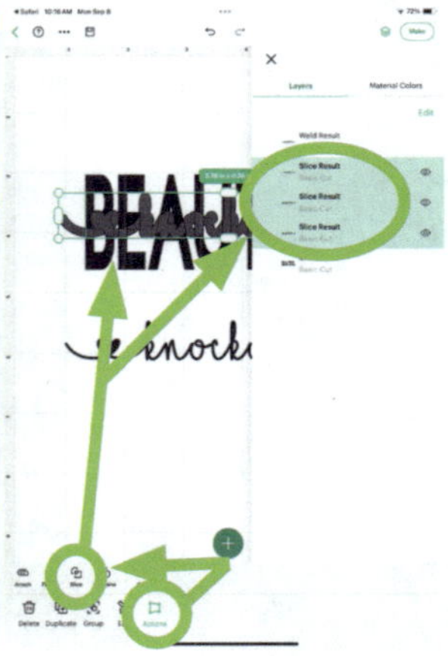

Step 6: The bold word will now have the Offset cut out from it. Drag the accent word inside the empty space Sliced out of the bold word.

Step 7: If desired, change the color of the accent layer (to differentiate it from the bold layer) and tap Make!

Practice this at jennifermaker.com/beautiful-knockout

KNOCKOUT TEXT (iOS)

iOS

HOW TO FIND FONTS

There are many fonts available in Cricut Design Space for iOS! Here's how to find them easier and faster in Cricut Design Space.

Step 1: Open your project (or start a new one), tap on your text to select it (or add new text), tap Edit, then tap Font Name.

Note: If you have text on your Canvas, double-tapping will let you change it.

Step 2: Select a font from the alphabetical list of Cricut fonts to apply it to your text immediately. If you cannot find your font, read the tips below.

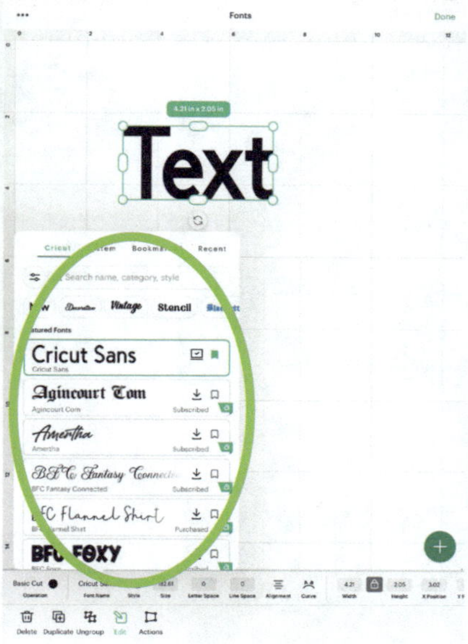

SEARCH: Type in the "Search" box to look for fonts by name. I recommend typing just the first few characters of the font name, as the list will start changing right away.

PREVIEW: A font preview appears here so you can see what it looks like. You're free to select it and see it in your own text on your Canvas without being charged for it.

SEE MORE: If you cannot see the entire alphabet and all of its numbers, tap, hold, and drag it to the right to see more.

ALL FONTS: Tap on "Cricut" to see all Cricut fonts available, or tap on "System" to see only fonts on your iPhone or iPad. By default, only Cricut fonts appear in your list. You can also see fonts that you have bookmarked and fonts you have recently used.

IDENTIFY: Font name, type(s), and price appear in the list. If you see a price, the font must be purchased before you can use it on your Cricut machine. A green "a" symbol indicates that it is a Cricut Access font.

FILTER: Click on the filter icon to further refine your search, such as finding only "Writing" fonts or "Free" fonts.

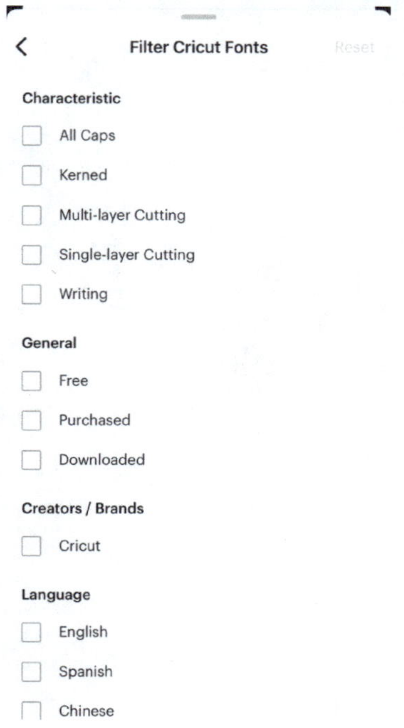

FIND FONTS

iOS

HOW TO CHANGE THE FONT FOR EXISTING TEXT

CHANGE THE FONT

Step 1: Open your project and select the text you want to change the font for. You can either single tap the text itself on the Canvas, or tap the text line in the Layers Panel.

Step 2: Tap the Edit button at the bottom.

Step 3: Tap the Font Name menu in the lower left corner.

Step 4: Choose a new font from the pop-up menu. You will see a preview in the font box.

Your font changes to your new selection!

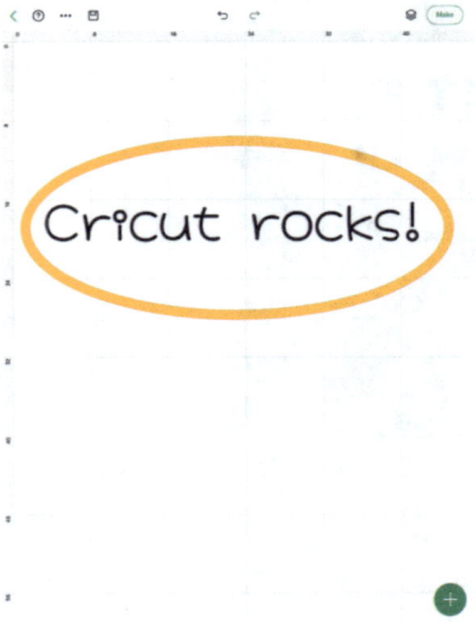

You can always change the color of your text by tapping the Edit button, then selecting the color circle next to the Operation panel.

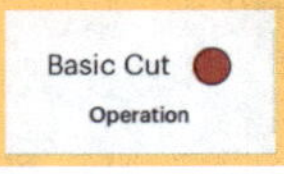

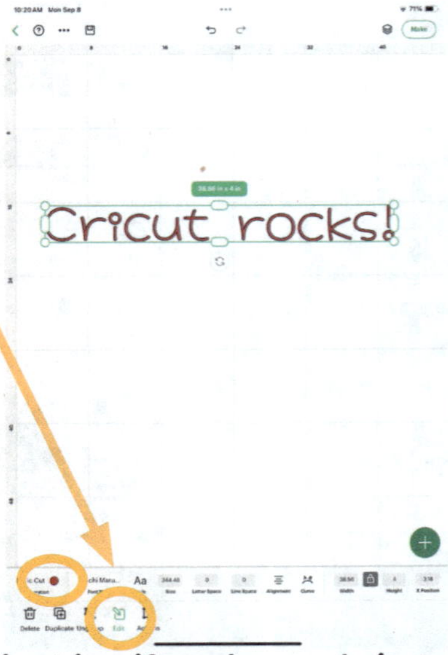

Practice this at jennifermaker.com/cricut-rocks

HOW TO CHANGE COLORS

Step 1: Select (tap) the layer you want to change, like the center of this flower.

Step 2: Tap Edit then tap the circle next to the Operation.

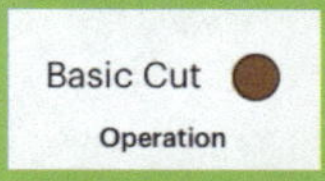

Step 3: Select (tap) the color you want. If you don't see the color you want, you can choose any custom color in the color picker below it. When done, tap Apply.

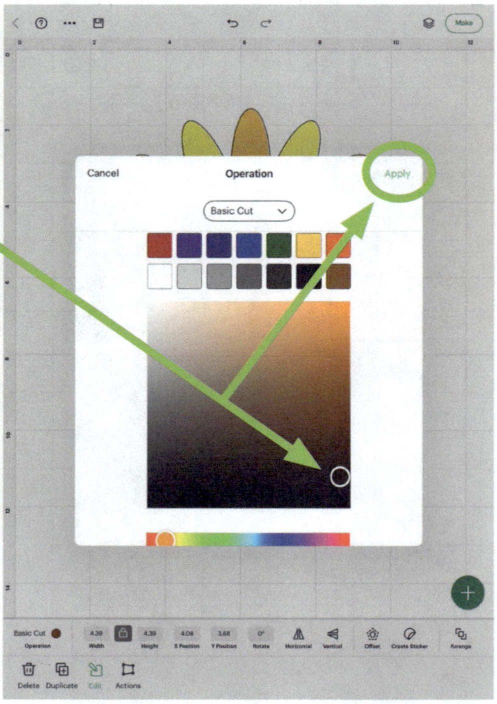

Your object changes to the color you selected!

Note: You cannot set pattern fills in the iOS version of Cricut Design Space. If you need to set pattern fills, use a desktop or laptop to access Cricut Design Space and see directions on page 22.

Practice this at jennifermaker.com/sunflower-colors

iOS

HOW TO CHANGE OPERATION AND TOOLS

The Operation menu lets you change a layer's type. Choices for the Cricut Joy and Joy Xtra are Basic Cut (default), Pen, Foil, and Guide. The Explores add Score and Print Then Cut. And the Cricut Makers add to this several more choices: Wavy, Perforate, Deboss, and Engrave. The Venture adds a large format cutting capability of 25 inches! You will only see the Makers' operation choices if you've set your machine to Maker, Maker 3, or Maker 4. Here's how to set your machine and change the operation.

Step 1: Tap the three lines menu in the upper left corner, tap Machine Selection, then tap your Cricut.

Step 2: Tap a layer, then tap Edit, then tap Operation.

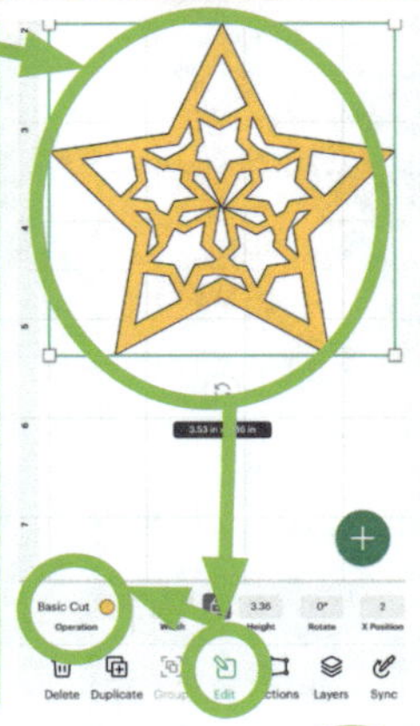

Tap Basic Cut then Apply to use the Fine Point, Deep Point, fabric, or rotary (Maker only) blades. You cannot use the knife blade with the iOS version.

Tap Pen then Apply to set a layer to write with pens and markers. You can choose the color and thickness, too.

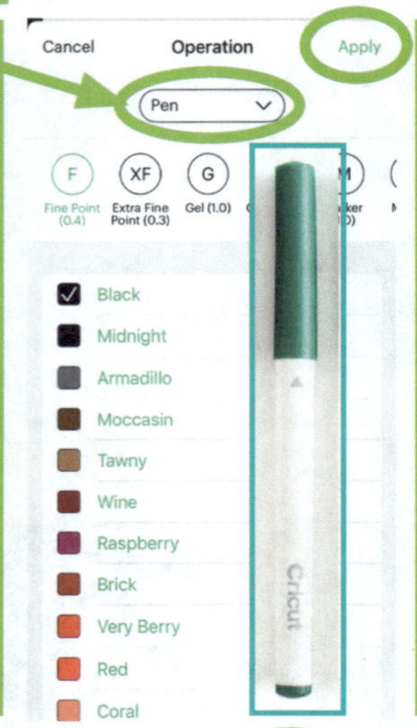

Tap Score then Apply to set a layer to score with the Stylus (Maker, Venture, or Explore) or Scoring Wheel Tools (Maker only).

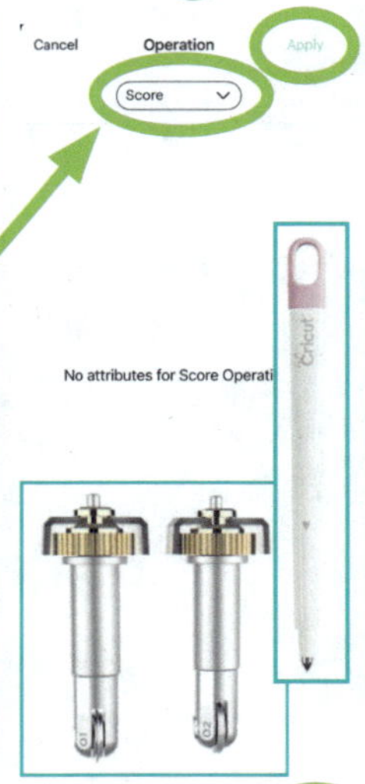

Tap Engrave then Apply to set a layer to use the Engraving Tool (Maker only).

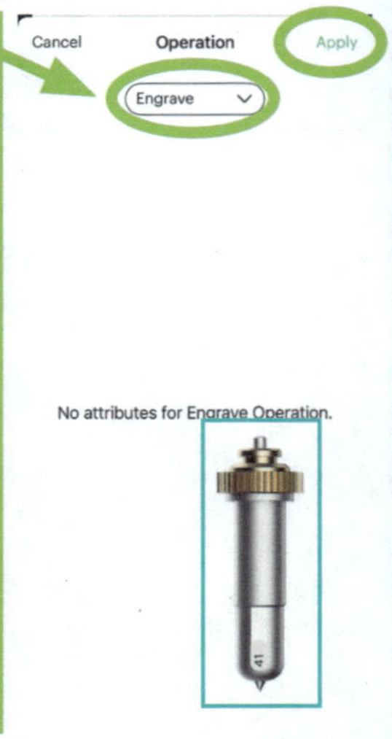

Tap Deboss then Apply to set a layer to use the Debossing Tool (Maker only).

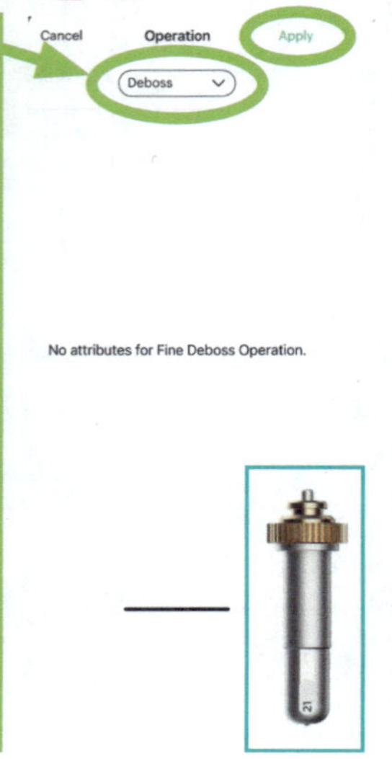

Tap Wavy then Apply to set a layer to use the Wavy Edge Tool (Maker only).

Tap Perforate then Apply to set a layer to use the Perforation Blade Tool (Maker only).

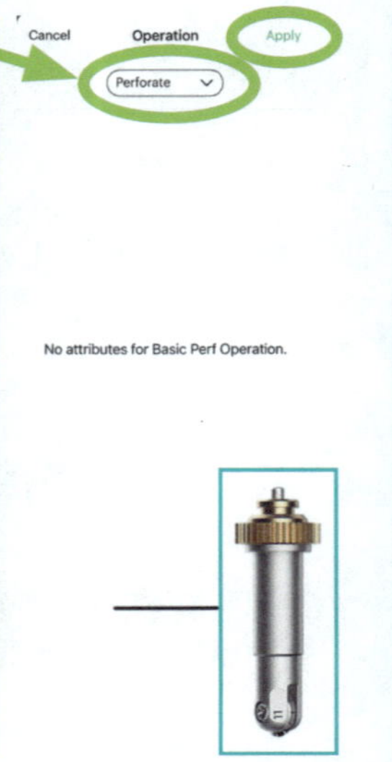

Practice this at jennifermaker.com/starry-star

OPERATION & TOOLS

HOW TO SET TEXT TO WRITE WITH A PEN

You can insert a Cricut pen or marker into any Cricut machine and have it draw with it, and many crafters like to use this feature with a writing font to mimic handwriting. Be sure to check your pen to make sure it is compatible, as pens are designed for specific machines. Here's how to choose a good font that looks like handwriting and set it to Draw in Cricut Design Space:

Step 1: Tap Font Name, tap the Filter icon, and tap Writing to see writing fonts.

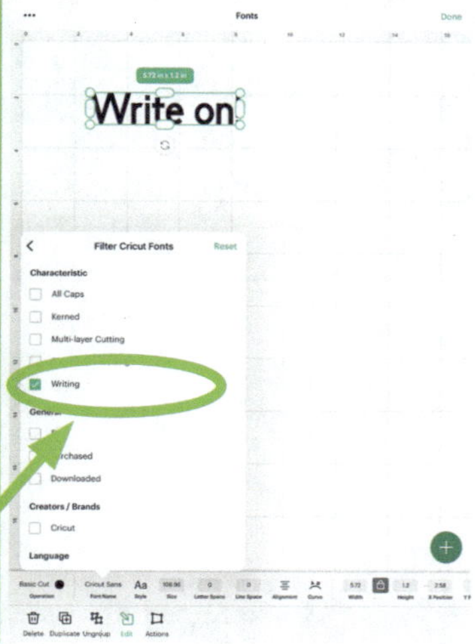

Step 2: Select a writing font (such as the free Cricut Sans or Cricut Alphabet). Some may have a fee or need a Cricut Access account.

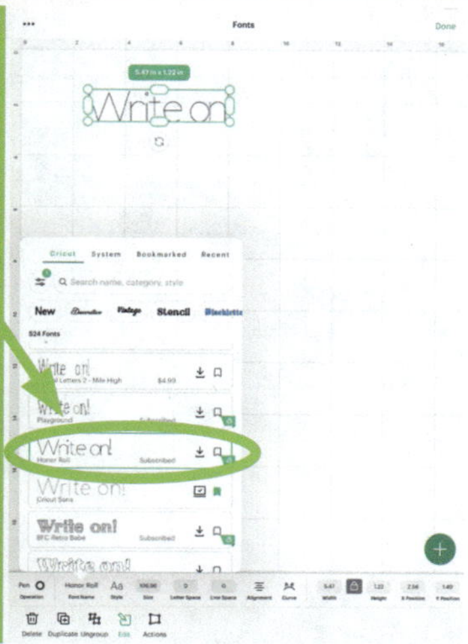

Step 3: Tap Edit, tap Style, then tap Writing to select the Writing style of the font.

Step 4: Tap Operation. Select Pen and tap a pen type and color, then tap Apply. Make any other desired changes, then tap Make.

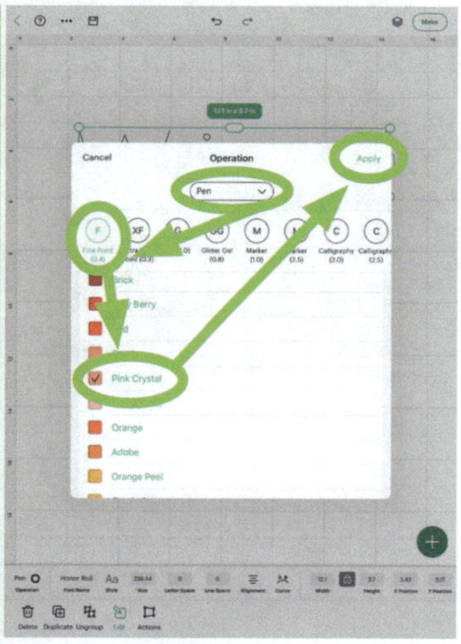

Step 5: Tap, hold and drag the text to the spot you want it to be on your material on the machine mat, then tap Next.

Step 7: Insert the pen in your Cricut's accessory clamp, position your material on the cutting mat, load your mat, and press the flashing button.

See my blog post at jennifermaker.com/cricut-writing-fonts for more tips on writing on your Cricut! I also have a free writing font you can use at jennifermaker.com/make-gift-tags-cricut

Practice this at jennifermaker.com/write-on

HOW TO SCORE WITH A STYLUS OR WHEEL

Step 1: Open or create a project with score lines. You can add a score line to any project by tapping Shape, then tapping Line.

Step 2: Tap the Layers icon and make sure any lines to be scored are identified as Score. If they are, skip to Step 4.

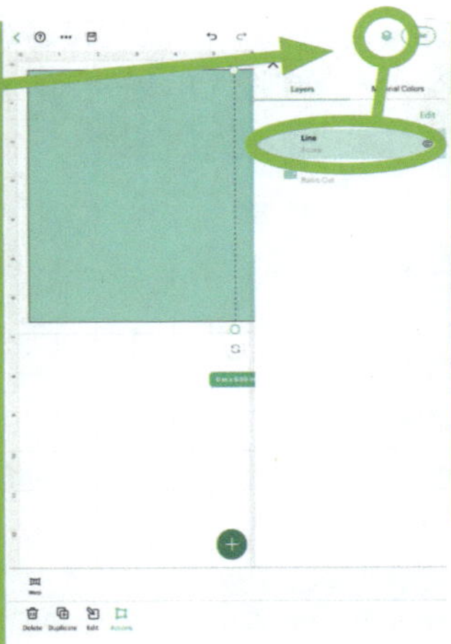

Step 3: Change lines to scores by tapping the Line, tapping Edit, then tapping Operation.

Step 4: Make sure your score line is attached to the layer you want scored (look for the word "Attach" above the score and base layers to confirm), then tap Make. If they are not attached, see page 55 for directions on how to attach layers.

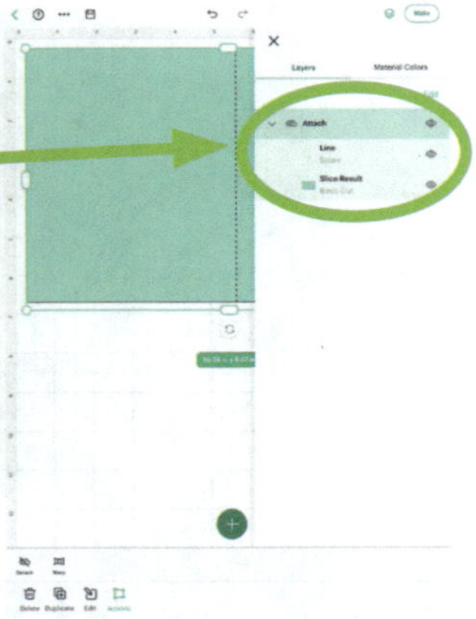

Step 5: Make sure the score line is on the same layer as the cut, then tap Next.

Step 6: Check the necessary tools. If the screen says to use a scoring wheel but you do not have one, tap Edit Tools.

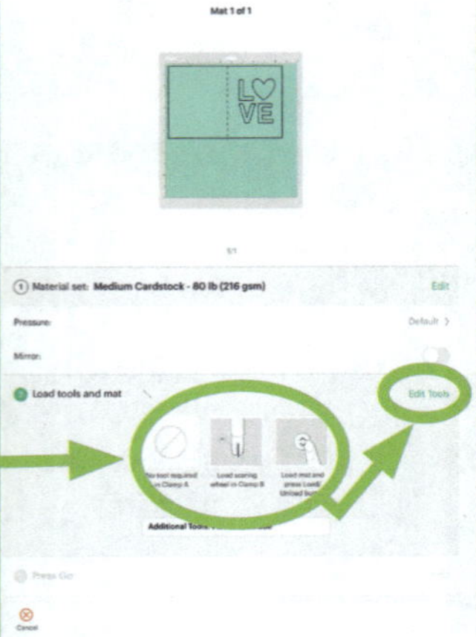

Step 7: Tap on the scoring tool of your choice, then tap Continue.

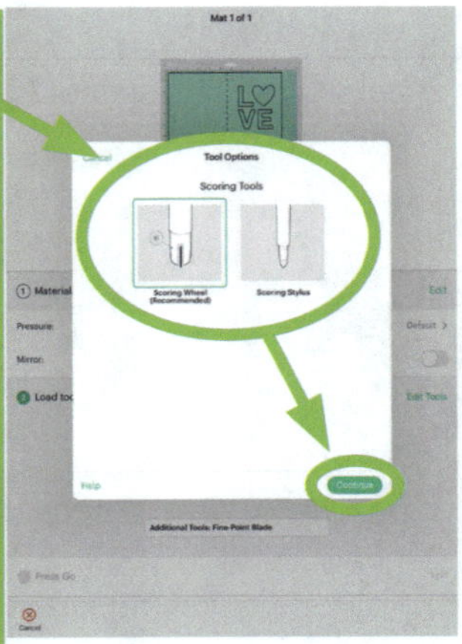

Step 8: Insert the scoring tool that matches Step 7, then press the flashing icon on your Cricut.

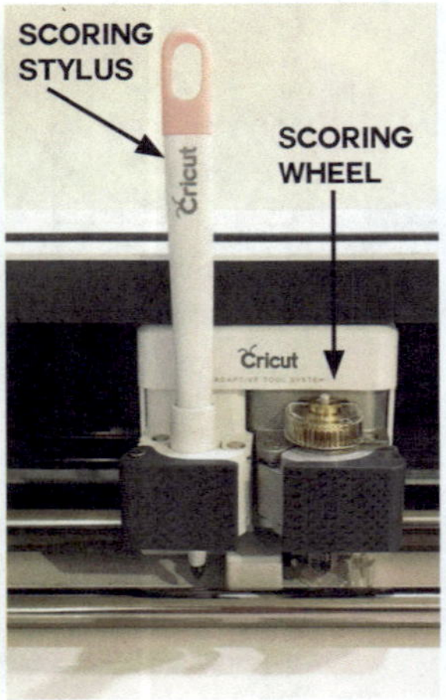

Practice this at jennifermaker.com/love-card

HOW TO USE THE CREATE STICKER TOOL

The Create Sticker tool is an easy way to turn any image into a sticker. It isn't absolutely required for sticker-making, but it does make it easier by telling your Cricut how much of a border to cut and whether to cut the sticker using the Die Cut method or the Kiss Cut method.

Step 1: Upload or create a design that you'd like to turn into a sticker.

Select the entire design, click Edit and click the Create Sticker button in the top menu.

Step 2: Choose whether you'd like your sticker to be Die Cut or Kiss Cut (die cut means the sticker and its backing will be cut out, and kiss cut means that just the sticker is cut out, not the backing).

Select your Border Width and Border Fill Color. Click Done.

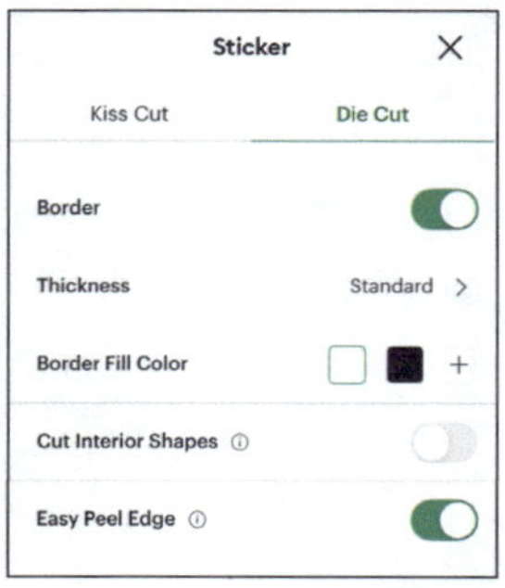

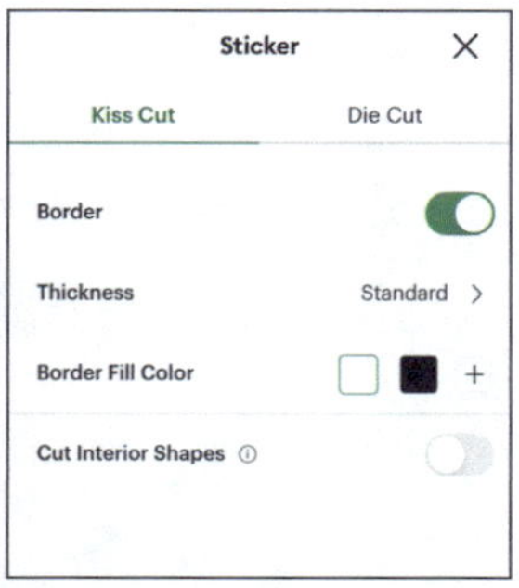

Your design will now be a single-layer Print Then Cut sticker! You will see a border around your design, and it will now be a Print Then Cut operation in the Layers Panel.

Print the sticker out on sticker paper using your color inkjet printer, then allow your Cricut to cut it out.

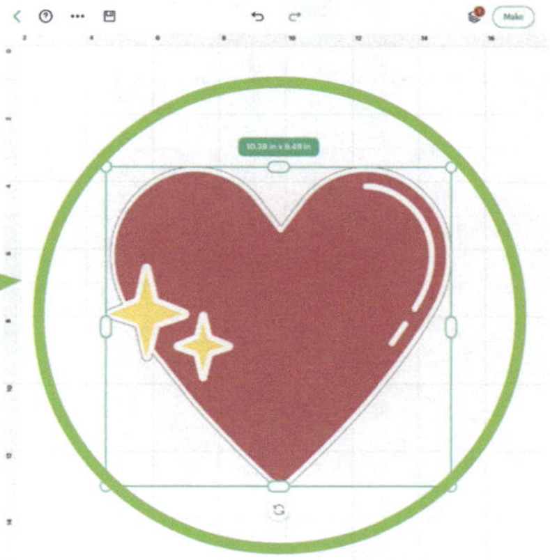

Warning: The Create Sticker tool is currently only a feature for Cricut Access members.

Practice this at jennifermaker.com/heart-sticker

HOW TO REPOSITION ITEMS ON MAT PREVIEW

Need exact control over where items on your mat are cut? Want to cut one mat with multiple pieces of material in different colors? You can do this if you reposition items on your mat before you cut! Here's how to do it on an iOS device:

Step 1: Open or create a project. Make anything you want to appear on the same mat the same color. Tap Make.

Step 2: Make sure the items you want to reposition are all on the same mat.

Tip: You can move objects from one mat to another by tapping the three dots and tapping Move object.

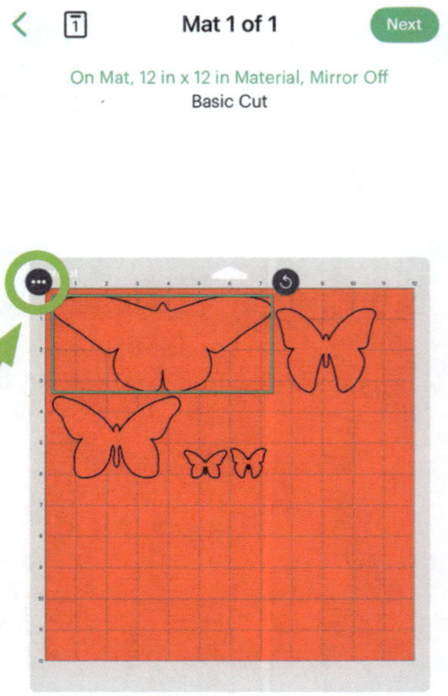

Step 3: Move each object on the mat by tapping, holding, and dragging to a new position. You can also move and hide by tapping the three dots.

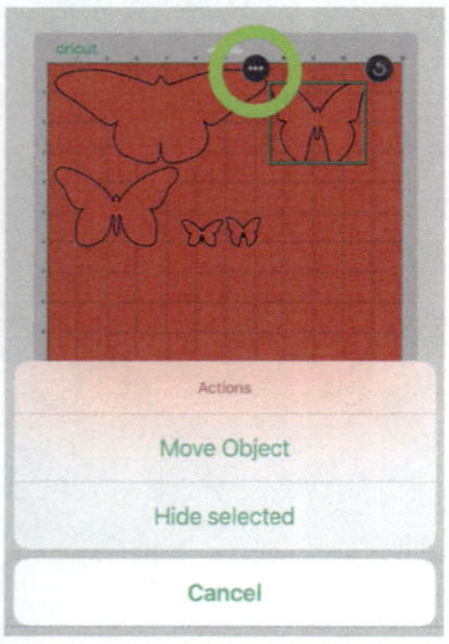

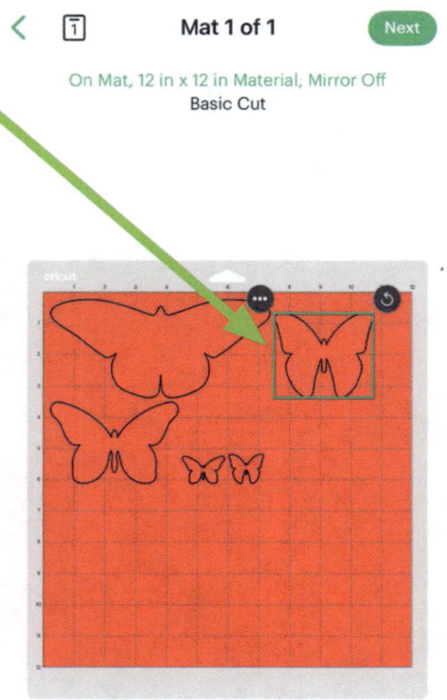

Step 4: Make sure the material on your actual mat matches the placement on this virtual mat, then tap Next.

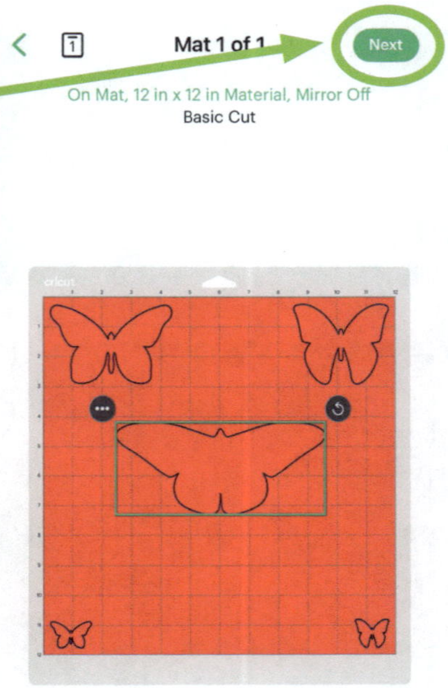

Practice this at jennifermaker.com/butterflies

HOW TO MIRROR AND CUT IRON-ON VINYL

Want to make a T-shirt or bag with iron-on vinyl? Here's how to mirror your image and position your vinyl on your mat for iron-on (heat transfer) vinyl!

Step 1: Select all the objects you want to iron-on, tap Actions, then tap Attach.

Attach

Step 2: Tap Make.

If asked how to make it, tap "On Mat" for regular iron-on.

Step 3: Tap the Mat icon in the upper left corner of the screen.

Step 4: Toggle Mirror to the on position and tap Close to close this window.

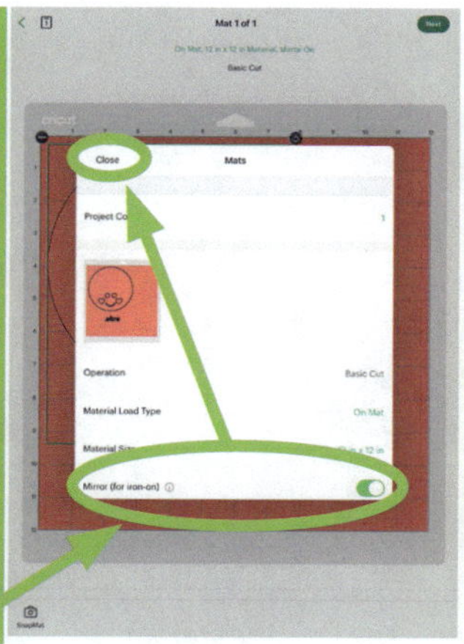

Step 5: Verify that your image is mirrored, then tap Next.

Step 6: Tap on All Materials.

All Materials

Step 7: Search on "Iron" and select the type of iron-on vinyl you plan to use.

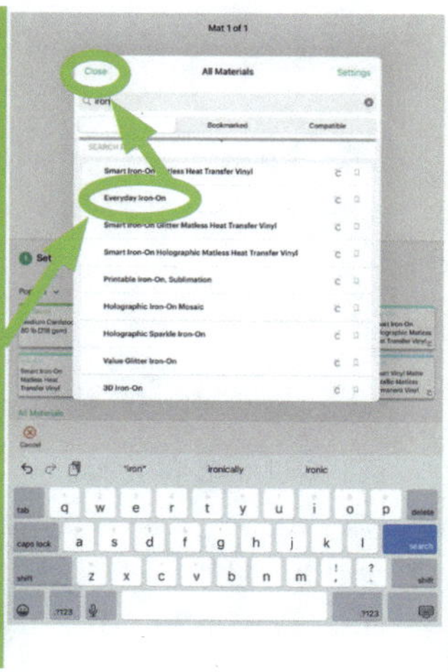

Step 8: Place your iron-on vinyl on your cutting mat shiny side down, load the mat, and press the flashing button on your Cricut cutting machine.

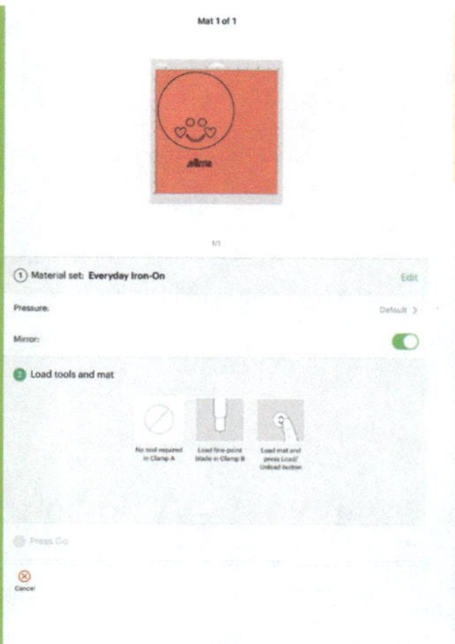

Remember, put the vinyl SHINY SIDE DOWN on your cutting mat!

Practice this at jennifermaker.com/simple-smile

HOW TO USE A LAYOUT

Step 1: Open a new project. Tap + (green circle), then tap Layouts.

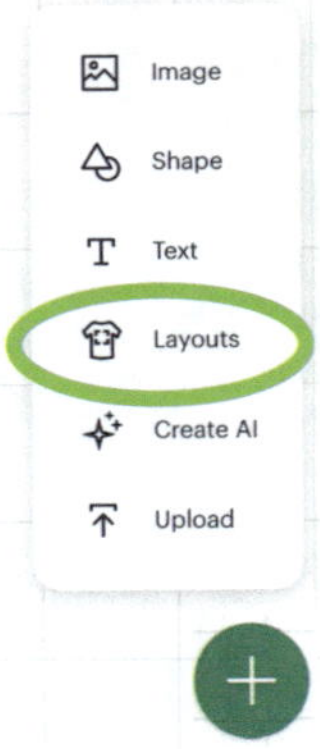

Step 2: Choose a layout that best fits your project. For example, to make a monogrammed bag, I will choose Tote Bag > Medium. Then close out of the panel.

Step 3: Tap the guide and tap Edit. Tap the lock icon to unlock it, then type in the dimensions of your actual item.

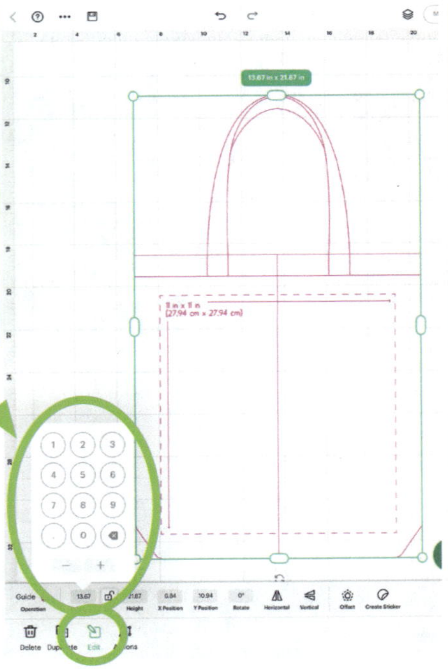

Tip: You can modify your template at any time by tapping on the layout. If you no longer want to view the template but still need it, click the eye icon located in the Layers panel to hide it.

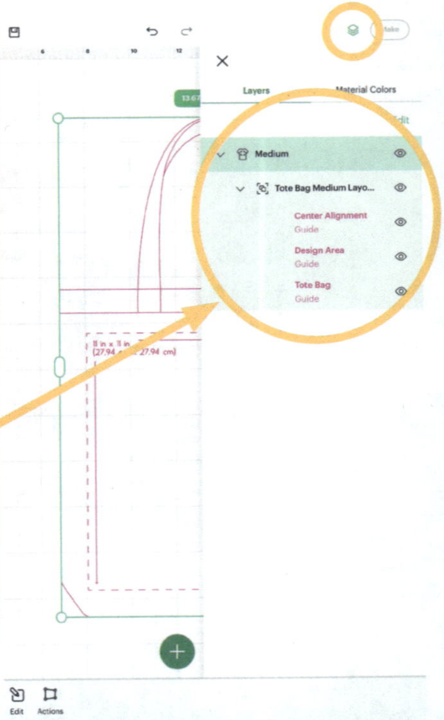

Need a layout but can't find it in the layout library? You can upload your own image (see page 83), resize it as needed using the dimension boxes in the edit panel, and then click Arrange > Send to Back. Be sure to hide the layer (click the eye icon) before you cut it to avoid cutting out the layout, too.

iOS

HOW TO USE SNAPMAT

A useful feature of Cricut Design Space on iOS is SnapMat, which allows you to take a photo of your material on the mat and then position your items on it. Here's how to use it:

Step 1: Start a new project and add images to the Canvas, or open an existing project. Tap Make.

Step 2: Tap the SnapMat icon.

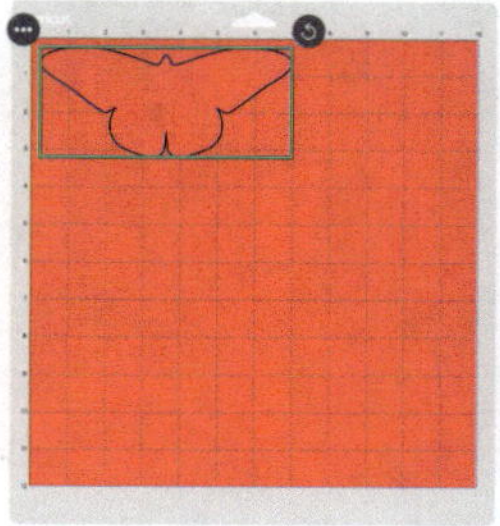

Step 3: Place your material on a mat and place the mat on a light or white colored surface. Center the mat in the border. When it is centered, the app will take a photo automatically.

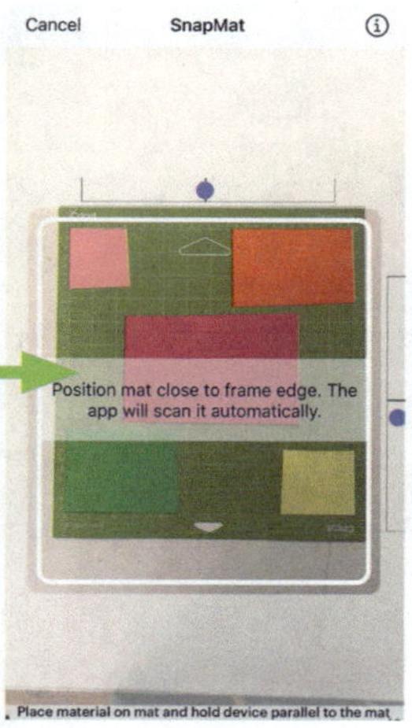

Step 4: Look at the photo taken. If you like it, tap Use. If you don't like it, tap Retake.

Step 5: Tap and drag elements on to the best spots on the mat.

SNAPMAT

Step 6: If you have multiple mats in your project, you'll need to repeat Steps 5-6 for each mat. (Yes, that means you need to take new SnapMat photos for each mat.)

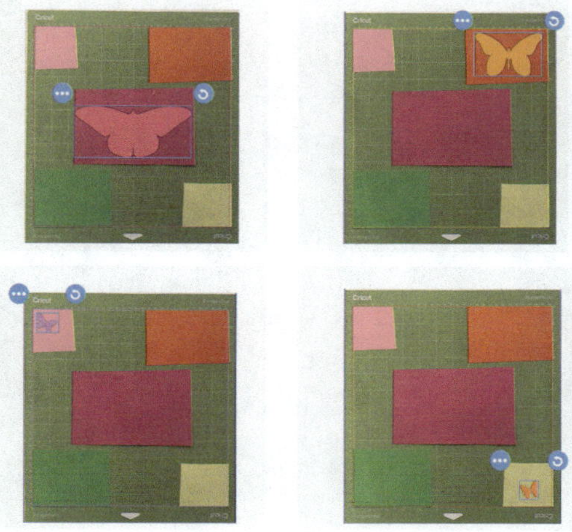

Step 7: When ready, tap Next, choose your materials, and make your cuts!

Tip: If SnapMat won't take a photo of your mat, make sure you've got good lighting and put something white (like a white sheet) under the mat for better contrast. Hold your device parallel to the surface.

Practice this at jennifermaker.com/butterflies

HOW TO SAVE WORK AND VIEW SAVED PROJECTS

Step 1: Create something and tap the Save icon.

Step 2: Tap Save from the drop-down menu that appears. If you see Save As appear, that means you saved it before and you have the option to save it with a different name to preserve the original save.

Step 3: Give the project a name and tap Save to the Cloud if you want to access it elsewhere, or Save to iPhone (or Save to iPad) if you want it only on this device.

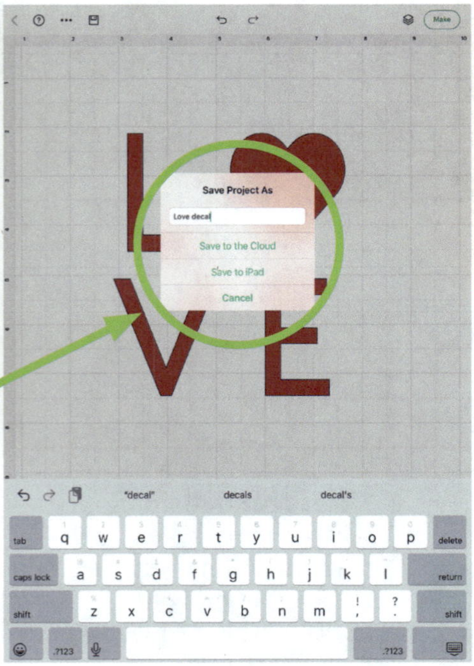

If Cricut is able to save your project, a confirmation window will appear.

Practice this at jennifermaker.com/love-decal

iOS

HOW TO
SAVE FOR OFFLINE WORK

With the Cricut Design Space for iOS app, you can save projects for offline and access them even when you aren't connected to the Internet. Here's how to do it:

Step 1: Save a project using the directions on the previous page (Page 78). If you've already saved this project before in the Cloud for online work, tap Save As instead of Save. If you're not sure where you've saved it, tap Save As.

Step 2: Type in a name if you haven't already given it one, then tap Save to iPhone or Save to iPad.

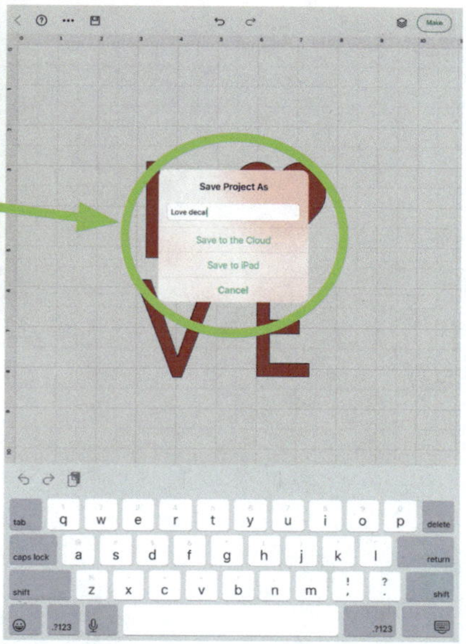

Step 3: If successful, Design Space tells you that your project was saved.

Step 4: To view your Saved Projects, tap the < (Back) icon in the upper left corner, then tap My Stuff and choose Projects, then select the filter and select On this iPhone (or iPad).

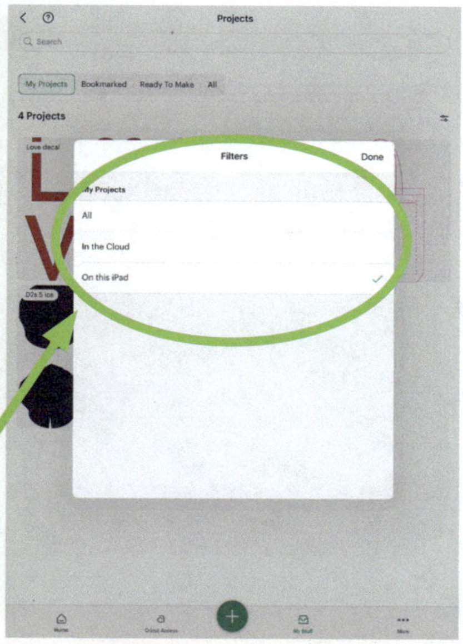

- There is currently no way to batch save all of your projects for offline. You must click each one and select "Save for Offline/Save to iPhone/Save to iPad" individually.
- If you go offline, you'll only be able to view and access projects saved on your iPhone or iPad.
- Any images you have in a project from Cricut Access will expire after 30 days if you do not go online at all during those 30 days (even if you have monthly access). So be sure to set a reminder to go online at least once every 30 days.
- You cannot upload anything new while offline (this means even from your iPhone/iPad or images within Design Space). So be sure to save all images you want in a project/Canvas before heading offline.

Practice this at jennifermaker.com/love-decal

HOW TO SHARE LINKS TO PROJECTS

Did you make an awesome design and now want to share it? You can, so long as there are no uploaded images in your project. (You cannot share projects with images you uploaded.)

Step 1: Open a project you saved in the Cloud by tapping My Stuff and choose either Projects or Images that have been previously saved in the Cloud or on this iPhone (or iPad).

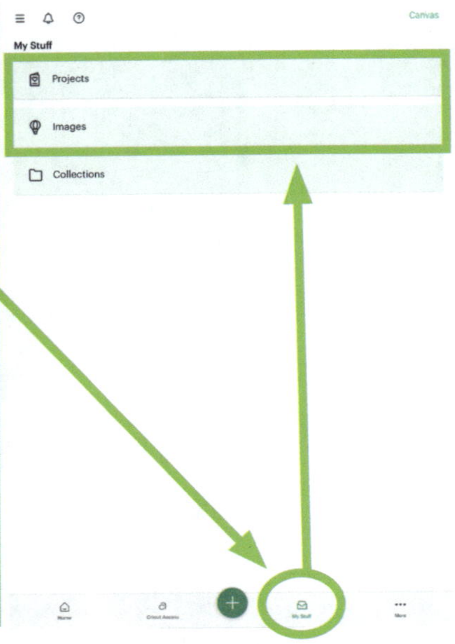

Step 2: To share a project, tap the Share icon that appears in the "Project Details" pop-up window.

Note: If your design has any purchased elements from Cricut Access or cartridges, anyone attempting to use your design either must also have them, and if they do not, they will be prompted to pay for them before cutting.

Note: Projects with images or fonts that must be purchased to use cannot be saved to your iPhone or iPad without first purchasing them.

Step 3: Add a project name, images, an optional description, and tags to describe the project you plan to share, then click Done.

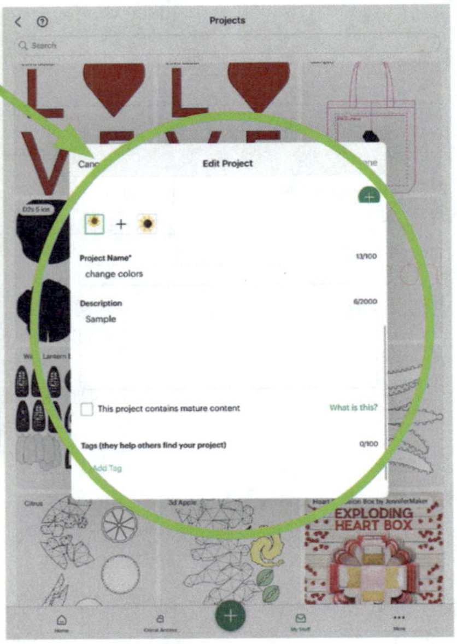

Step 4: Tap Share to Design Space to share your project publicly or tap Share Private Link to share your project to someone specific.

Note: The URL for these projects will look something like this: https://design.cricut.com/landing/project-detail/62c1b835a627c3f6397faa9e

iOS

HOW TO FLATTEN

Need to make a Print Then Cut project? Flatten is your friend! The Flatten tool allows you to turn any image into a single, printable layer for the Print Then Cut feature.

Step 1: Add two or more items to your Canvas that you want to flatten. Then tap and drag a selection box around all objects you want to flatten to select all of them.

Note: Flatten is used only for Print Then Cut.

Step 2: Tap Actions, then tap Flatten.

Actions

Flatten

Note that all items are now on one layer and now work only for Print Then Cut.

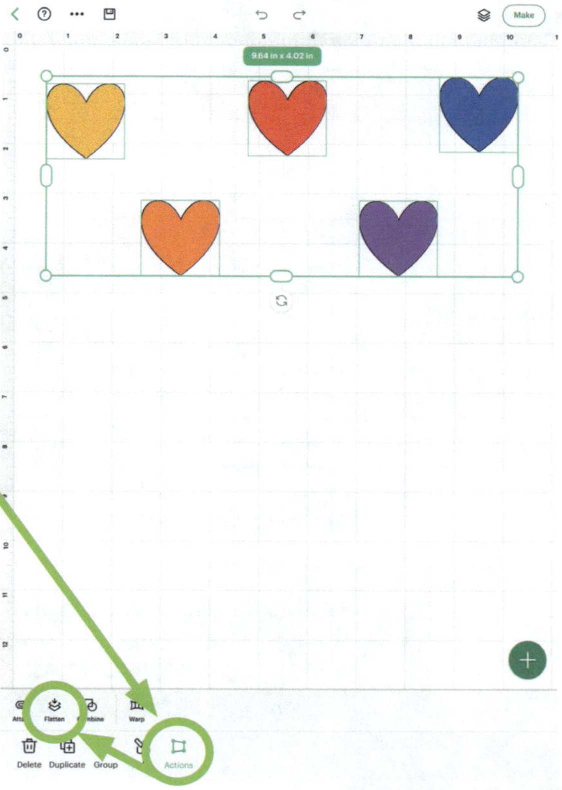

If you decide this isn't what you wanted to do, tap the Unflatten button.

Unflatten

Practice this at jennifermaker.com/five-hearts

HOW TO PRINT THEN CUT

Find or upload a printable image with one of these two methods:

Method A: Search for printable images in Design Space by tapping Image, then tap Filter and tap "Print Then Cut."

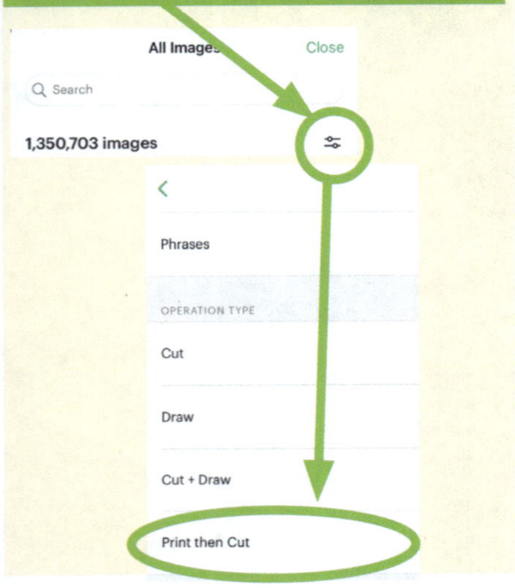

Method B:

Step 1: Upload a PNG with a transparent background. To remove the background from your image, follow the steps on "How to Erase a Background from an Image" (on Page 84). Your image should appear on your Canvas. Then move to Step 2.

Step 2: On the Canvas, tap Make to go to the mat preview screen. Make sure you see "Print, Basic Cut" click Next.

Step 3: Under "Print on" below the mat preview, tap Send to Printer.

Step 5: Select your printer, toggle on "Print in Color," and click Print.

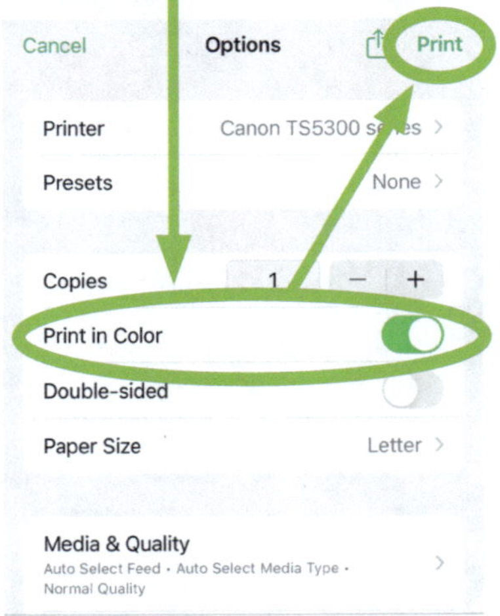

Step 6: Select your Material (i.e. Printable Vinyl).

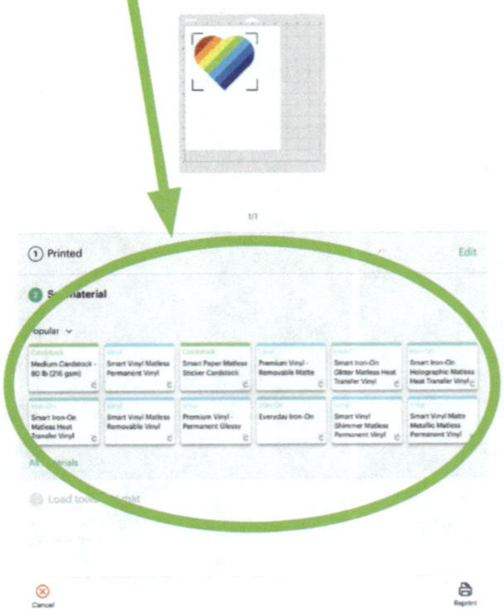

Step 7: Place your printed page on your cutting mat, load it, and tap the flashing button on your Cricut to begin.

Practice this at jennifermaker.com/rainbow-heart

HOW TO UPLOAD IMAGES IN IOS

Step 1: Tap the green + button to open a New Project.

Step 2: Tap the green + button and tap the Upload icon.

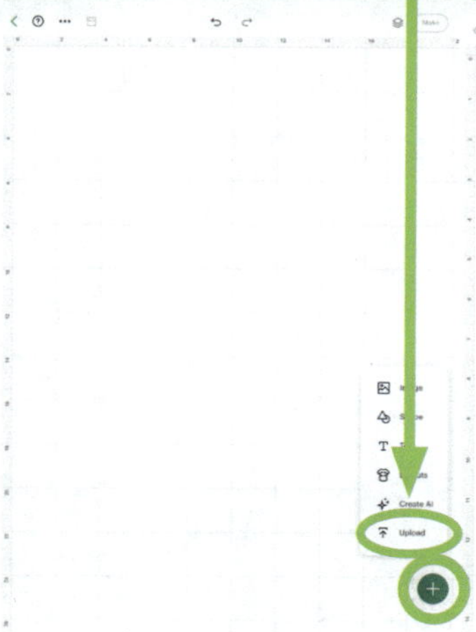

Step 3: Tap Browse Files or Select from Photo Library, depending on where you saved your file.

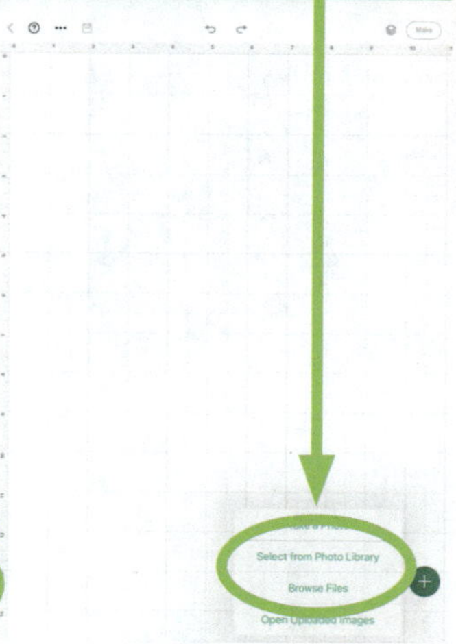

Note: If you want to use the Browse Files feature, be sure you are running iOS 16 or later on your device and upgrade if not.

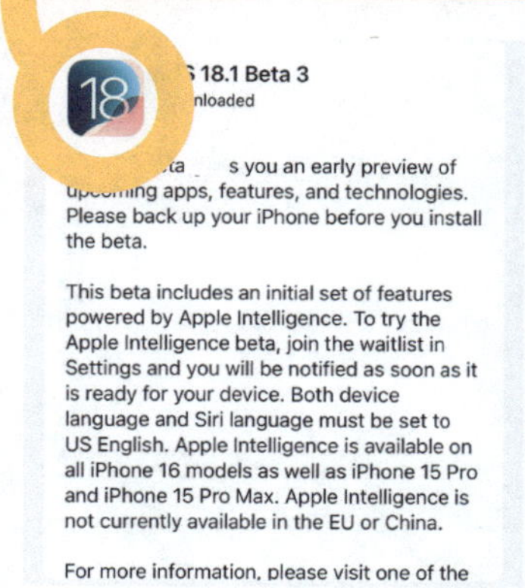

Step 4: Choose the method you want your image to upload as. Tap Next.

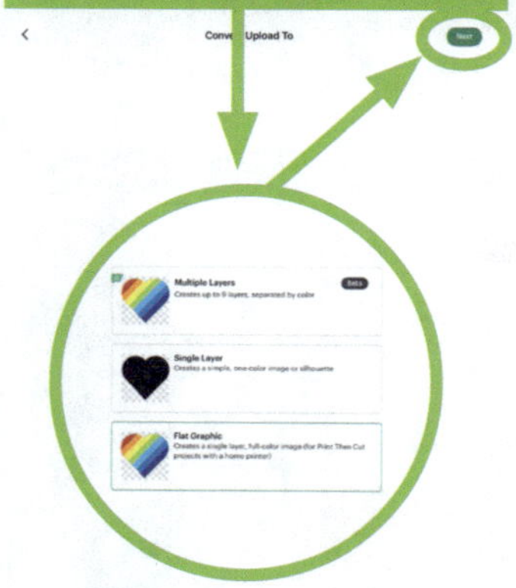

Step 5: Clean it up (if you want) and tap Apply.

Step 6: Choose an image type, name it, and tap Upload.

Tip: Type a word or two as a tag to help you find this image later in a search.

Step 7: The newly uploaded image appears on your Canvas!

UPLOAD IMAGES (IOS)

Practice this at jennifermaker.com/rainbow-heart

HOW TO ERASE A BACKGROUND FROM AN IMAGE

Step 1: Find or upload a JPG, PNG, GIF, BMP, or HEIC file that you want to use.

If you have Cricut Access, tap the Remove Background tool. If not, tap the x button.

Step 2: If you don't have Cricut Access and/or the background did not remove cleanly, tap the Select tool.

Step 3: Tap on the white background around your image to erase it. You may need to click in several areas to get it all. The box at the bottom right controls how much of a given color you remove.

Step 4: Check the cut lines of the object by tapping on ... then choosing Single Layer. If you need to fix it, tap Original and resume working. If it looks good, tap Apply.

Step 5: Decide what method you want to use for your image, tap Next, give it a name, then tap Upload.

Step 6: Once uploaded, the image appears on your Canvas.

Practice this at jennifermaker.com/rainbow-heart

HOW TO USE FILE/PHOTO TO LAYERS

The File/Photo to Layers function allows you to upload an image and let Design Space convert it into up to nine layers. It doesn't always work perfectly, but can be a really cool tool to use.

Step 1: Start a new project by tapping the green circle on the main screen.

Step 2: Tap the green + button and tap the Upload icon.

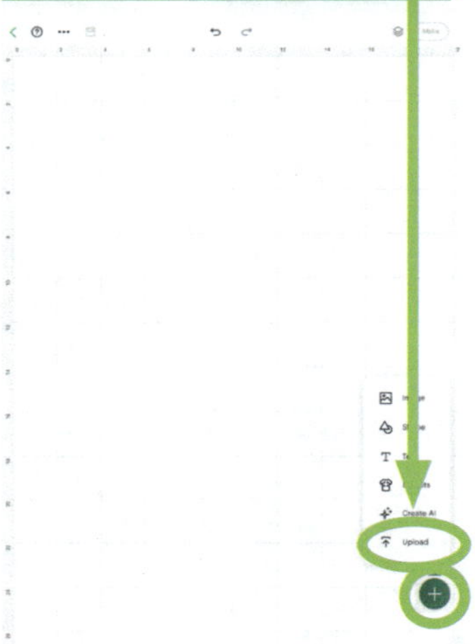

Step 3: Tap Select Photo From Library.

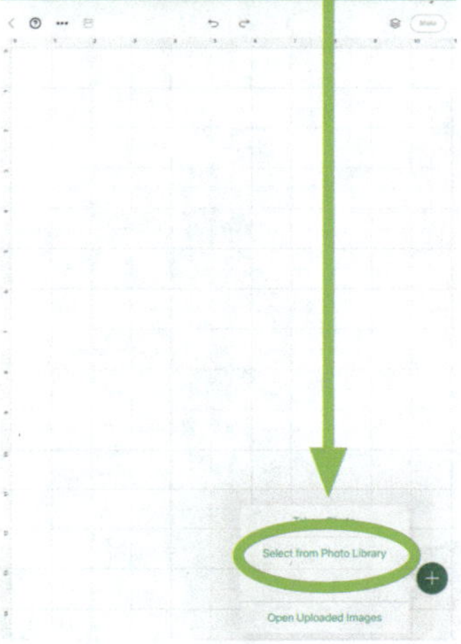

Step 4: Select an image. Erase the background and click Apply.

Step 5: Tap the Multiple Layers option, then tap Next.

Step 6: Tap Clipart or Photo. Tap the Output Style you want. Tap Next.

Step 7: Give your image a name, then tap Upload.

Step 8: Your new layered image will appear on the Canvas.

Practice this at jennifermaker.com/rainbow-heart

iOS

HOW TO
COMBINE MULTIPLE PROJECTS

While there is no built-in function in Design Space that allows you to combine projects, there is a workaround. Here's how you do it:

Step 1: Open a project you want to combine with another. Turn off the grid: tap the 3 dots at the top left > Canvas Settings and toggle the Grid off.

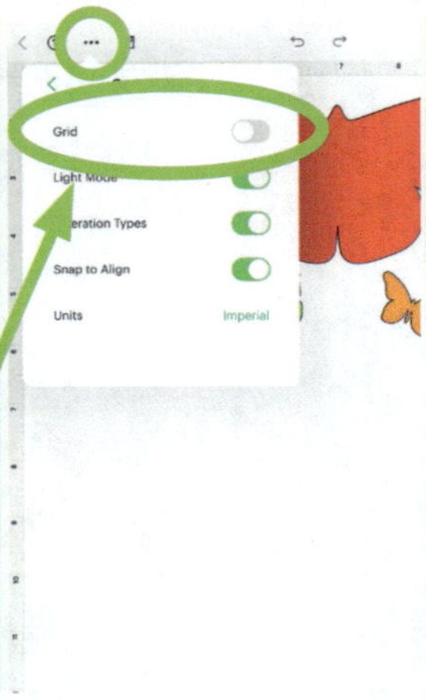

Step 2: If any individual elements in your design are touching and you need them separated, move them apart now.

Step 3: Take a picture of Design Space screen by pressing the Side button and the Volume up button at the same time. Quickly release both buttons. Tap the thumbnail of your screenshot that appears in the lower-left corner, and crop it (slide in the sides) to adjust the design.
Tap Done then Save to Photos.

Step 4: Open the project to which you want to add your other project. Allow it to replace your current Canvas.

Step 5: Follow previous pages to upload the image from Step 3 and remove the background. Tap Single Layer then tap Next.

Step 6: Insert the newly uploaded image onto your Canvas with the other image from step 4.

Step 7: Tap the first project's image, tap Duplicate, and make as many duplicates as there are elements in the project.

Step 8: Select each duplicate copy and tap Actions > Contour to separate out each element into its own layer.

Step 9: Recolor each element (see page 69) as needed and move back into position. Now your two projects are combined!

Practice this at jennifermaker.com/butterflies and jennifermaker.com/rainbow-love

iOS

HOW TO UPLOAD SVG FILES ON AN IPHONE OR IPAD

SVG files are special files that you can upload to Cricut Design Space and cut beautiful designs from. To use an SVG, first you must download and unzip an SVG file. You can practice downloading a file at jennifermaker.com/svg-heart. To unzip a file, go to the Files app on your iPhone or iPad, locate and tap on Downloads, tap and hold the downloaded ZIP filename, and choose Uncompress from the drop-down menu. Note that you will not see the folder in step 4 unless you do this first.

Uncompress

Be sure you are running iOS 16 or later on your device (check in Settings > General > Software Updates). If not, upgrade first.

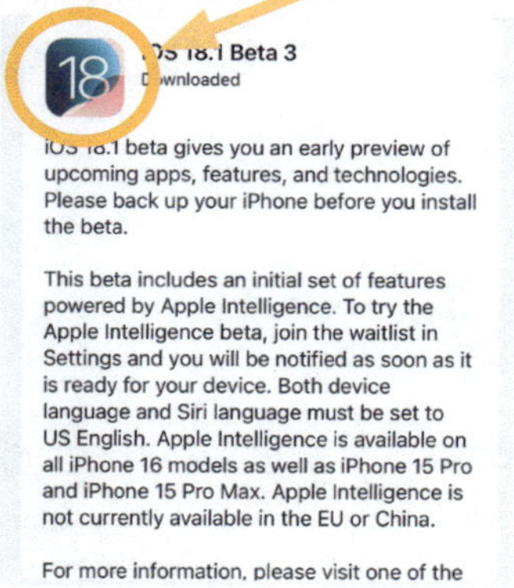

Step 1: Tap the + to start a new project.

Step 2: Tap the green + and tap Upload.

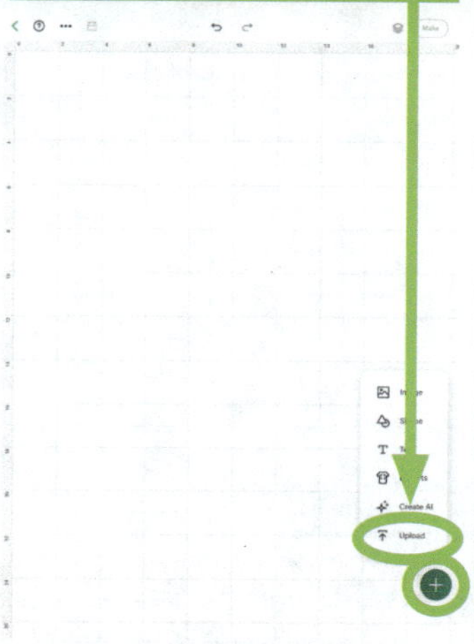

Step 3: Tap Browse Files.

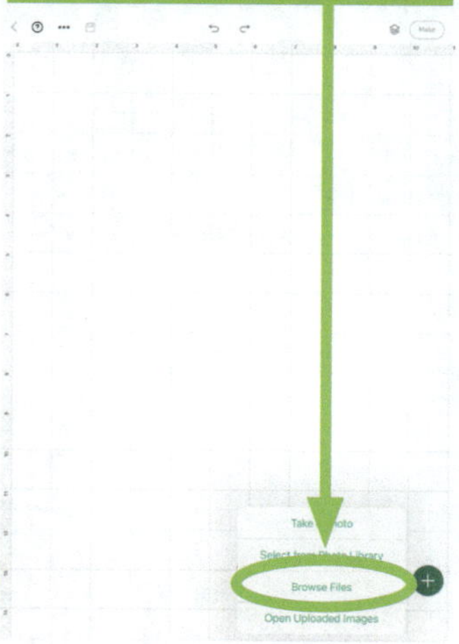

My Stuff

Step 4: Make sure to tap the actual file not the zip folder.

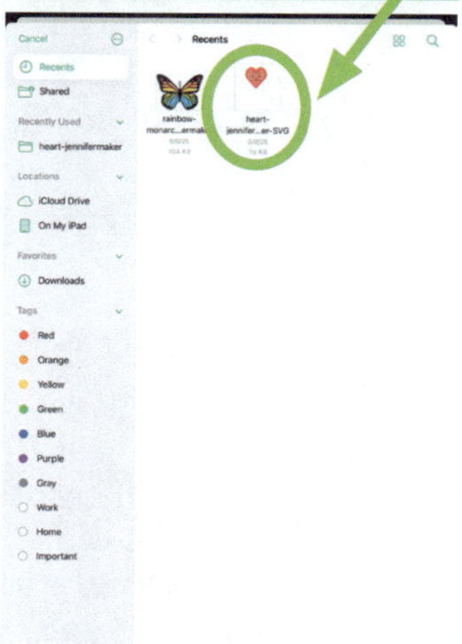

Step 5: Tap Upload to add it to your Canvas.

TIP: Type a word or two as a tag to help you find this image later in a search.

Once uploaded, your image appears on your Canvas, ready to be modified and/or made!

UPLOAD SVG FILES (IOS)

Practice this at jennifermaker.com/svg-heart

HOW TO
RESIZE A PROJECT

Have you ever uploaded an SVG design, cut it out, and realized it was too small or too big? Here's how to check the size before you cut it out:

Step 1: Insert, upload, or create an image on your Canvas in Design Space, then select all images you want to resize by tapping and dragging a selection box around them.

Step 2: Tap Edit, then note the size at the bottom of the window in the Width and Height boxes.

10		4.21
Width		Height

To determine if the sizing is right, compare it to the sizing in the original instructions or tutorial. If no sizing is provided, you'll have to use your best judgment. Here's how to resize a project:

Step 3: Be sure the lock icon indicates it is locked, then tap the Width or Height boxes and tap on the number pad to enter the proper size.

locked

The entire selected image(s) is resized and retains its proportions.

6.23		2.62
Width		Height

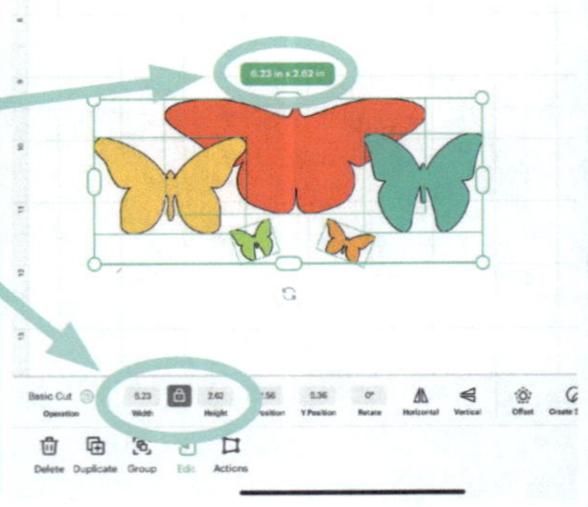

You can also resize images using the resize icon by dragging any corner of a selection box. Just hold and drag to resize.

Note that Cricut Design Space has been known to automatically resize any SVG file that measures over 12" (either wide or high) down to 12" on its longest side, and there may be no notification that an image was resized. So if you ever place an image on your Canvas and notice that one side measures exactly 12," that is a strong indicator that your image has been resized for you. To learn how to fix this, visit https://jennifermaker.com/resize-svg.

Practice this at jennifermaker.com/butterflies

iOS

HOW TO USE CREATE AI

Create AI is a feature in Design Space that lets you describe what you want, and Cricut will generate original art for you. Here's how to use it:

Step 1: Tap the + icon for a new project.

Step 2: Tap + (green circle), then Create AI.

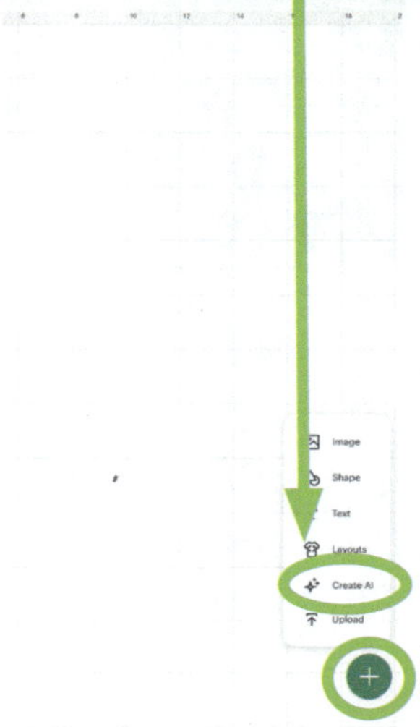

Step 3: Describe the image you want. Be clear and specific!

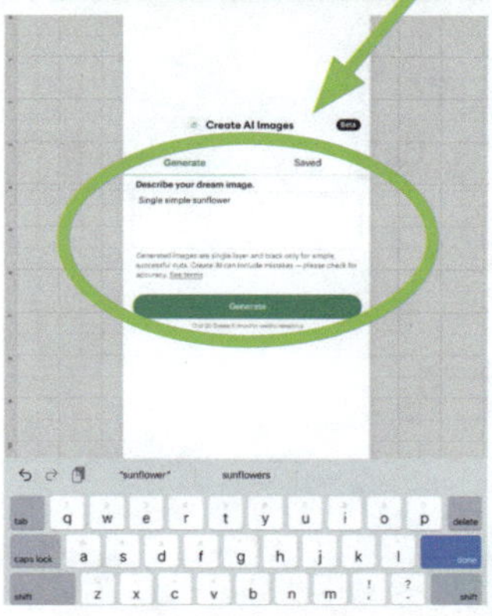

Step 4: Click Generate.

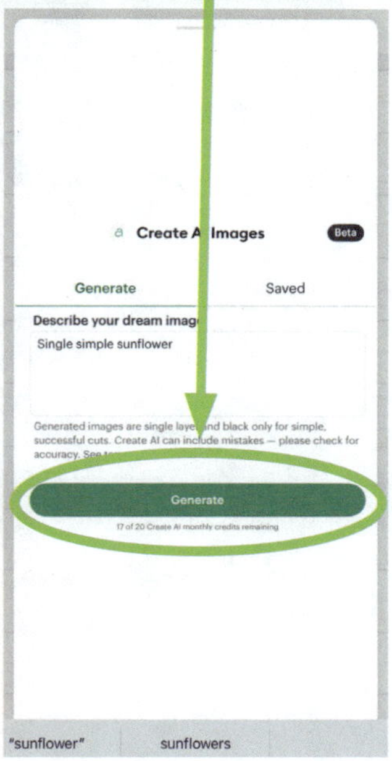

Note: Create AI images generated in the iOS App are single layer and black only for simple, successful cuts.

Step 5: Wait for your image to generate.

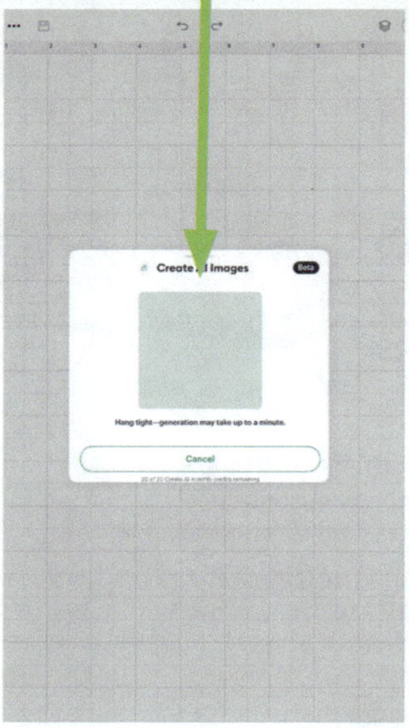

Step 6: Once your image is generated, Tap the + (green circle), to add it to your canvas.

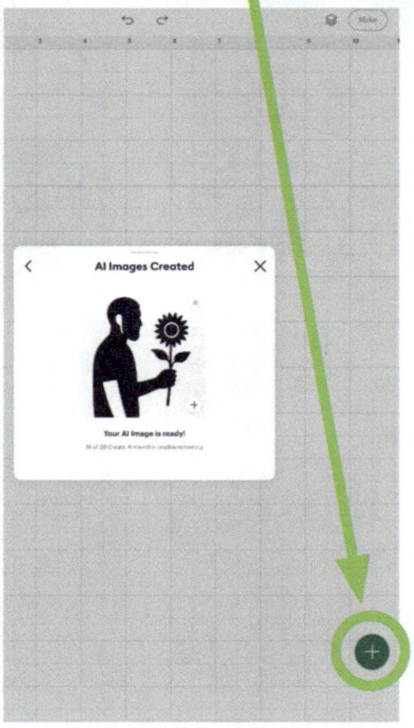

Step 7: Resize your image if desired.

All images generated by Create AI can be found under "Saved" in the Create AI Images panel.

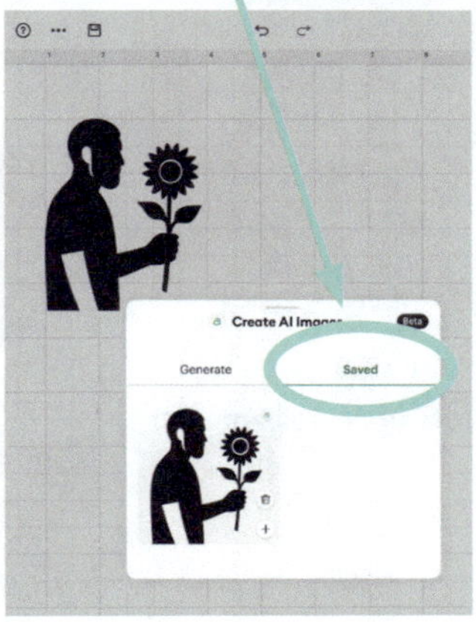

Note: The Create AI tool is currently only a feature for Cricut Access members, who receive 20 AI credits each month to generate new designs.

CREATE AI

HOW TO FOLLOW SOMEONE IN DESIGN SPACE

You can follow your friends and other Cricut crafters in Design Space, and even get notifications on their new projects! Here's how to follow someone and how to set your notification settings.

Step 1: Ask a friend for their profile link and go to the link in Safari. My link is at jennifermaker.com/follow-me-on-cricut. Then tap on Open in App.

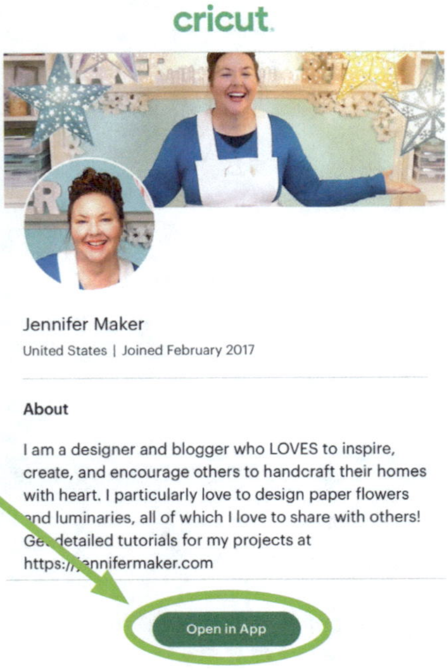

Step 2: Tap the Follow button to begin following that friend on Design Space.

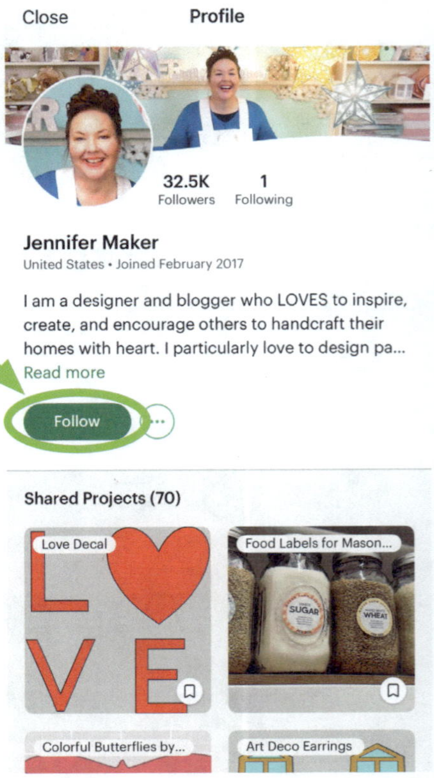

You may also find people to follow by going to the main Home screen and scrolling down to The Contributing Artist or Top Publishers this Month and select the profile name.

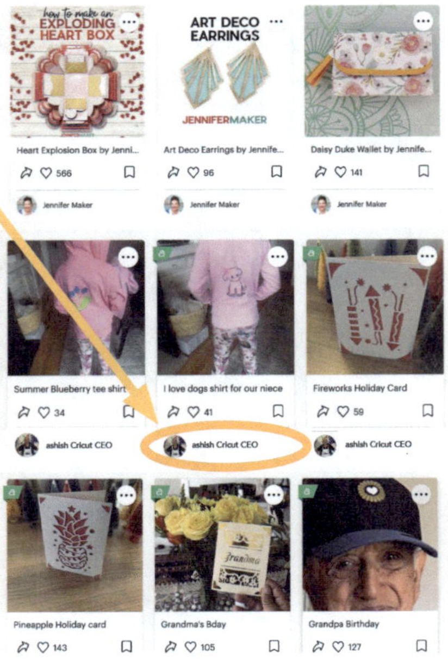

Once their profile is open, you may click the Follow button to begin following them.

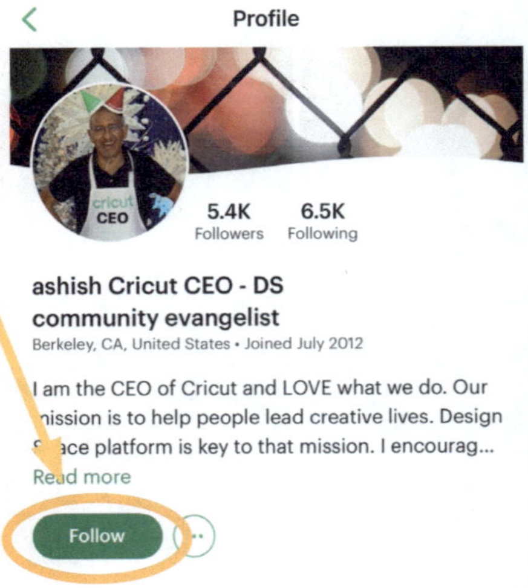

Follow me at jennifermaker.com/follow-me-on-cricut

HOW TO USE AND MODIFY CUSTOM MATERIALS SETTINGS

You can use and modify settings for MANY materials using the Custom Materials settings in Design Space. Here's how you access and change them:

Step 1: On the home screen, tap the three lines in the upper left corner, then tap Settings, then Custom Material Settings.

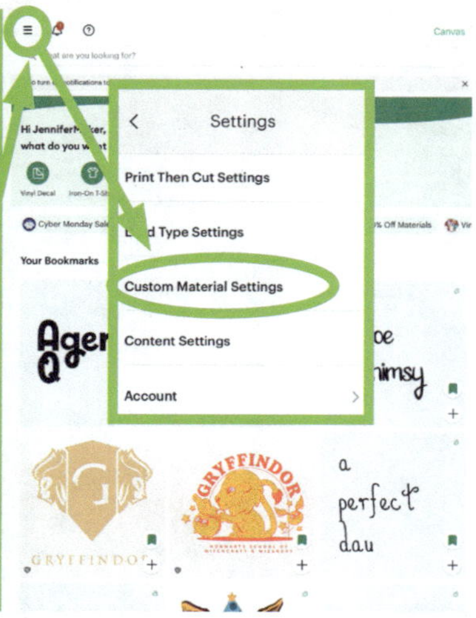

Step 2: If prompted, tap your Cricut in the "Select Device" pop-up. Then scroll through the list of materials, find one to edit, and click the arrow button to the right of it.

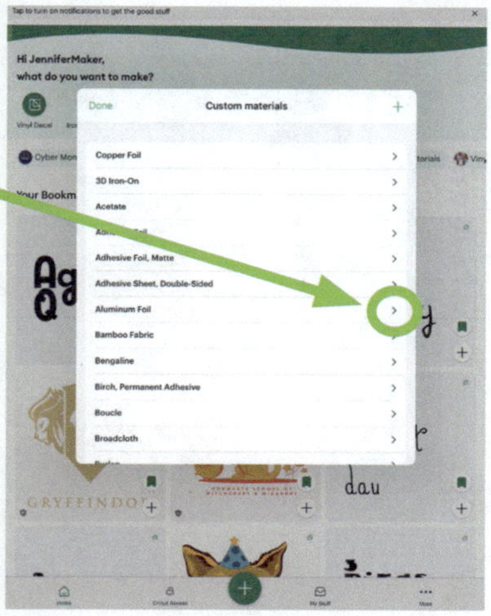

Step 3: Tap the setting you want to change. There may be only one option here.

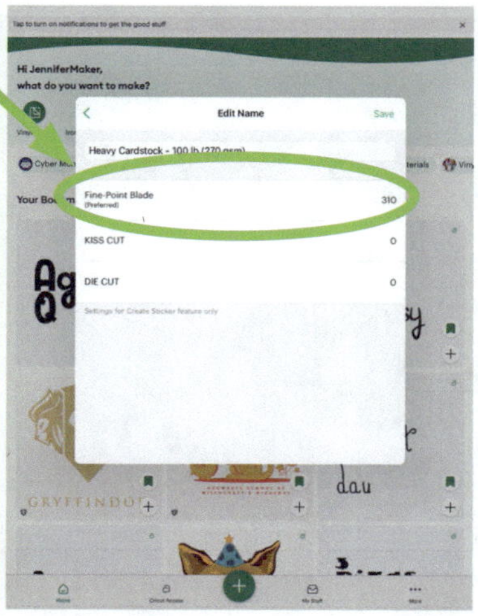

Step 4: Change the settings here as needed. Usually I just adjust pressure, but you can change how many times it cuts, too. Tap Save.

Step 5: If you want to create an entirely custom material, tap the + sign in the top right corner, type a name for it, then tap Add.

+

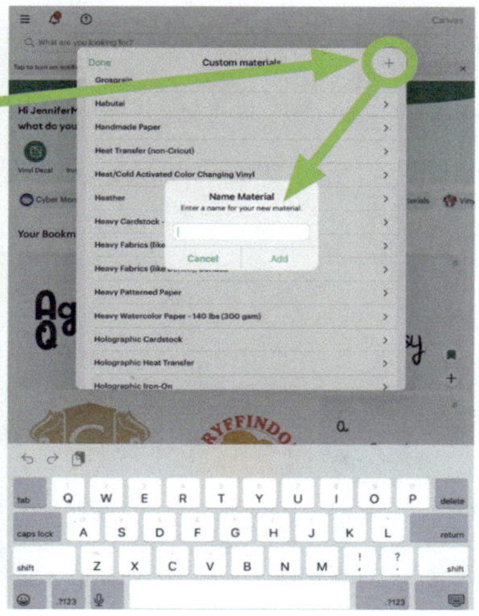

Step 6: Change the settings here as needed, then tap Save. You may need to test to get the right settings.

Save

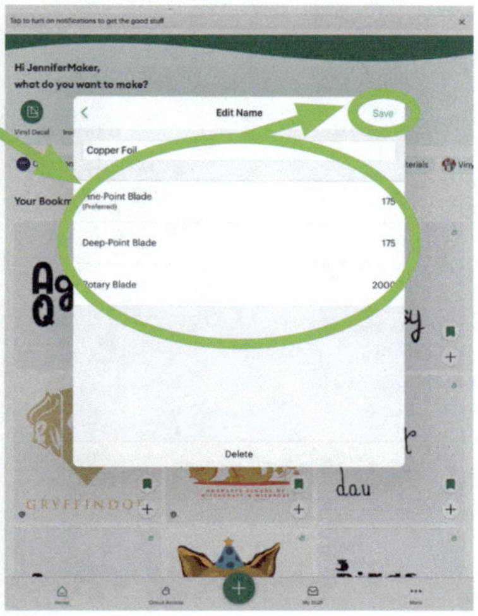

CUSTOM MATERIALS

HOW TO UPDATE THE CRICUT APP IN IOS

Step 1: Go to the Home screen and tap the App Store to check for updates.

Step 2: Once in the App Store, tap the Search icon and search on Cricut Design Space.

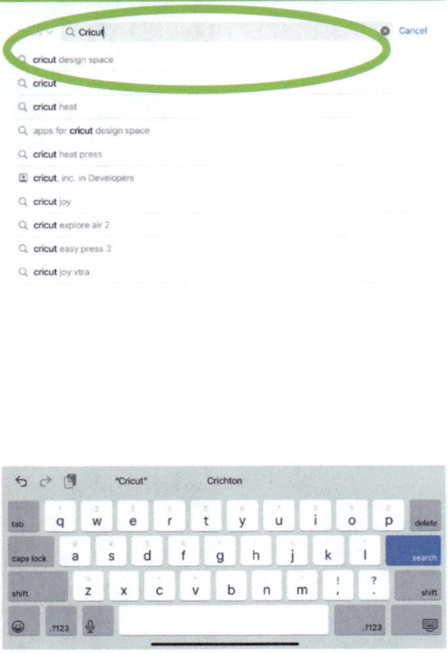

Step 3: Tap Update. Make sure you have a good Internet signal for the best results.

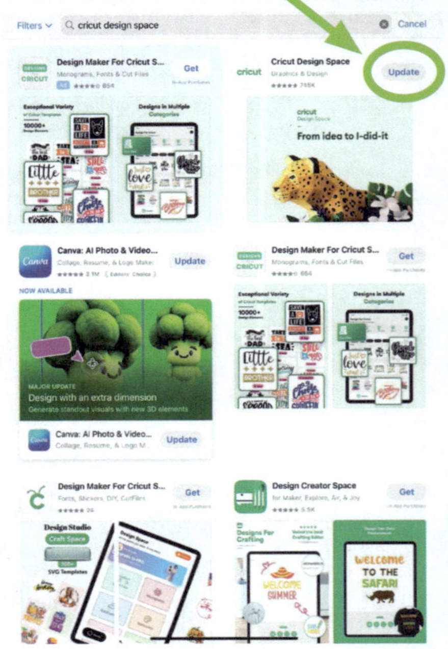

Step 4: Wait for Cricut Design Space to update, usually no more than a few minutes.

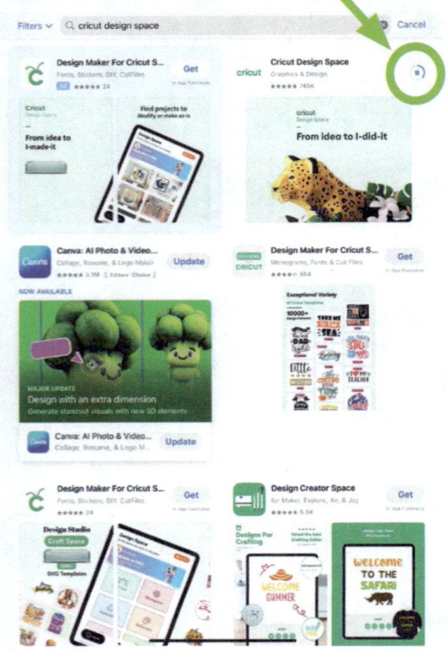

Step 5: Tap Open to launch the updated version of the Cricut Design Space app.

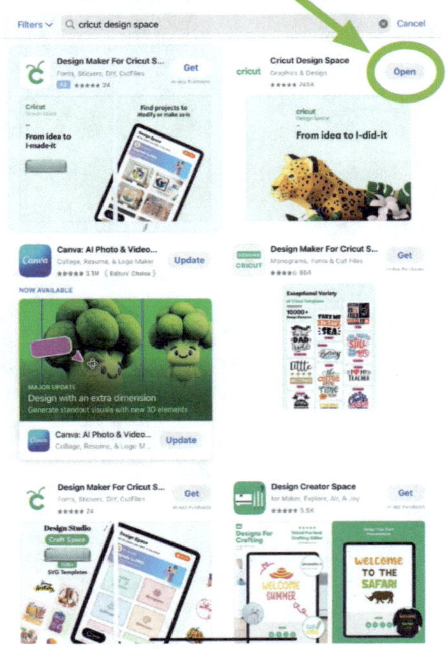

Note: If Cricut Design Space does not need updated, you will not see the "Update" button when you open the app in the App Store.

iOS

HOW TO TROUBLESHOOT DESIGN SPACE PROBLEMS

Your ability and willingness to troubleshoot problems is a high factor in your success with your Cricut (and really, most things in life). Problems happen, but you CAN solve them. Here are the steps I take when I encounter problems with Cricut Design Space:

Cricut Design Space is acting weird or not working at all.

Is it down?

- Yes → Watch for it to come back.
  - Still having problems?
    - Yes → Do you have a strong Internet connection?
    - No → Have fun and make something awesome!
- No → Is it installed and up-to-date?
  - Yes → Restart your device.
    - Are you still having problems?
      - Yes → Do you have a strong Internet connection?
      - No → Have fun and make something awesome!
  - No → Have fun and make something awesome!

Do you have a strong Internet connection?

- Yes → Keep the app with Design Space open and don't move away while cutting.
  - Are you still having problems?
- No → Connect to Internet & move your Cricut and device closer to router.
  - Still having problems?
    - Yes → Close any other apps running on your device.
    - No → Have fun and make something awesome!

Close any other apps running on your device.

Are you still having problems?

- Yes → Make sure your Cricut is actually connected via Bluetooth.
- No → Have fun and make something awesome!

Are you still having problems?

- Yes → Disconnect your Cricut, restart your device, and reconnect your Cricut.
- No → Have fun and make something awesome!

Are you still having problems?

- Yes → Contact Cricut Member Care at help.cricut.com. Cricut Member Care is very helpful!
- No → Have fun and make something awesome!

Having different problems? Here are more solutions:

Machine problems:
Check the Cricut site at help.cricut.com

Cutting problems:
Check my ideas at jennifermaker.com/cricut-cutting-problems-tips-cleaner-cuts

Mat problems:
Check my mat tips at jennifermaker.com/cricut-cutting-mats-sticky

Blade problems:
Check my blade tips at jennifermaker.com/cricut-blades-cutting-tips

Contact Cricut Member Care at help.cricut.com. Cricut Member Care is very helpful!

HOW TO INSTALL CRICUT DESIGN SPACE

Step 1: Connect your Android device to the Internet, go to the Home screen, and tap **Play Store**.

Step 2: Tap in the search bar at the top and type "Cricut," then tap **Cricut Design Space app**.

Step 3: Tap **Install** and wait for it to download & install.

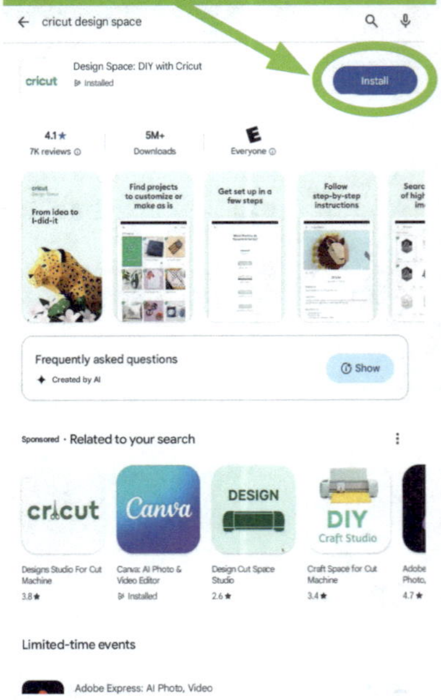

Step 4: Tap **Open**. Make sure you have a good Internet signal for the best results.

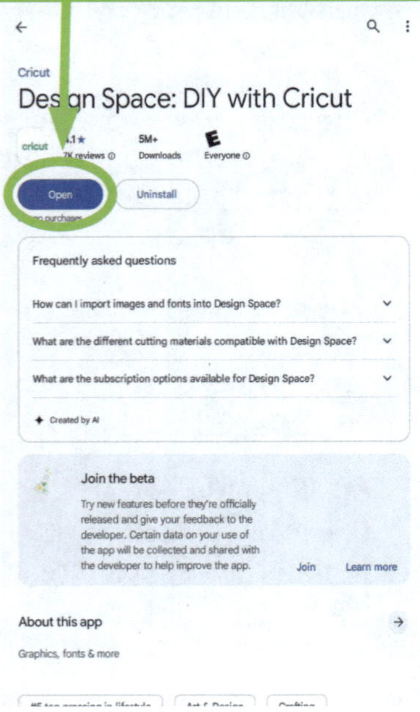

Step 5: Tap **Sign In** (if you already have an account). If not, tap **Machine Setup**.

Step 6: Enter your Cricut sign in email and password to begin using the app.

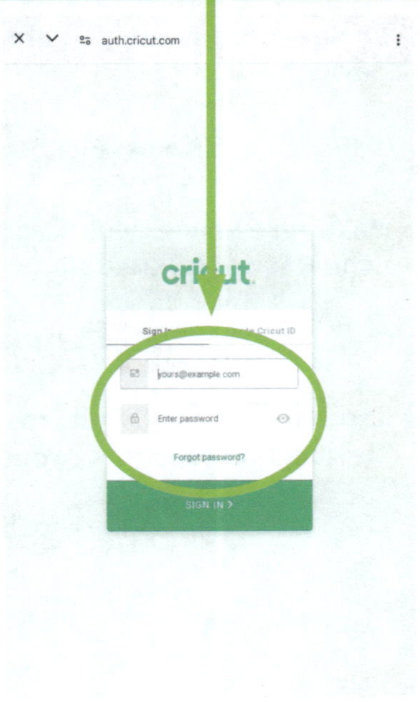

HOW TO OPEN AND START A NEW PROJECT

Step 1: Tap the Cricut Design icon on your device. If you cannot find it, scroll up, tap in the search area, then type and search for "Cricut."

Tip: If this is your first time using Cricut on your device, see page 94 for details on how to install it.

Step 2: Tap the green + button for a new project, then choose "Blank Canvas."

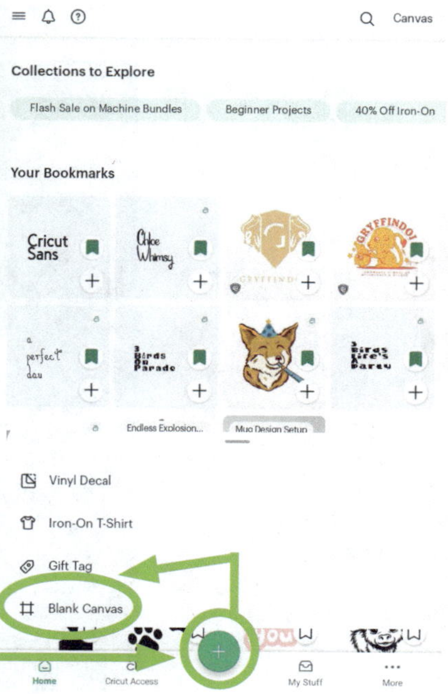

Warning: If you get an error message upon opening the Cricut app, it probably means your WiFi connection is missing or not strong enough for Cricut to retrieve your account information. Move within range and try again.

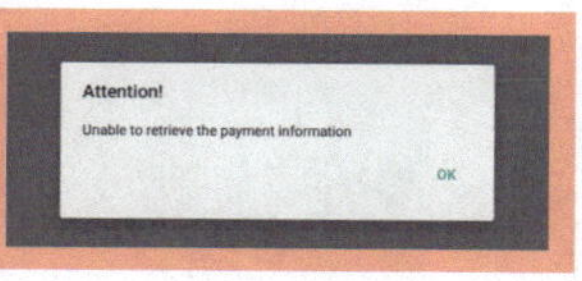

Step 3: If you see this message, it means you left something on your Canvas the last time you used the app. So either tap Cancel (if you want to see what you left there) or tap Replace for a new, blank Canvas.

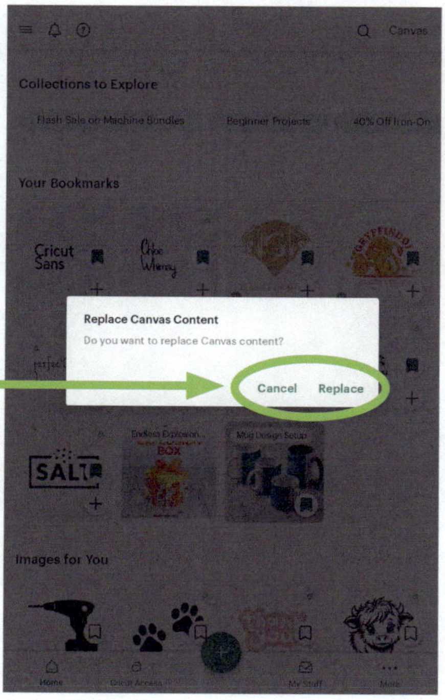

You will get a new Canvas, ready for you to add images, shapes, text, and projects!

HOW TO CONNECT VIA BLUETOOTH

Step 1: Tap the Settings app.

Note: Your Cricut must be within 10-15 feet of your device. If you need to use a Wireless Bluetooth Adapter, make sure it is inserted.

Step 2: Tap Connections, then tap Bluetooth. Turn on Bluetooth if it is off, then look for your Cricut in this list and tap it. If you do not see it listed, make sure your Cricut is turned on and no other Bluetooth device is connected to it.

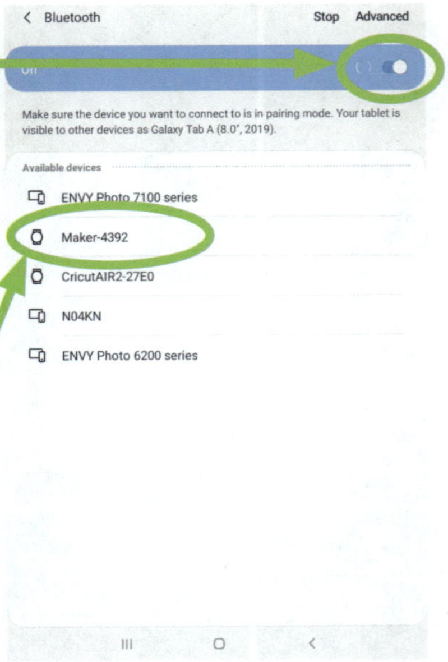

Step 3: If you get a pairing request, type 0000 (that's four zeros) or 1234 as the passcode and tap OK.

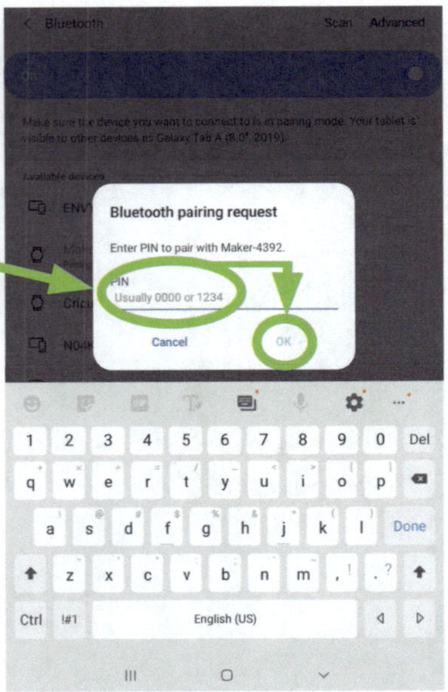

Once paired, it will appear in your Bluetooth window under Paired Devices.

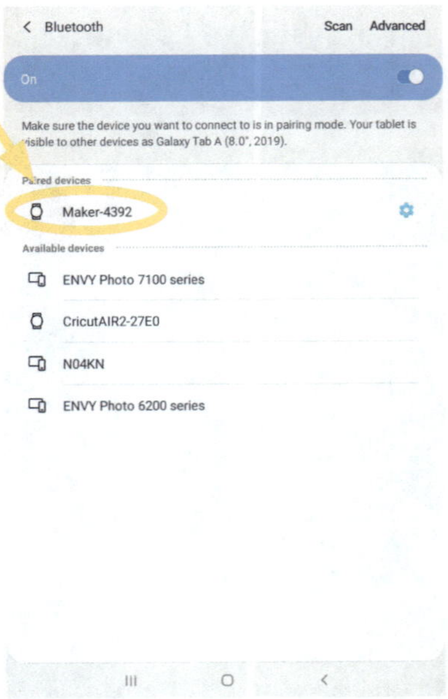

HOW TO ATTACH TO KEEP THINGS TOGETHER

Did you tap Make It and find all of your elements re-ordered and out of place? Fix this and keep everything exactly where you want with the Attach button. Use Attach to hold your cuts in the same position relative to each other on the cutting mat. The Attach feature also helps you affix a writing or score layer to a cut layer.

Step 1: Add all of your elements to the Design Space Canvas on your Android device, including text, SVG designs, score lines, write lines, etc.

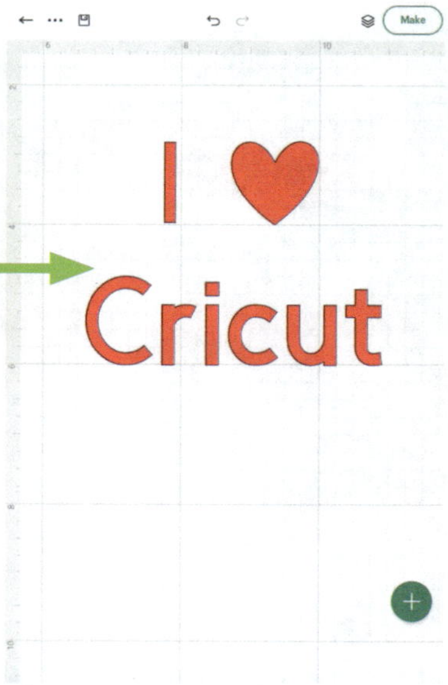

Step 2: Tap and drag a selection box around all of the images you want to attach together, tap on Actions at the bottom of the screen, then tap Attach.

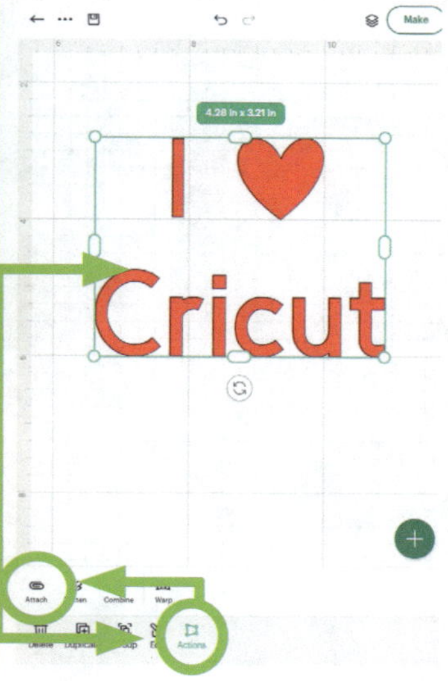

Note that attached layers will take on the same color. So only attach layers that you really want to be the same color!

Tip: If you are having a problem attaching layers, try ungrouping layers first.

You can verify that your images are attached by tapping Layers and noting that they are now labeled "ATTACH."

Score lines must be attached with the appropriate cut layer in order for them to score on the right layer, as shown below.

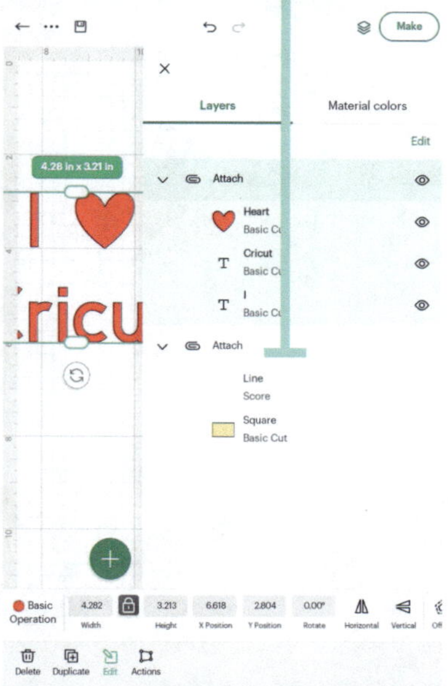

Practice this at jennifermaker.com/i-love-cricut

HOW TO GROUP AND UNGROUP

Grouping lets you keep objects together in your design but not necessarily on your mat (you still need to use the Attach function to keep things together on the mat). Sometimes projects and uploaded images will be grouped when you open/insert them, and you'll need to ungroup them so you can make changes.

GROUP / UNGROUP

HOW TO GROUP:

Step 1: Tap and drag a rectangle to select objects. Alternately, tap Layers and select each layer you want to group together.

Step 2: With all objects you want to be in a group selected, tap the Group button in the bottom toolbar.

Tip: Once your objects group, they will be nested under a new line item in your Layers Panel called "Group." ▼ GROUP

HOW TO UNGROUP:

Option 1: Tap the Layers button in the top toolbar and look for "Group." Tap on it, then tap the icon at the bottom of the screen.

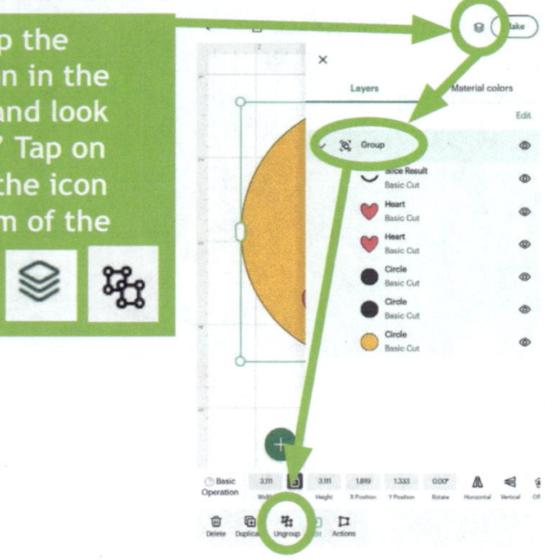

Option 2: Select the grouped layers, then tap the Ungroup icon in the bottom toolbar.

You often need to ungroup before you can attach objects. Sometimes, a project or image set has multiple groups. So if you want to attach and have an issue, look for ALL groups and ungroup them first.

Practice this at jennifermaker.com/smiley-face

HOW TO WELD

Need to join elements to create a new image? Do it with the Weld tool! The Weld tool can simplify a design, keep the letters of a word connected, and combine shapes to create new designs.

Step 1: Insert any images you want to weld onto your Canvas.

Note: If you are trying to create a single image with Weld, make sure all elements are overlapping.

Step 2: Select all the images you want to weld. Tap Actions, Combine, then Weld. This will weld the images together as just one image.

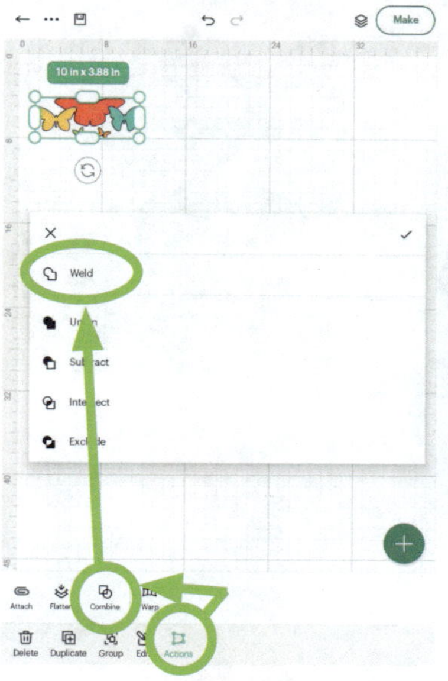

Tip: You can select items within groups to weld by tapping on their names in the Layers Panel.

WELD

Once your images weld, they will change to the same color and a new image appears in the Layers Panel.

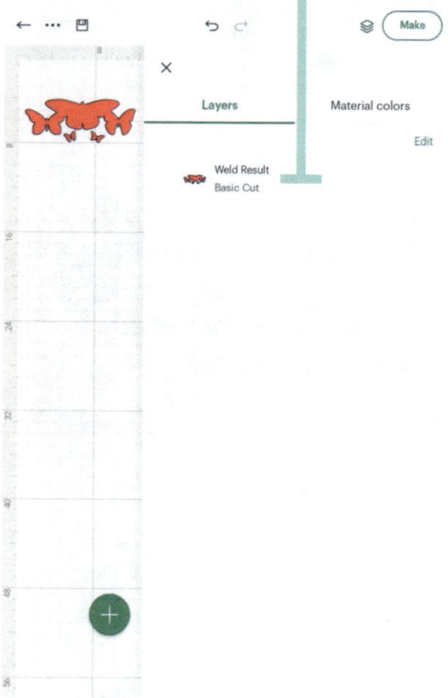

Note: You can unweld ONLY if it is the current project on your Canvas and you recently welded it. If so, tap Undo until you unweld the image(s).

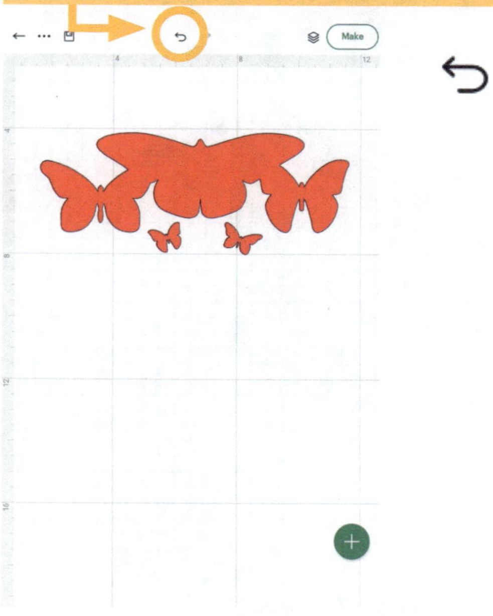

Practice this at jennifermaker.com/butterflies

HOW TO USE UNION, SUBTRACT, INTERSECT, & EXCLUDE

Need to join elements to create an image? These tools are similar and can be found when you select Combine! The Union tool is similar to Weld (previous page) but it is not permanent! Your layers will still be accessible individually! Subtract is similar to Slice (next page) but it does not leave you with remaining pieces; it subtracts the bottom layer and top layer. Intersect takes two overlapping layers and combines them, leaving only the parts that intersect. Exclude is the opposite of intersect; it takes two overlapping layers and cuts what overlapped, leaving behind what did not overlap.

Step 1: Insert your images onto your Canvas so that they are overlapping.

UNION: Select your images and tap Actions > Combine > Unite. This action combines the items together.

SUBTRACT: Select your images. Tap Actions > Combine > Subtract. This subtracts the top layer from the bottom layer.

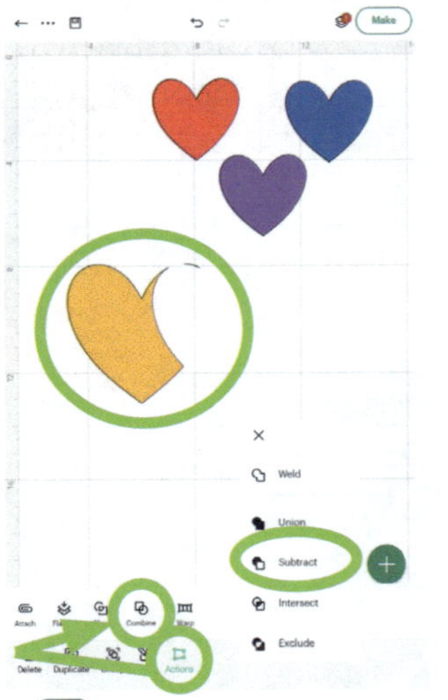

EXCLUDE: Select your images and tap Actions > Combine > Exclude. This action removes the parts that intersected.

INTERSECT: Select your images and tap Actions > Combine > Intersect. This action leaves only the parts that intersected between the two images.

Tip: If you don't like how the action operated on your images, press the undo button and try a different one!

Practice this at jennifermaker.com/five-hearts

HOW TO SLICE
(CUT AN IMAGE OUT OF ANOTHER)

Want to cut out parts or even make your own custom designs? If so, Slice is the tool for you! Slice lets you cut out parts of another object. If you keep slicing, you can make some pretty amazing designs!

Step 1: Insert your images onto your Canvas so that they are overlapping.

Step 2: Tap and drag a selection box around all of the images you want to Slice, tap on Actions at the bottom of the screen, then tap Slice.

After you tap Slice, new layers called "Slice Result" will appear.

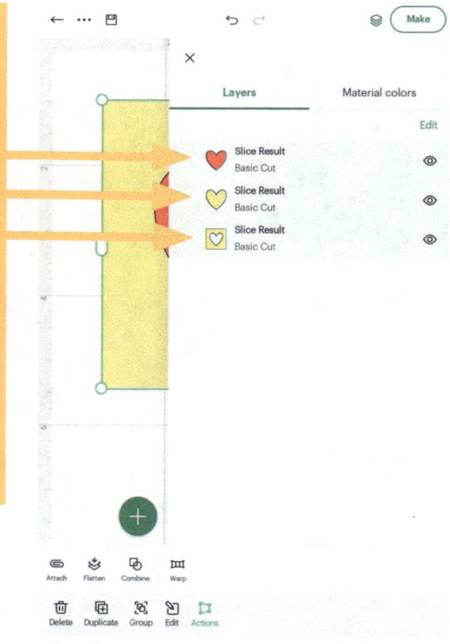

Step 3: Move, hide, or delete the layers you do not want, then you're good to go!

Slice Tips:

- You can Slice both images and text.
- Layers in groups can be Sliced if you select just the individual layers, not the entire groups.
- If you use Slice with hidden layers, all hidden layers will be removed.
- If text is multi-layered and one layer is hidden, you can use the Slice tool. However, if you ungroup text from its shadow layer, it becomes an image and will no longer work with the Slice tool unless the text is ungrouped to individual letters.

Practice this at jennifermaker.com/heart-slice

HOW TO REMOVE PARTS WITH CONTOUR

Need to erase parts of an existing design? Don't want that word or that circle, but can't ungroup or hide a layer? Use Contour to remove existing parts from projects.

Step 1: Choose an image with elements you'd like to remove then tap Actions, then tap the Contour tool in the lower right corner of the app window.

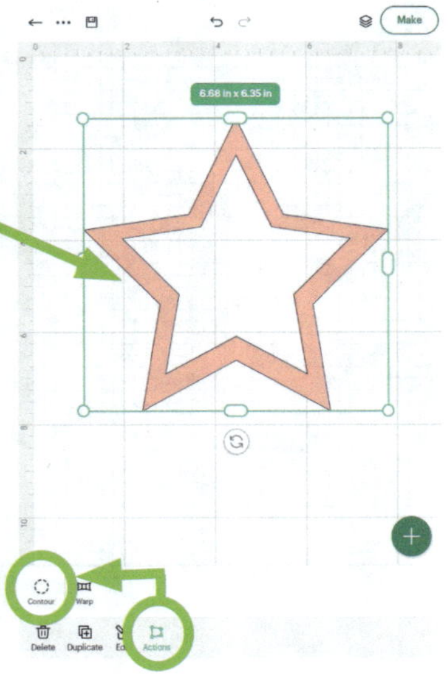

Step 2: Tap on the elements you want to remove. You can make the image larger (to see detail) by pinching to zoom.

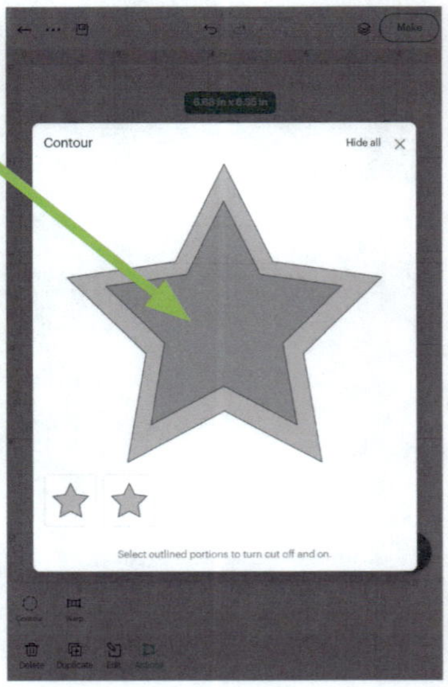

Step 3: Elements that appear darker are those that you can remove. When your image looks the way you want it to, click the X icon in the upper left hand corner to return to your Canvas.

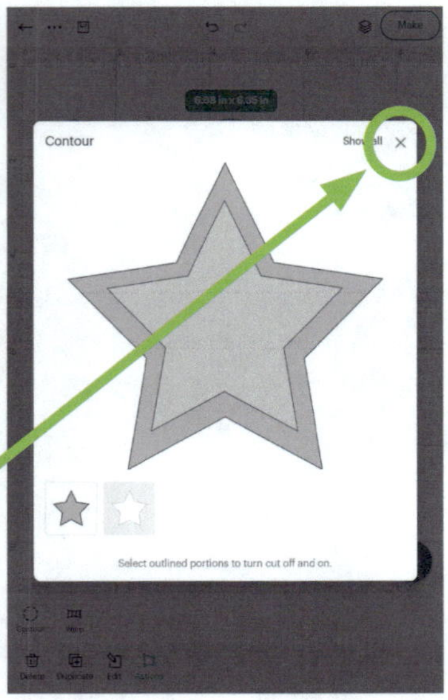

Step 4: Confirm that your image looks the way you want it. If you need to make more changes, just click the Contour tool again.

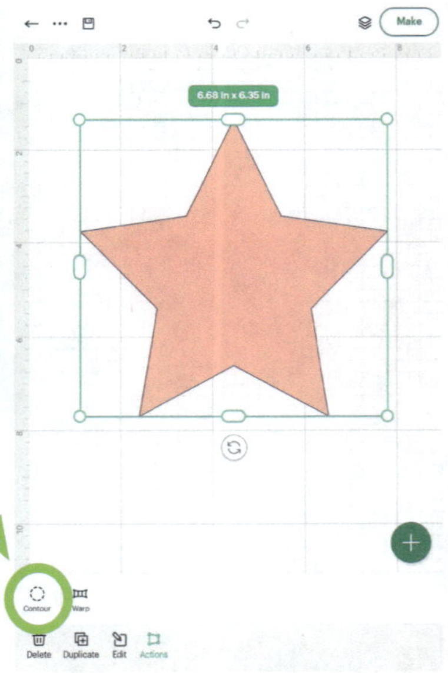

Tip: Contour isn't permanent so long as you don't Weld your images! If you decide later you want a Contoured image to go back the way it was, or simply edit it further, all the hidden parts are retained!

Practice this at jennifermaker.com/pink-star

HOW TO CURVE TEXT

Step 1: Tap the + sign (green circle), then tap Text. Add some text.

Step 2: Select your text by tapping on it, then tap the Curve icon in the menu at the bottom of the screen.

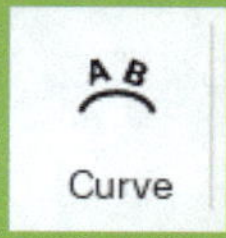

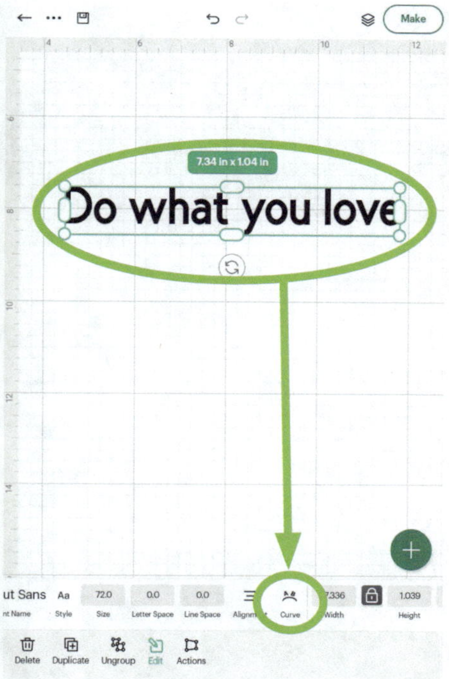

Step 3: To curve your text downward, drag the sliding bar to the right or type in a number above zero. Tap the checkmark in the corner of the pop-up when finished.

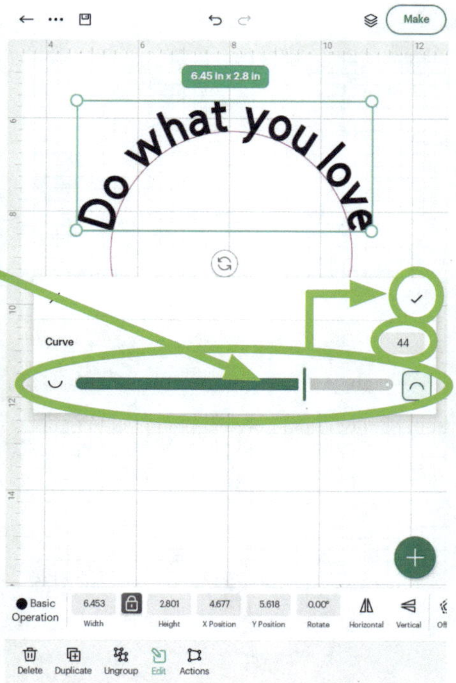

Step 4: To curve your text upward, drag the sliding bar to the right or type in a number below zero. Tap the checkmark in the corner of the pop-up when finished.

Tip: If you have difficulties moving the letters into position, it may be because SmartGuides are turned on. To turn them off, tap Settings in the bottom toolbar and toggle off SmartGuides.

Practice this at jennifermaker.com/rainbow-love

HOW TO WARP TEXT, SHAPES, AND IMAGES

Step 1: Tap the + sign (green circle), then tap Shape and add a rectangle to the Canvas, unlocking and stretching it to make it wider.

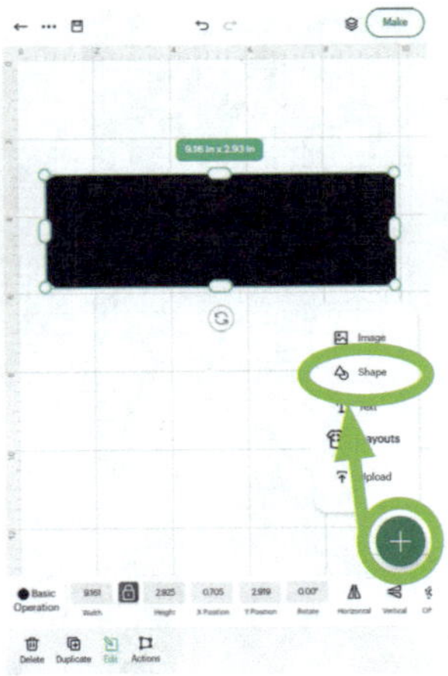

Step 2: Add some text on the Canvas, resize it, and move it on top of the rectangle.

Step 3: With your shape and text selected, click Actions > Warp.

Step 4: Choose a warp style. You can also choose how much you want the warp effect by sliding the bar or using the number box at the bottom of the screen.

Step 5: Your text changes to the warp style you selected!

Tip: If you decide that you want to use a different warp style other than the one you originally selected, just select your text and shape, click the Warp button again, and choose a new style.

Note: There are some fonts that cannot be warped, as well as Print Then Cut images. Design Space will notify you about it if you try to warp a font that cannot be warped.

Warning: Warp is currently available for Cricut Access members only.

HOW TO ALIGN AND DISTRIBUTE OBJECTS

Step 1: Add two or more items to your Canvas that you want to align or distribute evenly.

Step 2: Tap and drag a selection box around all items you want to align and/or distribute.

Step 3: Tap on the Edit tool in the bottom toolbar, tap Align, and tap Align Bottom.

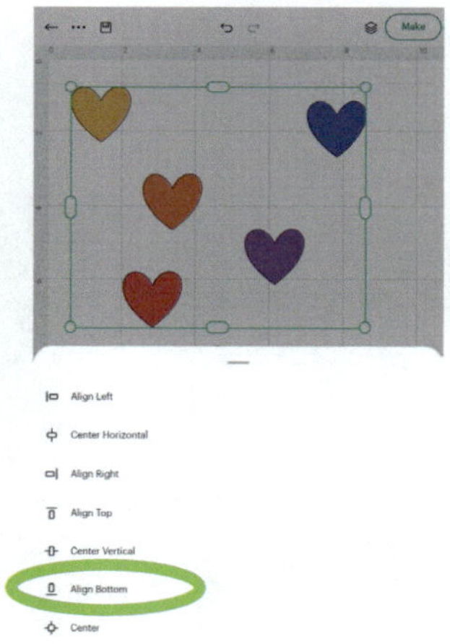

Step 4: All selected items are aligned with the bottom-most object. Next, let's space them out evenly.

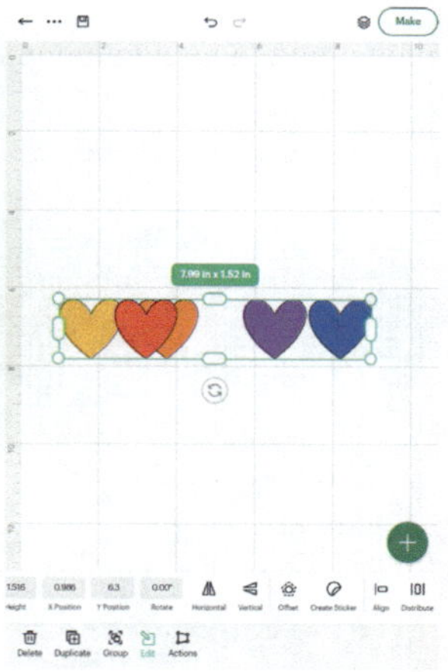

Step 5: Tap on the Edit tool in the bottom toolbar, tap the Distribute tool, and choose Distribute Horizontally.

Step 6: Note that all the hearts are now in a perfect row with the same spacing.

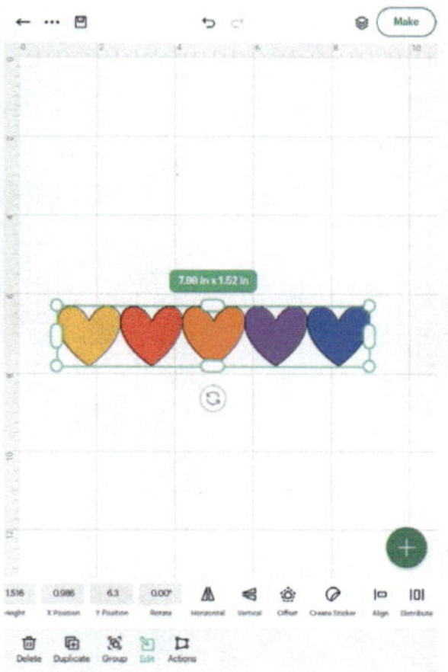

Practice this at jennifermaker.com/five-hearts

HOW TO CHANGE LETTER SPACE

Step 1: Tap the + (green circle), then tap Text. Choose a font and type something onto the Canvas. Note how the letters are spaced widely apart. Let's fix that.

Step 2: Select the text, tap Edit, tap Letter Space, adjust using the sliders or the number pad until the letters look better.

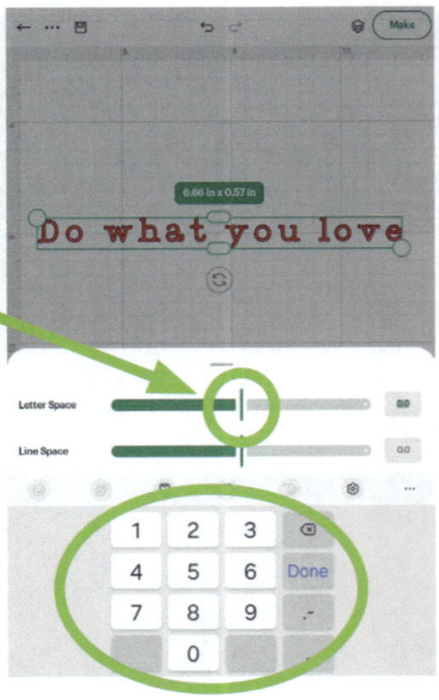

Step 3: If you have letters that are too close to each other (like the letter "D" and "o" in the example here), select the text and tap Action, then tap Isolate Letters.

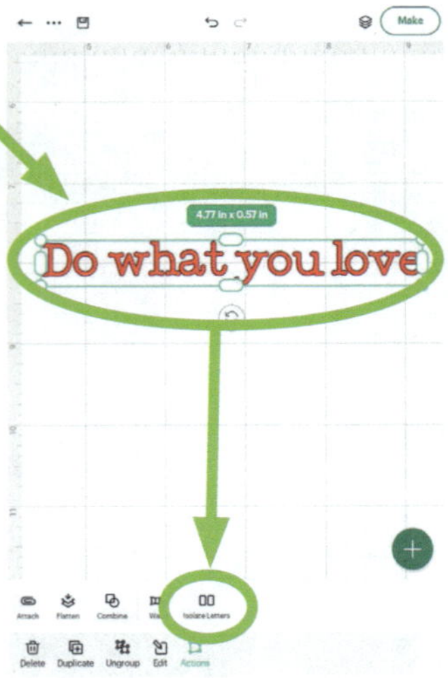

Step 4: Select just the letter "D" and move it until it is properly spaced.

Important: Select all letters and then tap Group to make sure your letters stay together when you cut them.

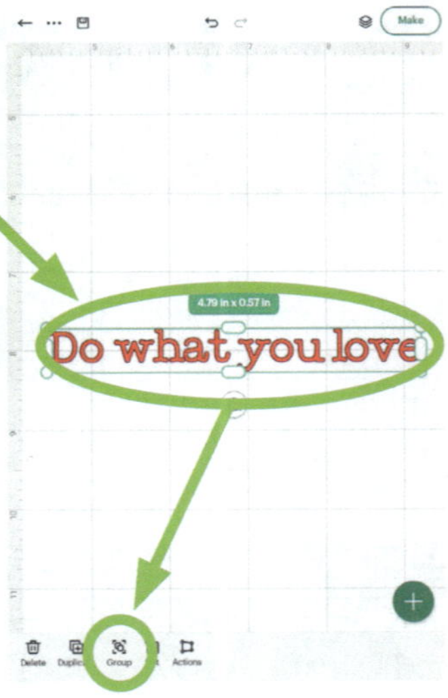

Tip: If you have difficulties moving the letters into position, it may be because SmartGuides are turned on. To turn them off, tap Settings in the bottom toolbar and toggle off SmartGuides.

Practice this at jennifermaker.com/rainbow-love

HOW TO WELD TEXT AND KEEP LETTER CENTERS

Welding text can be a little tricky. Typically, you weld script fonts (which can have overlapping letters) so words cut out as single units. Sometimes when you weld, the centers fill in—here's how to fix that:

Step 1: Type in some script text, change your letter spacing so the letters overlap a bit (see previous page), select all, then tap Actions > Combine > Weld.

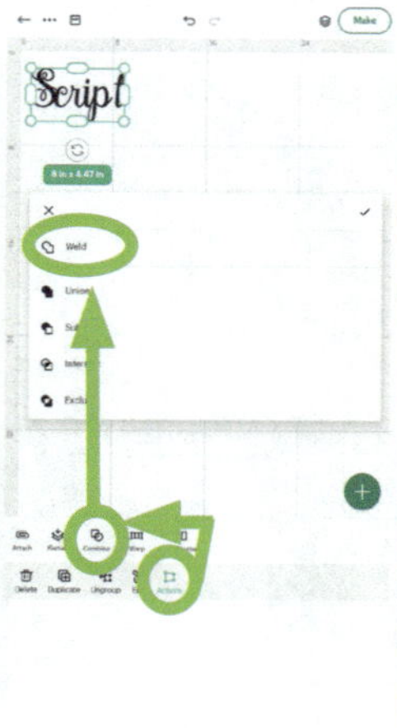

Step 2: If you get a center filling in (like the p here), tap Undo, then use the Resize handle to make your text MUCH larger, then tap Actions > Combine > Weld again.

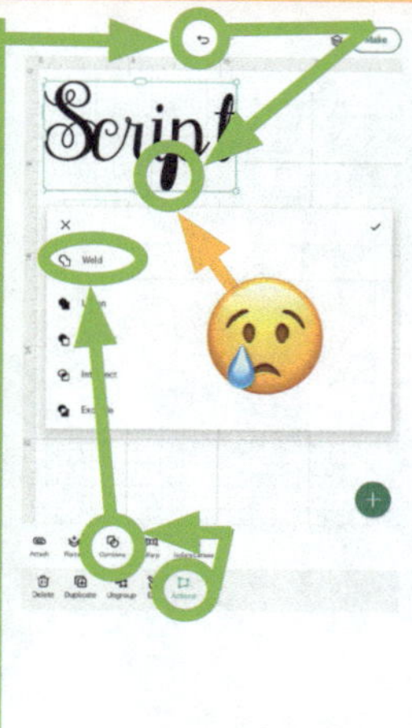

Step 3: Repeat step 2 until you can weld and the letter center does not fill in (you may have to get REALLY big), then resize back down to the right size.

Another thing that can happen with text is that letter centers (the interior white space) can disappear when you cut them out. But you can connect the spaces and keep the centers! Here's how to fix that:

Step 1: Type some text and look for letters & numbers with interior white space (counters), like A, B, D, O, P, Q, R, a, b, d, e, g, o, p, q and 0, 4, 6, 8, and 9.

Step 2: Add a square by tapping + (green circle), then Shape. Unlock it and resize it so it forms a rectangle about the width of the letter's strokes.

Step 3: Tap and drag the rectangle over a letter with interior white space so it's connecting the space inside to the space outside, like this:

Step 4: Select the word and the rectangle, then tap Actions > Slice.

Step 5: Delete all layers except the layer with the word in it.

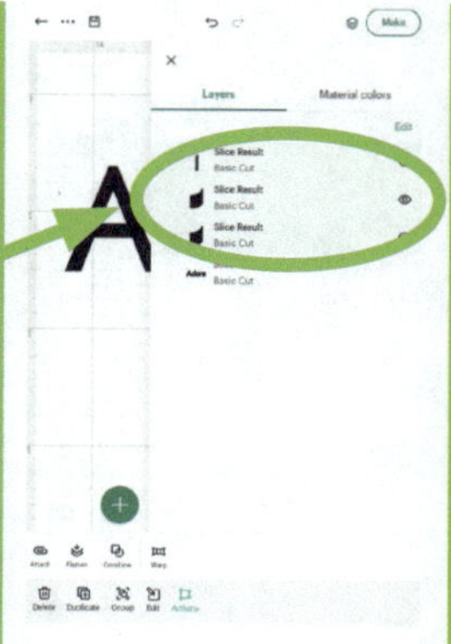

Repeat steps 2-5 for all letters as needed.

Practice this at jennifermaker.com/script-text and jennifermaker.com/adore-text

HOW TO OFFSET AND KNOCKOUT TEXT

Knockouts are a popular decorative effect and can create beautiful projects. Here's how to do them on Android:

Step 1: Type your main word in a bold chunky font like Cricut Sans Bold. Unlock it, resize it to make it taller, and tap Actions > Combine > Weld.

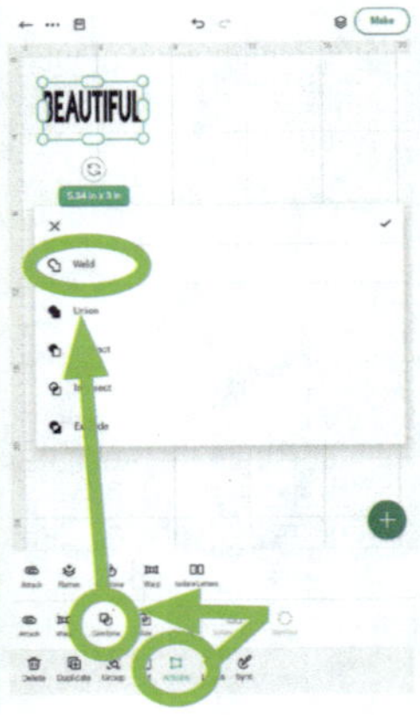

Step 2: Type an accent word in a script font (i.e., I Love Glitter). Adjust letters as needed, unlock it, resize it, and tap Actions > Combine > Weld.

Step 3: With the Script font still selected, tap Edit, then Tap Offset.

Step 4: Choose your Offset dimensions by using the slider or tapping the box and typing it directly in.

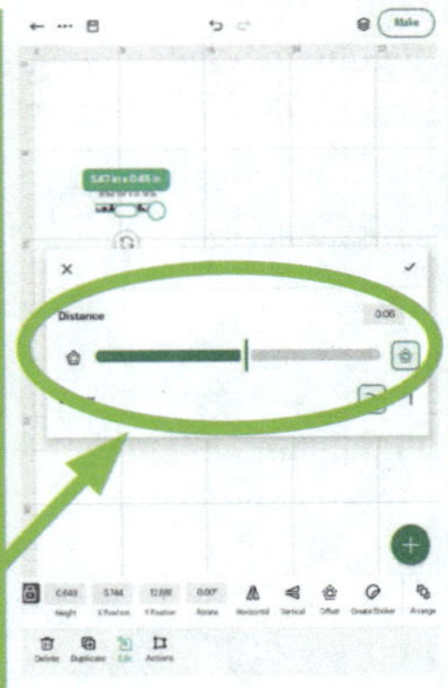

Step 5: Decide whether you want rounded or straight corners. Then tap the checkmark in the top right corner.

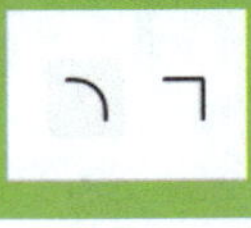

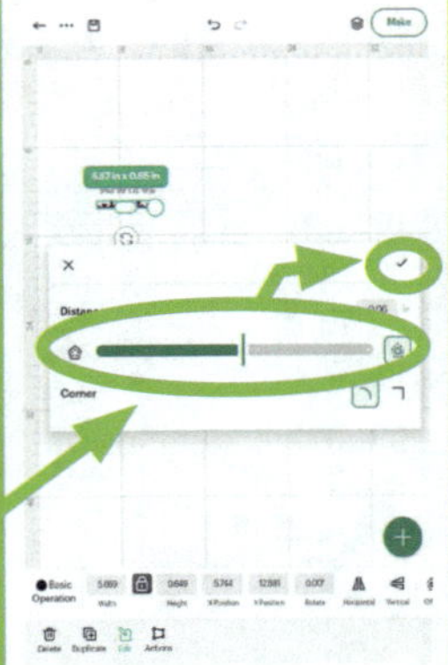

Step 6: Move the Offset text (not the original text) up into the larger word. Select both the larger word and the offset, then tap Actions, then Slice.

Step 7: Delete the new Sliced layers so that you only have the original larger word layer remaining, like in this example:

Step 8: Move the smaller word into the space created within the larger word.

Step 9: Change the color of one of the words so the two words stand apart.

KNOCKOUT TEXT

Practice this at jennifermaker.com/beautiful-knockout

HOW TO FIND AND BOOKMARK FONTS

Find and bookmark your favorite fonts so you can come back to them whenever you need them. This can save you a lot of time, especially when you want to recreate projects.

Step 1: Tap + (green circle), then tap Text. Tap the Font Name in the bottom left corner.

Step 2: Search for a font you want to bookmark.

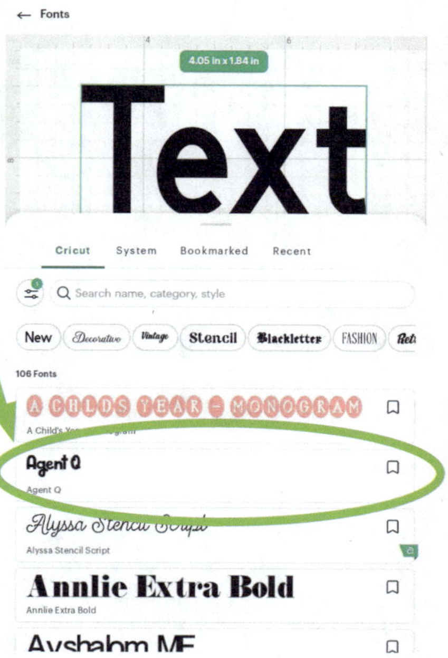

Step 3: Tap the bookmark icon to the right of your chosen font. The bookmark icon will turn green.

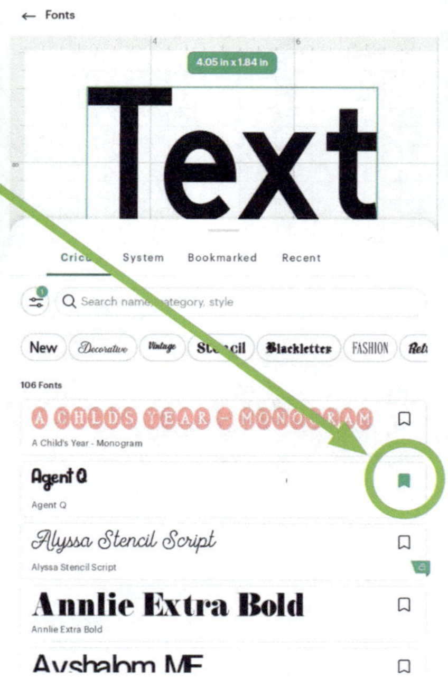

Step 4: Tap on the Bookmarked tab to find your bookmarked fonts. Tap on Recent to find fonts you recently used.

FIND & BOOKMARK FONTS

HOW TO CHANGE THE FONT FOR EXISTING TEXT

Step 1: Open your project and double-tap the text you want to change the font for so that there is a selection box around it.

Step 2: Tap the font name menu in the lower left corner to view the font list.

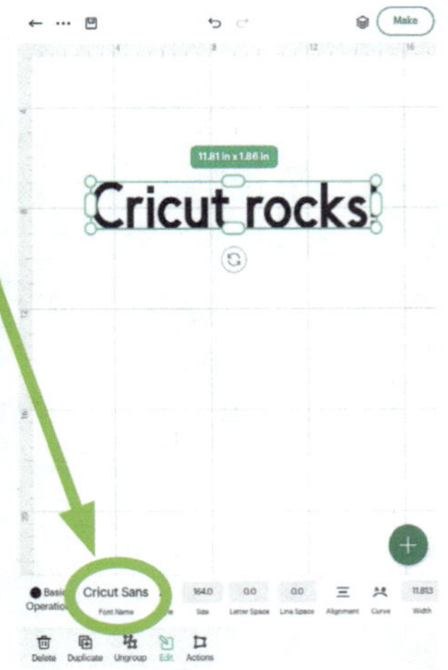

Step 3: Scroll through the list and tap the new font you want to use, then tap the back arrow in the top left corner.

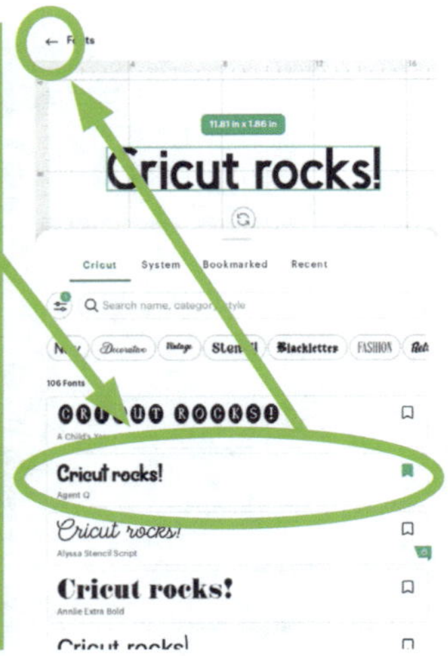

Your font changes!

If you ever type NEW text and cannot find it on your Android, zoom out and check the upper left corner — that's usually where you'll find it!

HOW TO CHANGE COLORS

Step 1: Select (tap) the layer you want to change, like the center of this flower.

Step 2: Tap Edit then tap the circle next to the Operation.

Step 3: Select (tap) the color you want. If you don't see the color you want, you can choose any custom color in the color picker below it. When done, tap the back arrow.

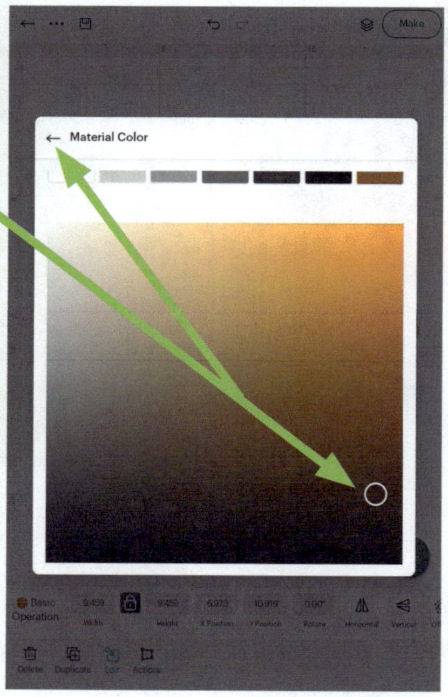

Your object changes to the color you selected!

Note that you cannot set pattern fills in the Android version of Cricut Design Space. If you need to set pattern fills, use a desktop or laptop to access Cricut Design Space and see directions on page 22.

CRICUT® COACH PLAYBOOK

HOW TO CHANGE OPERATION AND TOOLS

The Linetype menu lets you change the tool for a layer. Choices for the Cricut Joy and Joy Xtra are Cut (default) and Draw. The Cricut Explores add Score. The Cricut Makers add Engrave, Deboss, Wave, and Perforate. The Venture adds a large format cutting capability of 25 inches! You will only see the Maker linetype choices if you've set your machine to Maker or Maker 3. (Note: You cannot use the Knife or Foil Transfer tools from Android devices.) Here's how to set your machine and change the linetype.

OPERATIONS & TOOLS

Step 1: On the home page, tap the three lines in the upper left, tap Machine Selection, then tap your Cricut.

Step 2: Open a project, tap a layer, tap Edit, then tap Operation.

Tap Basic under Cut, then tap the back arrow to use the fine point, deep cut, fabric, or rotary blades. You cannot use the knife blade with Android.

Tap Draw then Pen Type and Color to set a layer to write with pens and markers. You can choose the color and thickness.

Tap Score, then tap the back arrow to set a layer score with the Stylus (Maker or Explore) or Scoring Wheel Tools (Maker only).

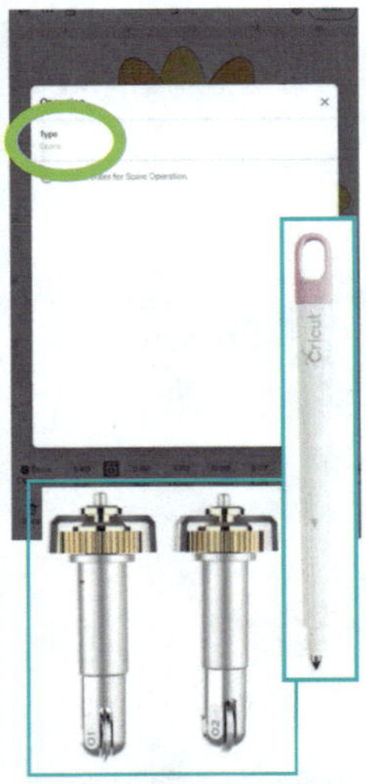

Tap Engrave, then tap the back arrow to set a layer to use the Engraving Tool (Maker only).

Tap Deboss, then tap the back arrow to set a layer to use the Debossing Tool (Maker only).

Tap Wavy Cut, then tap the back box to set a layer to use the Wavy Edge Tool (Maker only).

Tap Perforate, then tap the back arrow to set a layer to use the Perforation Blade Tool (Maker only).

Practice this at jennifermaker.com/starry-star

HOW TO SET TEXT TO WRITE WITH A PEN

First, be sure to check your pen to make sure it is compatible, as pens are designed for specific machines. You can insert a Cricut pen or marker into any Cricut machine and have it draw with it, and many crafters like to use this feature with a writing font to mimic handwriting. Here's how to choose a good font that looks like handwriting and set it to Draw in Cricut Design Space:

Step 1: Select your text, tap Font Name, then tap the Filter icon, then look for the category called Characteristic.

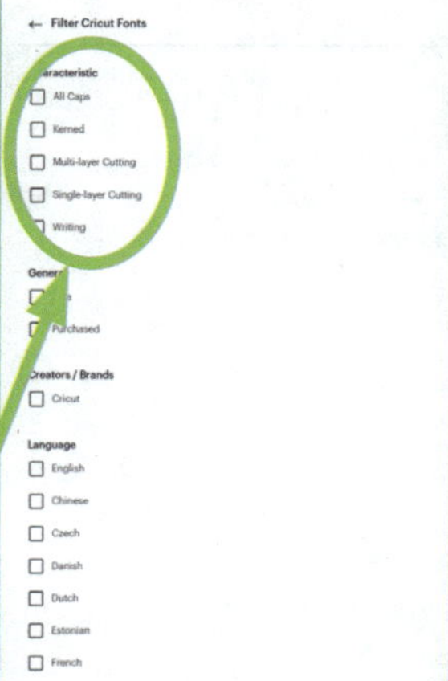

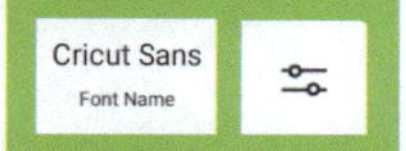

Step 2: Tap the checkbox next to Writing, then tap the back arrow.

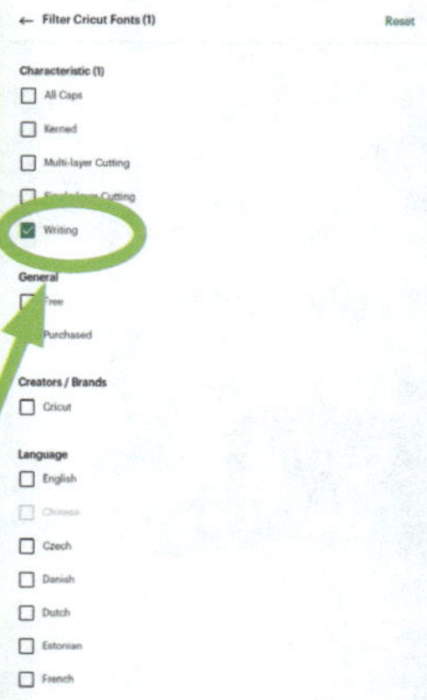

Step 3: Choose your writing font, then tap the back arrow in the top left corner.

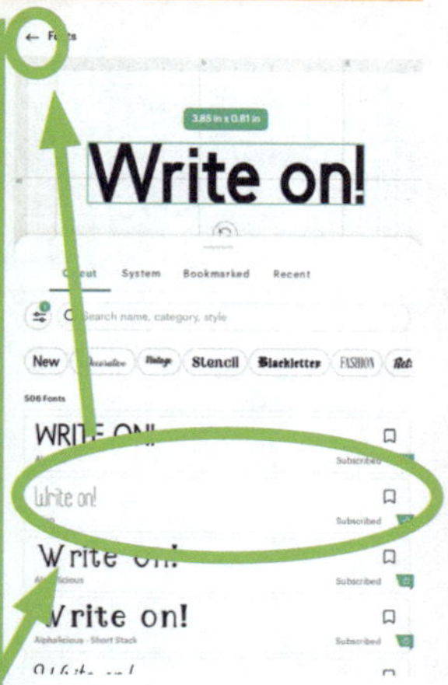

Step 4: To change pen type and color, tap Operation, then Pen, then Pen Type & Color.

Step 5: Tap a pen type and color, then tap the back arrow.

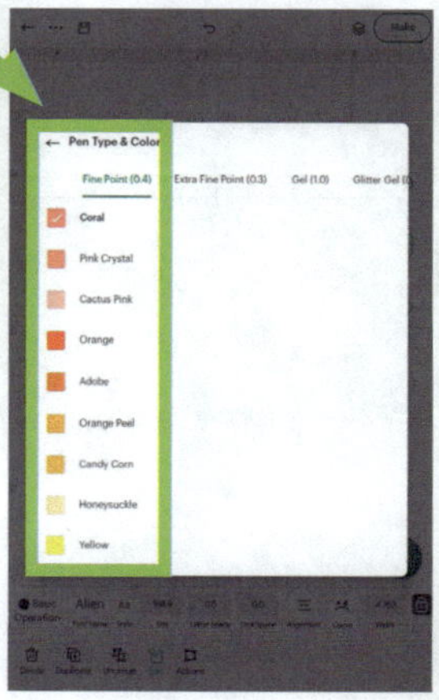

Step 6: Adjust the Font Size and Letter Space as necessary so it looks the way you want it to look, then click Make.

Step 7: Tap, hold and drag the text to the exact spot you want it to be written on your material on the cutting mat (see page 116), then click Next.

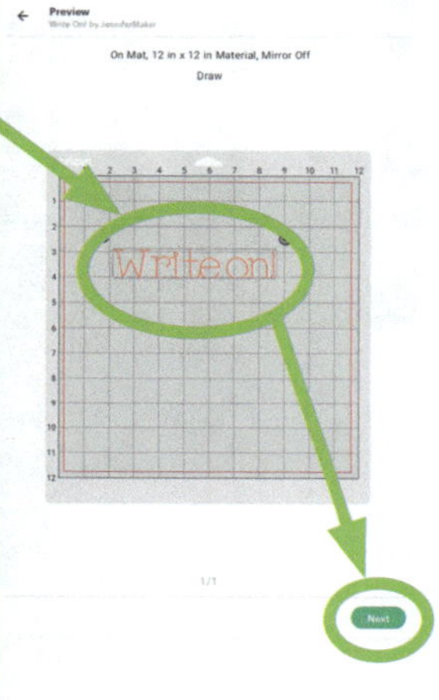

Step 8: Insert the pen in your Cricut's accessory clamp, position your material on the cutting mat, load your mat, and press the flashing button.

See my blog post at jennifermaker.com/cricut-writing-fonts for more tips on writing on your Cricut! I also have a free writing font you can use at jennifermaker.com/make-gift-tags-cricut

Practice this at jennifermaker.com/write-on

HOW TO SCORE WITH A STYLUS OR WHEEL

Step 1: Open or create a project with score lines. You can add a score line to any project by tapping the + (green circle), then Shape, then tap Line.

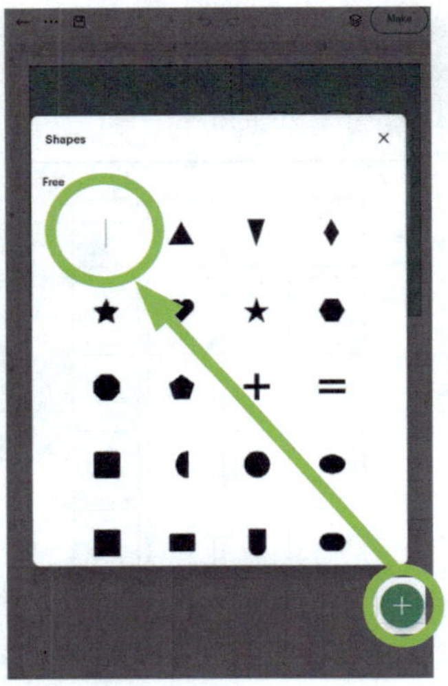

Step 2: Make sure any lines you want to be scored are attached to the layer that should have the score line (tap the arrow on the layer to change). Tap the X in the top left corner, then click Make.

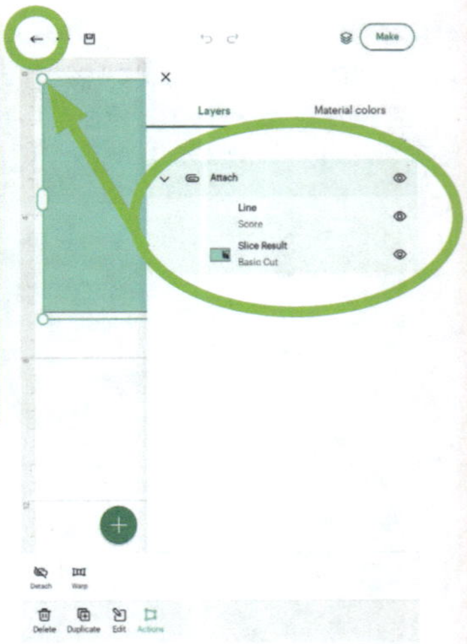

Step 3: Make sure the score line is on the same layer as the cut, then tap Next.

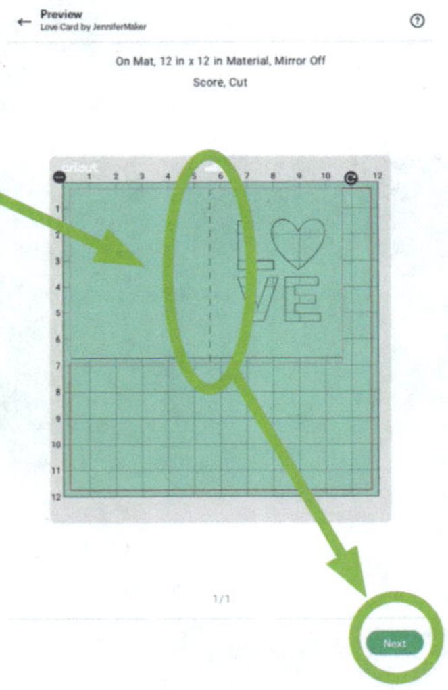

Step 4: Check the necessary tools. If the screen says to use a scoring wheel, but you do not have one, tap Edit > Tools.

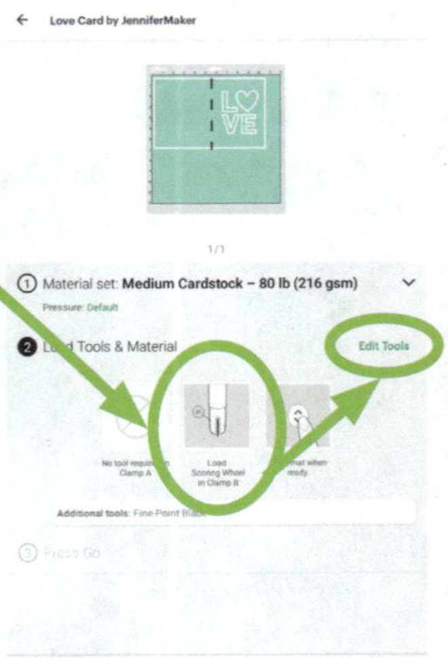

Step 5: Tap on the scoring tool of preference, then tap the back arrow.

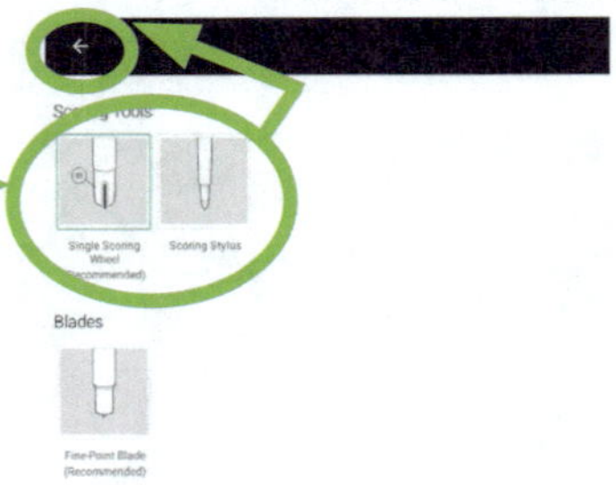

Step 6: Insert the scoring tool that matches step 5, then click the flashing icon on your Cricut.

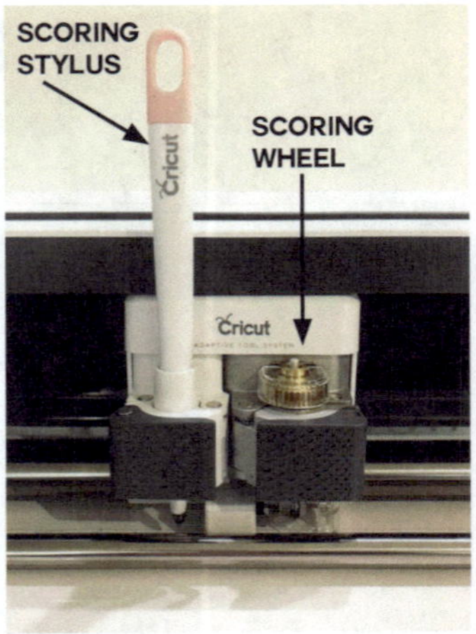

Practice this at jennifermaker.com/love-card

HOW TO USE THE CREATE STICKER TOOL

The Create Sticker tool is an easy way to turn any image into a sticker. It isn't absolutely required for sticker-making, but it does make it easier by telling your Cricut how much of a border to cut and whether to cut the sticker using the Die Cut method or the Kiss Cut method.

Step 1: Upload or create a design that you'd like to turn into a sticker.

Select the entire design and click the Create Sticker button in the top menu.

Step 2: Choose whether you'd like your sticker to be Die Cut or Kiss Cut (die cut means the sticker and its backing will be cut out, and kiss cut means that just the sticker is cut out, not the backing).

Select your Border Width and Border Fill Color. Click Apply.

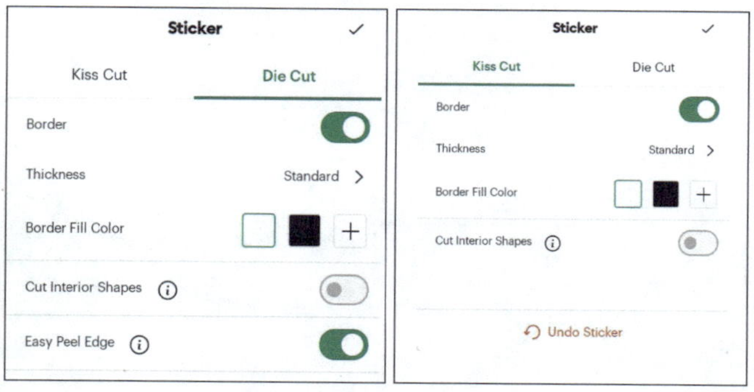

Your design will now be a single-layer Print Then Cut sticker! You will see a border around your design, and it will now be a Print Then Cut operation in the Layers Panel.

Print the sticker out on sticker paper using your color inkjet printer, then allow your Cricut to cut it out.

Warning: The Create Sticker tool is currently available for Cricut Access members only.

Practice this at jennifermaker.com/heart-sticker

CREATE STICKERS

Android

HOW TO REPOSITION ITEMS ON MAT PREVIEW

Need exact control over where items on your mat are cut? Want to cut one mat with multiple pieces of paper in different colors? You can do this if you reposition items on your mat before you cut! Here's how to do it on an Android device:

Step 1: Open or create a project. Make anything you want to appear on the same mat the same color. Tap Make.

Step 2: Make sure the items you want to reposition are all on the same mat.

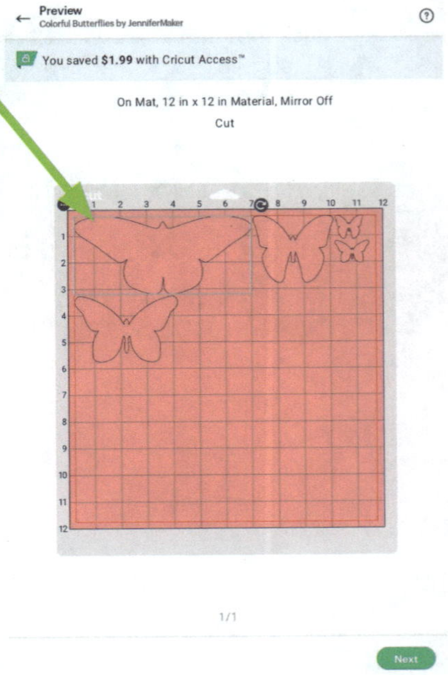

Step 3: Move each object on the mat by tapping and dragging to a new position. You can also rotate.

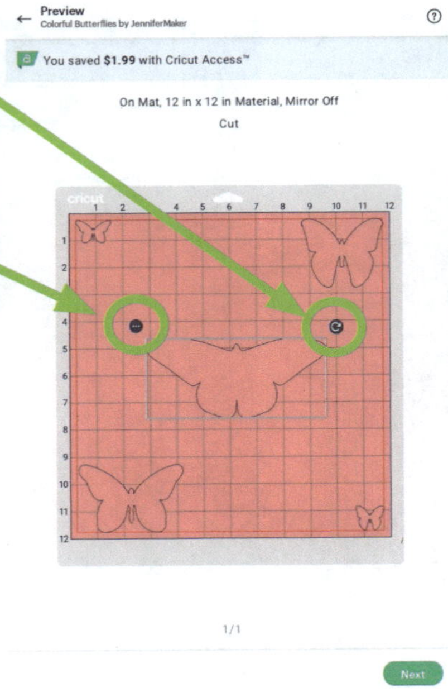

Step 4: Once you have each object where you want it to be on the mat, tap Next. Continue with cutting your design following the prompts on the screen.

REPOSITION ON MAT

Practice this at jennifermaker.com/butterflies

HOW TO MIRROR AND CUT IRON ON VINYL

Want to make a T-shirt or bag with iron-on vinyl? Here's how to mirror your image and position your vinyl on your mat for iron-on (heat transfer) vinyl!

Step 1: Insert your images and text. Select everything you would like to group, tap Actions, then tap Attach.

Step 2: Tap Make in the top right corner.

Step 3: Toggle the switch to mirror your design. The switch will turn green. Tap Next.

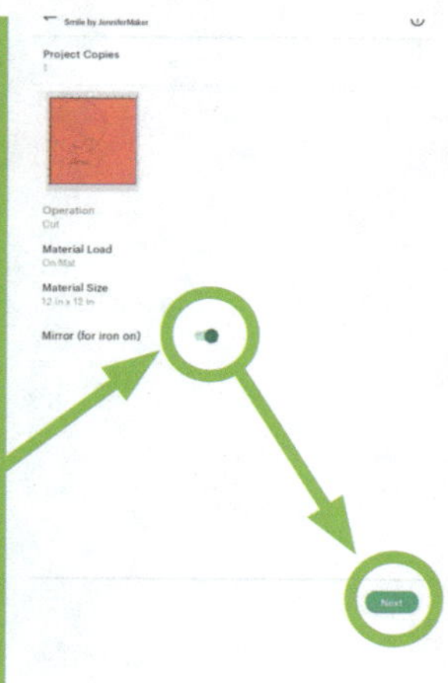

Step 4: Check to make sure that your design is mirrored on the preview. Tap Next.

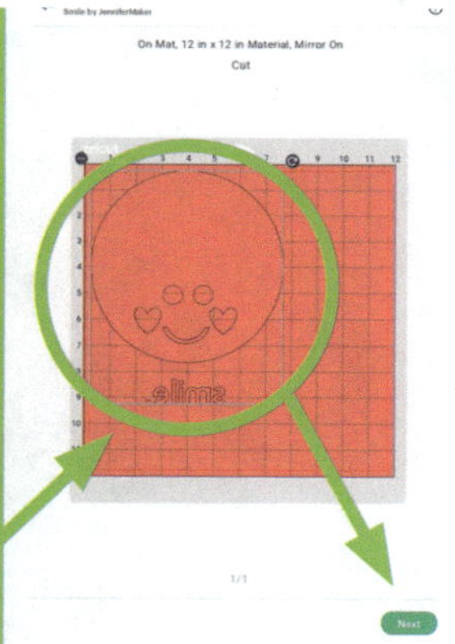

Step 5: Tap All Materials.

Step 6: Choose the type of iron-on vinyl you are using by tapping on the name.

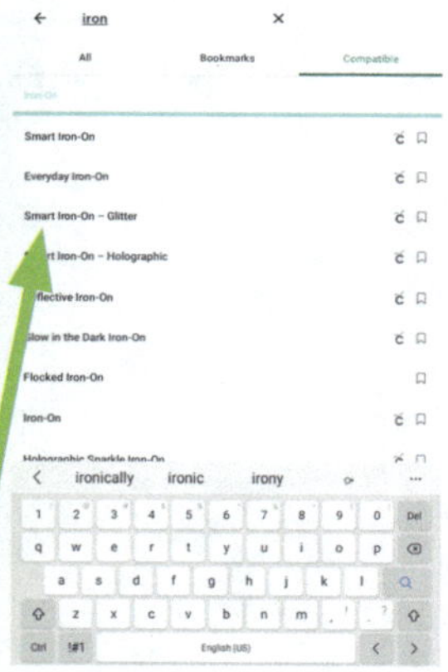

Step 7: Make sure your tools and materials are loaded. Follow the prompts to cut.

Remember, put the vinyl SHINY SIDE DOWN on your cutting mat!

Practice this at jennifermaker.com/simple-smile

HOW TO USE A LAYOUT

Step 1: Open a new project. Tap the + (green circle), then tap Layouts.

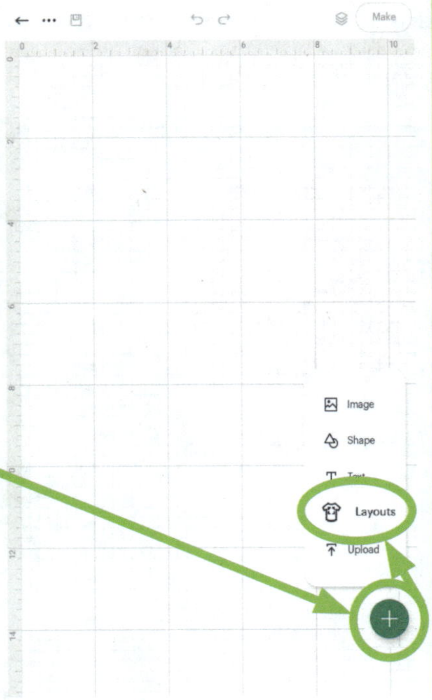

Step 2: Choose a layout that best fits your project. For example, to make a design for a T-Shirt, tap T-Shirt, then tap the size you want. Then slide the panel down.

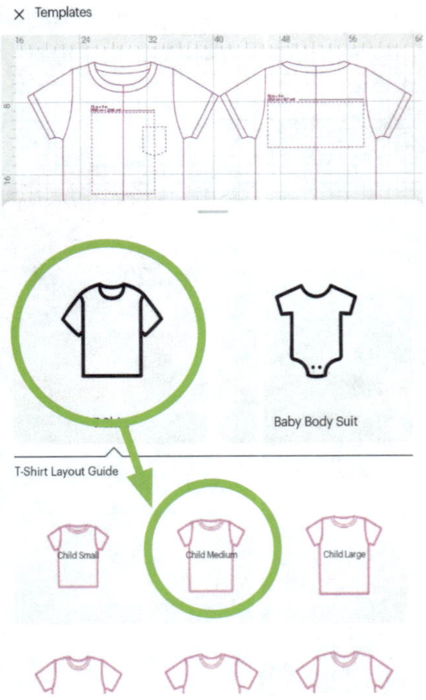

Step 3: Your layout will appear on the Canvas. Zoom in to the area where you want to create your design. For example, I want to place my design in the large tall rectangle on the front of the shirt.

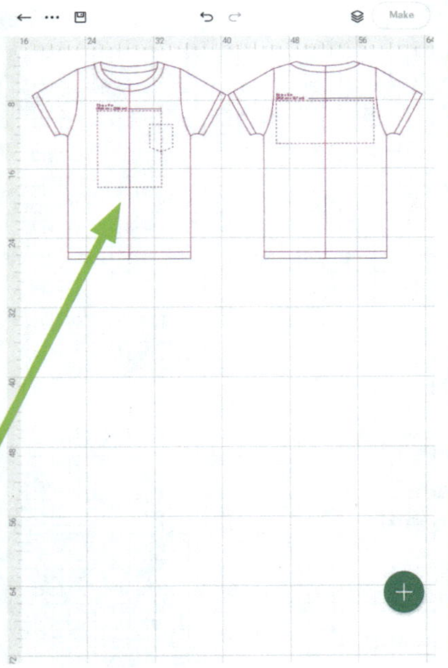

Step 4: Place your design within the dashed template area of your choice. Tap Make to cut your design. Be aware that the layout itself will not appear on the mats.

Need a layout but can't find it in the layout library? You can upload your own image (see page 83), resize it as needed using the dimension boxes in the edit panel, and then click Arrange > Send to Back. Be sure to hide the layer (click the eye icon) before you cut it to avoid cutting out the layout, too.

HOW TO SAVE WORK AND VIEW SAVED PROJECTS

Step 1: Create something and tap the Save icon.

Step 2: Give the project a name and tap Save.

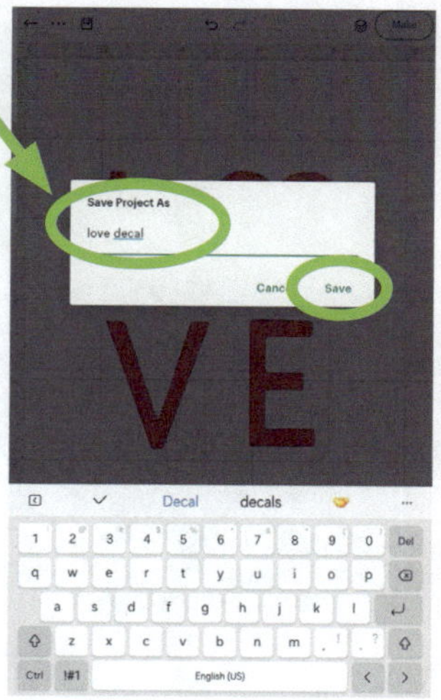

Step 3: Give your device time to save the project. Make sure you are near your Wi-Fi source for the best results.

If Cricut is able to save your project, a confirmation notice will appear at the bottom.

To view your Saved Projects, go to the home screen, tap My Stuff, then tap Projects.

Note that you cannot currently share a project from the Android version of Cricut Design Space, but you can save a project on Android and then access and share it from the desktop version.

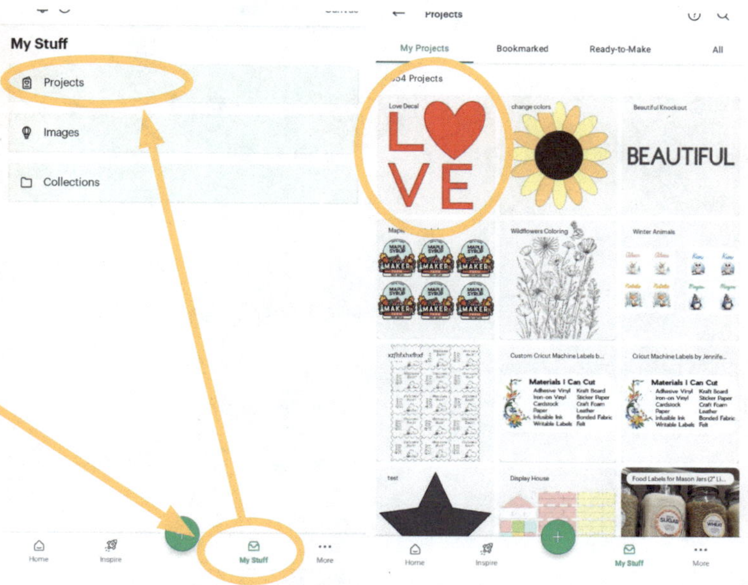

SAVE WORK/PROJECTS

Practice this at jennifermaker.com/love-decal

HOW TO FLATTEN

Need to make a Print Then Cut project? Flatten is your friend! The Flatten tool allows you to turn any image into a single, printable layer for the Print Then Cut feature.

Step 1: Add two or more items to your Canvas that you want to flatten.

Note: Flatten is used only for Print Then Cut.

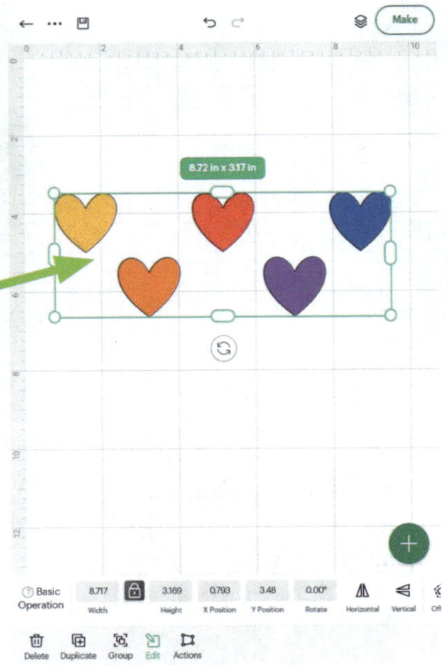

Step 2: Tap and drag a selection box around all objects you want to flatten to select all of them.

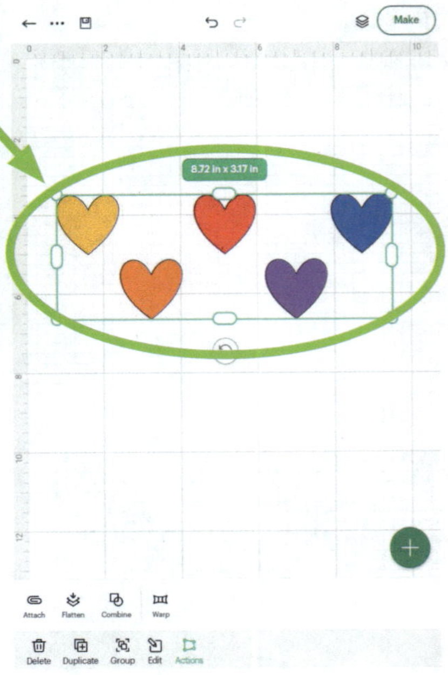

Step 3: Tap Actions, then tap Flatten.

Note that all items are now on one layer and now work only for Print Then Cut.

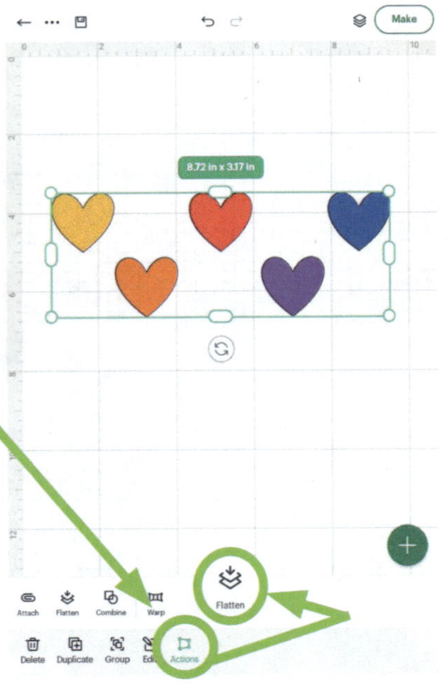

If you decide this isn't what you wanted to do, tap the Unflatten button.

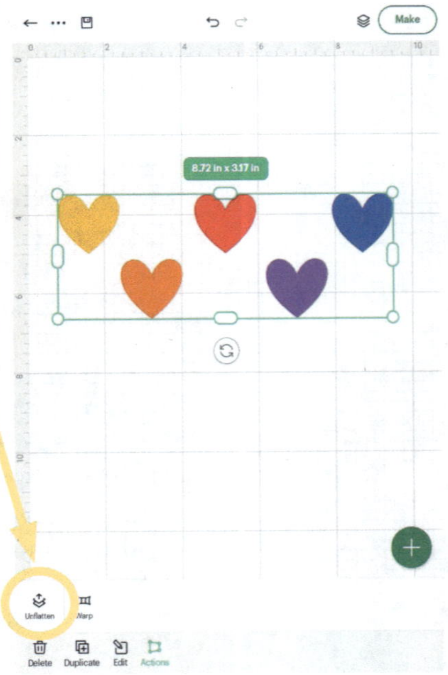

Practice this at jennifermaker.com/five-hearts

HOW TO USE PRINT THEN CUT

Use the Print Then Cut feature to create full-color designs. You must have a printer to use the Print Then Cut feature. Remember to flatten your design if necessary (see the previous page for how to flatten).

Step 1: Open a new project, then tap the + (green circle). Tap Image.

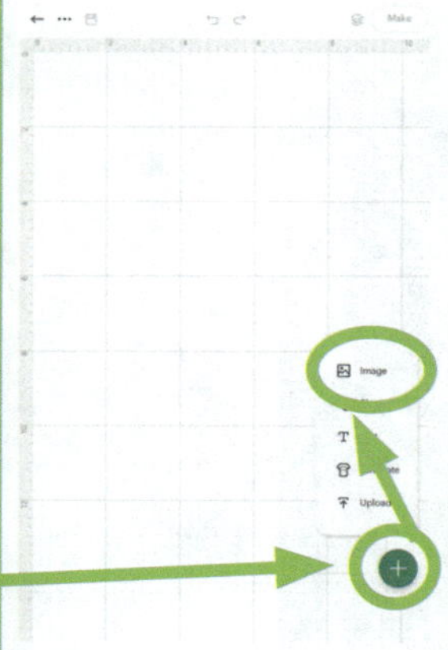

Step 2: Tap the filter icon on the top right.

Step 3: Under Operation Type, tap the checkbox next to Print then Cut.

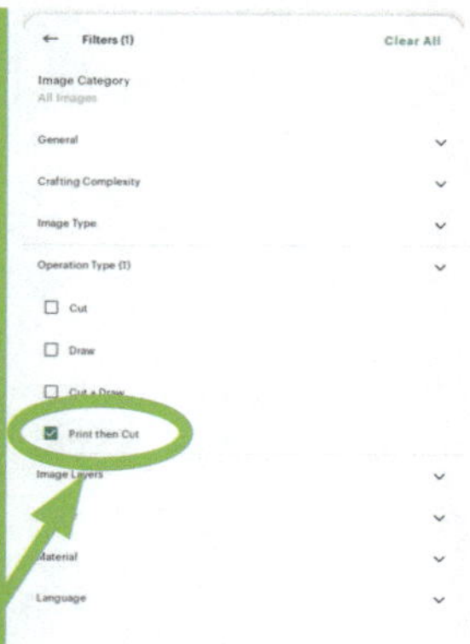

Step 4: Tap on the Print Then Cut image you want for your project, then tap the + (plus icon) on the bottom right.

Step 5: Your Print Then Cut image will appear on your Canvas. Resize it to your desired size. Tap Make.

Step 6: On the Prepare screen, make sure your settings are correct, then tap Next. Your project will print from your printer.

Step 7: Once your project has printed, let the ink dry on the paper. Then, adhere the paper to a mat using a brayer. Insert the mat into your Cricut, tap Next, and press the flashing button on your Cricut when prompted. Your Cricut will identify where to cut by using the black lines printed on the paper.

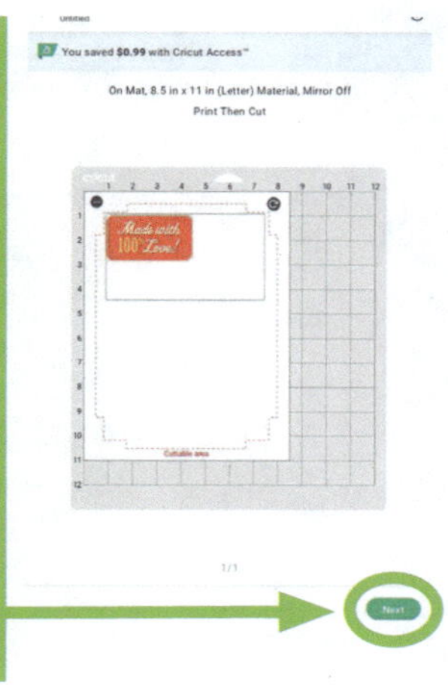

Use the highest quality print and color options on your printer for the best results.

HOW TO UPLOAD IMAGES

Step 1:
Tap the green + button for a new project.

Step 2: Tap the + (green circle), then tap Upload.

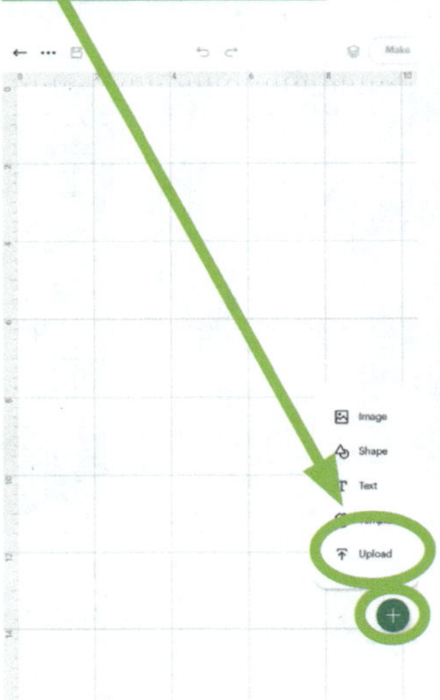

Step 3:
Tap Select from Photo Library to locate an image you already saved there.

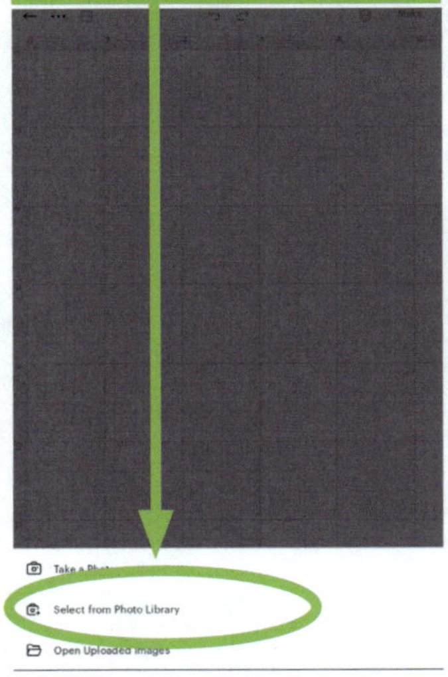

Step 4:
Tap the image file, such as PNG, JPG, GIF, or BMP.

Step 5:
Crop your image if necessary and tap Apply.

Step 6:
Clean it up (if you want) and tap Apply.

Step 7:
Choose your image upload type, then tap Next.

Step 8: Name your image, then tap Upload. Your image will appear on your Canvas.

Practice this at jennifermaker.com/rainbow-heart

HOW TO ERASE A BACKGROUND FROM AN IMAGE

Step 1: Upload a JPG, PNG, GIF, or BMP file that you want to use. Tip: You'll need to save to your Photos library in order to upload it. Use Google Drive or something similar to transfer files if necessary.

Step 2: Tap the Remove tool of your choice: Automatic, Select or Erase. You can also Restore and Crop.

Step 3: Tap on Select and tap the white background around your image to erase it. You may need to click in several areas to get it all. The color tolerance at the bottom controls how much of a given color you remove. When it looks good, tap Apply.

Step 4: Choose the upload method you'd like for your image. Then tap Next.

You can choose to save your image as a solid cut image or a Print Then Cut image.

Step 5: Give your image a name, then tap Upload. Now you can add the image to your Canvas.

Practice this at jennifermaker.com/rainbow-heart

Android

HOW TO USE FILE/PHOTO TO LAYERS

The File/Photo to Layers function allows you to upload an image and let Design Space convert it into up to nine layers. It doesn't always work perfectly, but can be a really cool tool to use.

Step 1: Start a new project by tapping the green circle on the main screen.

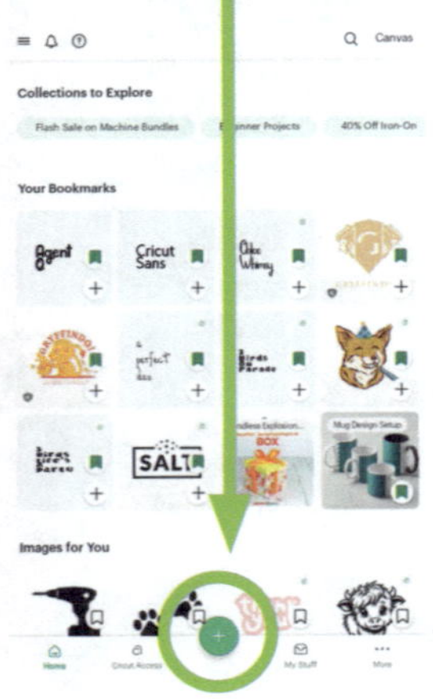

Step 2: Tap the + (green circle), then tap Upload.

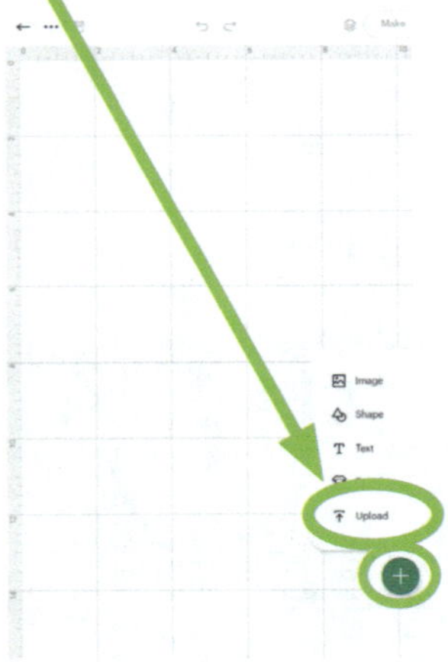

Step 3: Tap Select from Photo Library.

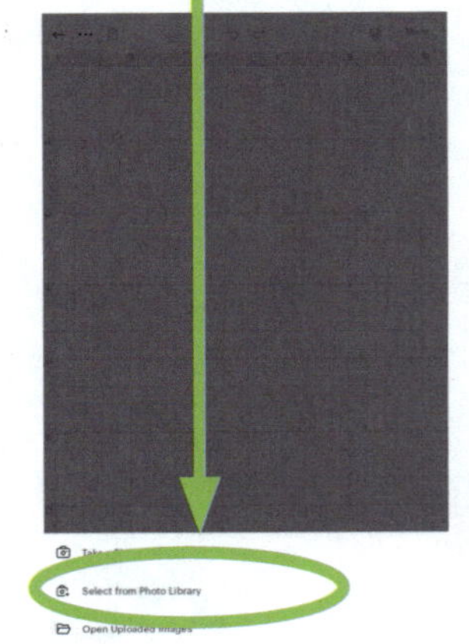

Step 4: Select an image. Erase the background and click Apply.

Step 5: Tap the Multiple Layers option, then tap Next.

Step 6: Tap Clipart or Photo. Tap the Output Style you want. Tap Next.

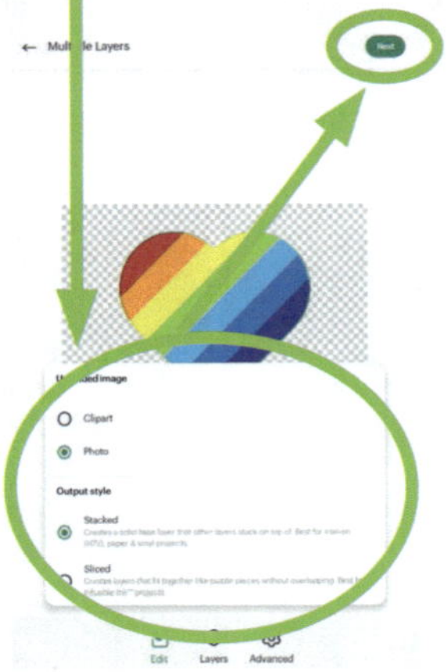

Step 7: Give your image a name, then tap Upload.

Step 8: Your new layered image will appear on the Canvas.

Practice this at jennifermaker.com/rainbow-heart

HOW TO
COMBINE MULTIPLE PROJECTS

Step 1: Open the project you want to add to another and turn off the grid by tapping Settings and toggle the Grid off.

Step 2: If any individual elements in your design are touching and you need them separated, move them apart now.

Step 3: Take a picture of the Design Space screen by taking a screenshot. Then, go to Home screen and tap Gallery, find the image, tap the Pencil icon, and crop it (slide in the sides) to just the design, and tap Save.

Step 4: Open the project to which you want to add your other project. Allow it to replace your current Canvas.

Step 5: Follow previous pages to upload the image from Step 3 and remove the back-ground. Tap Single Layer, then tap Next.

Step 6: Insert the newly uploaded image onto your Canvas with the other image from Step 4.

Step 7: Tap the first project's image, tap Duplicate, and make as many duplicates as there are elements in the project.

Step 8: Select each duplicate copy and tap Actions > Hide (see Contours on page 60) to separate out each element into its own layer.

Step 9: Recolor each element (see page 111) as needed and move back into position. Now your two projects are combined!

Practice this at jennifermaker.com/butterflies and jennifermaker.com/rainbow-love

HOW TO UPLOAD SVG FILES ON AN ANDROID

SVG files are special files that you can upload to Cricut Design Space and cut beautiful designs from. To use an SVG, first you must download and unzip an SVG file. You can practice downloading a file at jennifermaker.com/svg-heart. To unzip a file, go to My Files on your Android, tap on Downloads, tap to select the downloaded ZIP file, click on the three dots in the upper right corner of your screen, and choose Extract. Note that you will not see the folder in step 4 unless you do this first.

Step 1: Tap the + icon for a new project

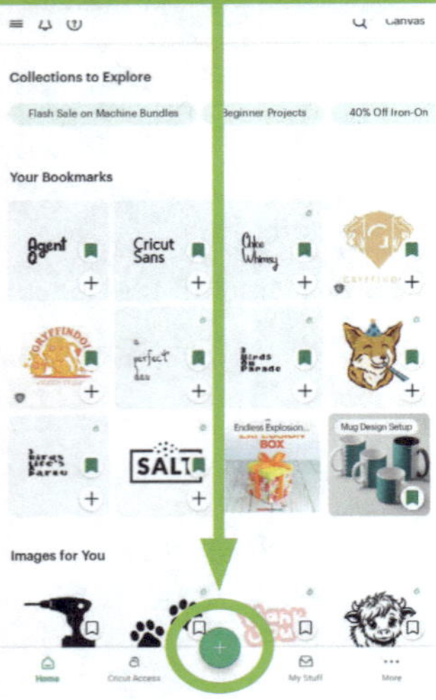

Step 2: Tap + (green circle), then Upload.

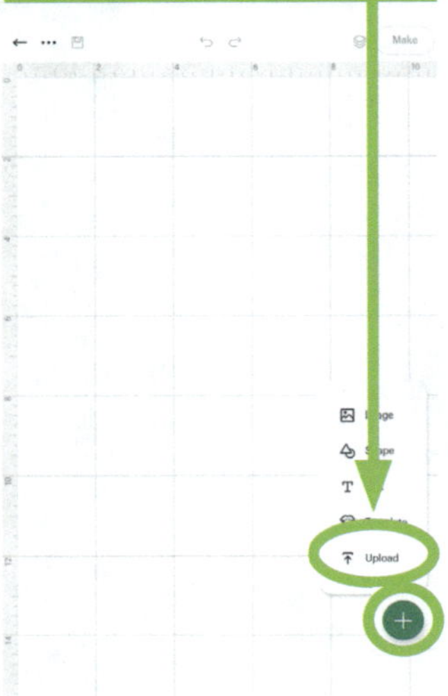

Step 3: Tap Select from Photo Library

Step 4: Tap the ☰ menu and open Downloads

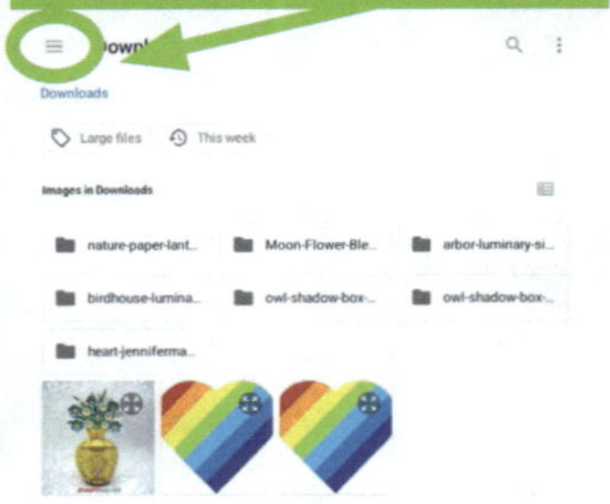

Step 5:
Tap the SVG file (do NOT tap the ZIP file—it will give you an error).

Step 6:
Enter a name for your image, then tap Upload.

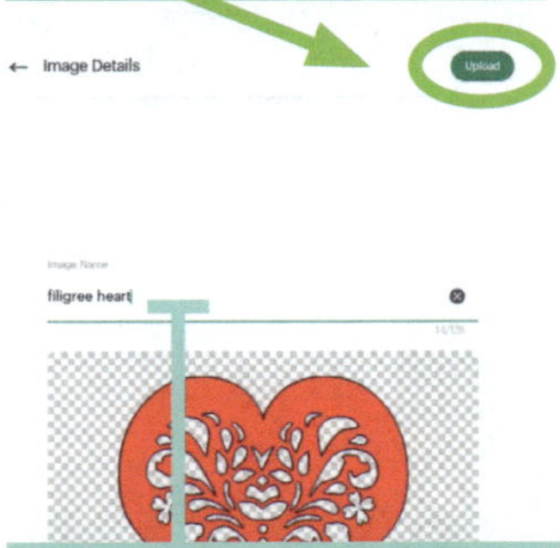

Tip: Type a word or two as a tag to help you find this image later in a search.

Once inserted, your image appears on your Canvas, ready to be modified and/or made!

Practice this at jennifermaker.com/svg-heart

HOW TO RESIZE A PROJECT

Have you ever uploaded an SVG design, cut it out, and realized it was too small or too big? Here's how to check the size of a project before you cut it out:

Step 1: Insert, upload, or create an image on your Canvas in Design Space, then select all images you want to resize by tapping and dragging a selection box around them.

Step 2: Tap Edit, then note the size at the bottom of the window in the Width and Height circles.

To determine if the sizing is right, compare it to the sizing in the original instructions or tutorial. If no sizing is provided, you'll have to use your best judgment. Here's how to resize a project:

Step 3: Be sure the lock icon indicates it is locked, then tap the Width or Height circles and tap on the number pad to enter the proper size, then tap Done.

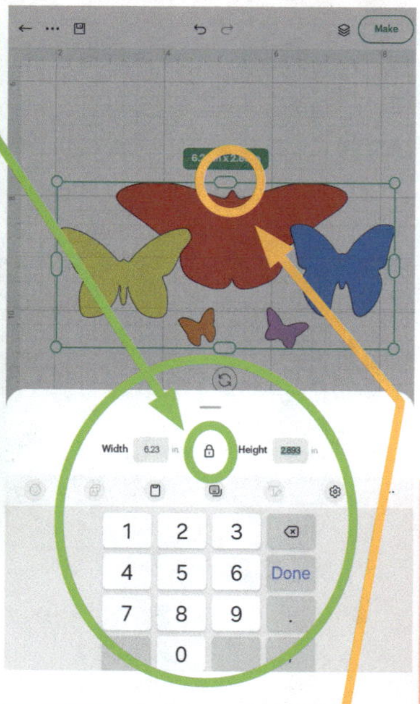

The entire selected image(s) is resized and retains its proportions.

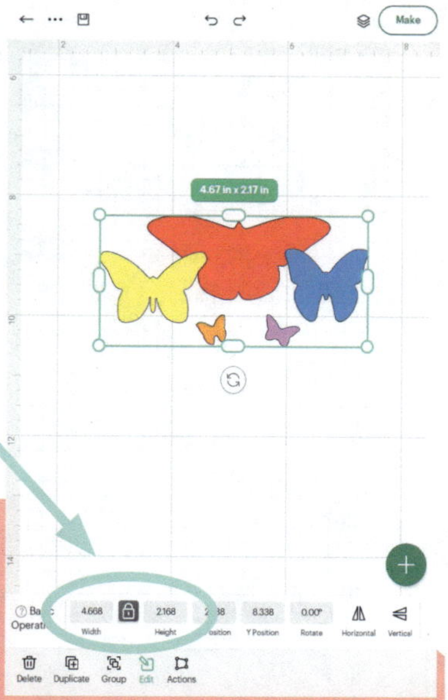

Note that Cricut Design Space may automatically resize any SVG file that measures over 12" (either wide or high) down to 12" on its longest side, and there is no notification that an image was resized. So if you ever place an image on your Canvas and notice that one side measures exactly 12," that is a strong indicator that your image has been resized. To learn how to fix this, visit jennifermaker.com/resize-svg.

You can also resize images using the resize icon in the lower right corner of a selection box. Just click, hold, and drag to resize.

Practice this at jennifermaker.com/butterflies

RESIZE A PROJECT

HOW TO USE CREATE AI

Create AI is a feature in Design Space that lets you describe what you want, and Cricut will generate original art for you. Here's how to use it:

Step 1: Tap the + icon for a new project.

Step 2: Tap + (green circle), then Create AI.

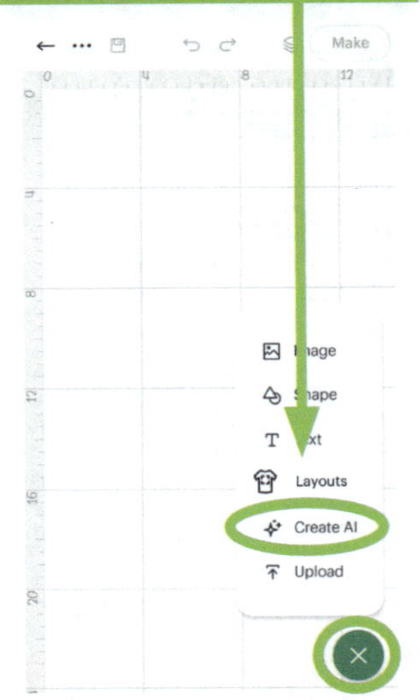

Step 3: Describe the image you want. Be clear and specific!

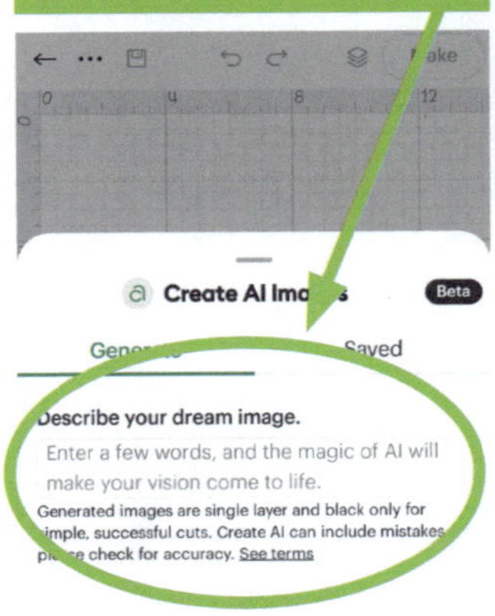

Step 4: Click Generate.

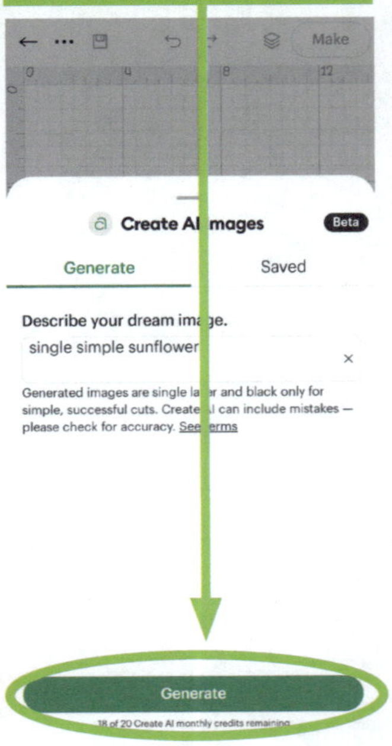

Note: Create AI images generated in the Android App are single layer and black only for simple, successful cuts.

Step 5: Wait for your image to generate.

Step 6: Once your image is generated, Tap the + (white circle), to add it to your canvas.

Step 7: Resize your image if desired.

All images generated by Create AI, can be found under "Saved" in the Create AI Images panel.

Note: The Create AI tool is currently only a feature for Cricut Access members, who receive 20 AI credits each month to generate new designs.

HOW TO FOLLOW SOMEONE IN DESIGN SPACE

You can follow your friends and other Cricut crafters in Design Space, and even get notifications on their new projects! Here's how to follow someone and how to set your notification settings.

Step 1: Ask a friend for their profile link and go to the link using your Internet browser. My link is at jennifermaker.com/follow-me-on-cricut. Then tap on Open in App.

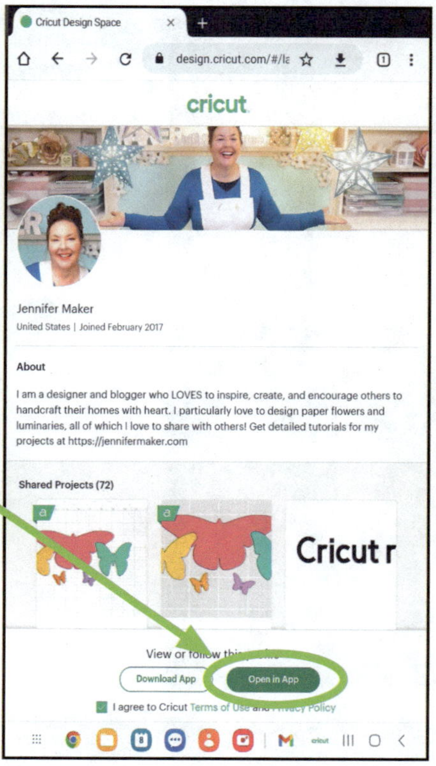

Step 2: Click the Follow button to begin following that friend on Design Space.

You may also find people to follow by going to the main Home screen and scrolling through the project categories, then clicking on a community member name.

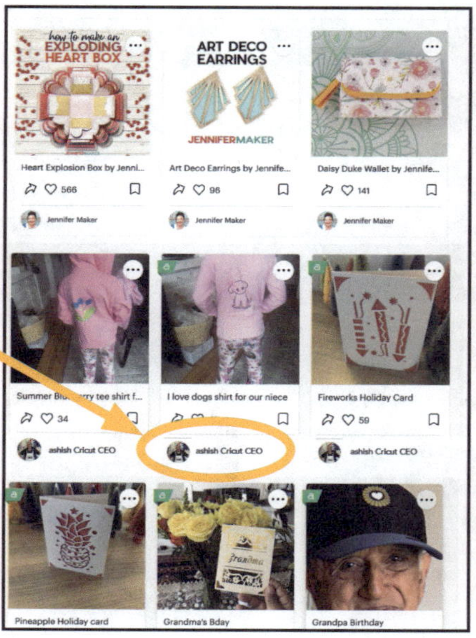

Once their profile is open, you may click the Follow button to begin following them.

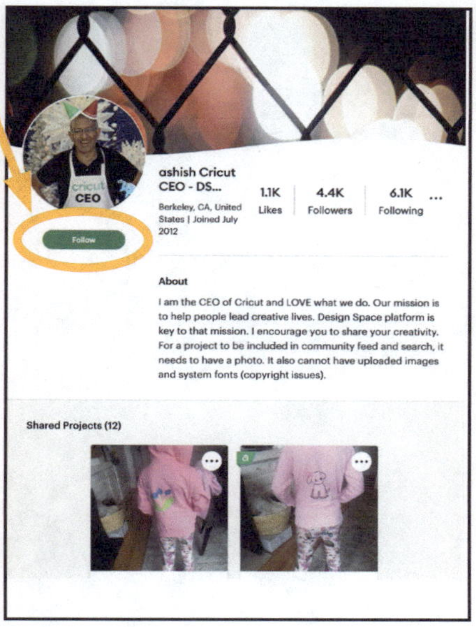

Follow me at jennifermaker.com/follow-me-on-cricut

HOW TO UPDATE THE CRICUT APP ON ANDROID

Step 1: Open your Cricut Design Space app. If a new version is available, it will tell you. Tap Update.

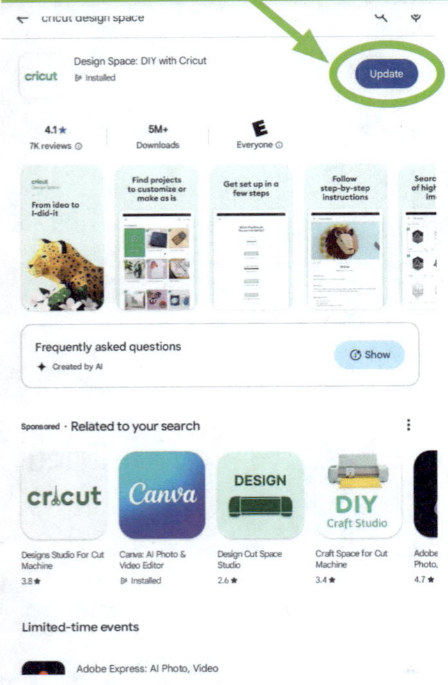

Alternatively, you can go to the Home screen and tap the Play Store to check for updates.

Once in the Play Store, tap the Search bar and search on Cricut Design Space.

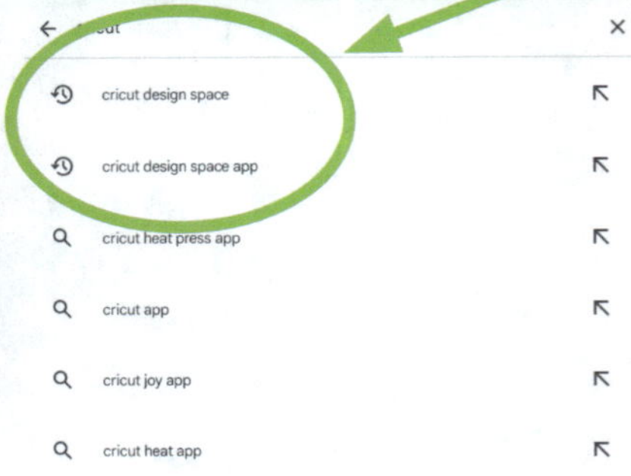

Step 2: Tap Update. Make sure you have a good Internet signal for the best results.

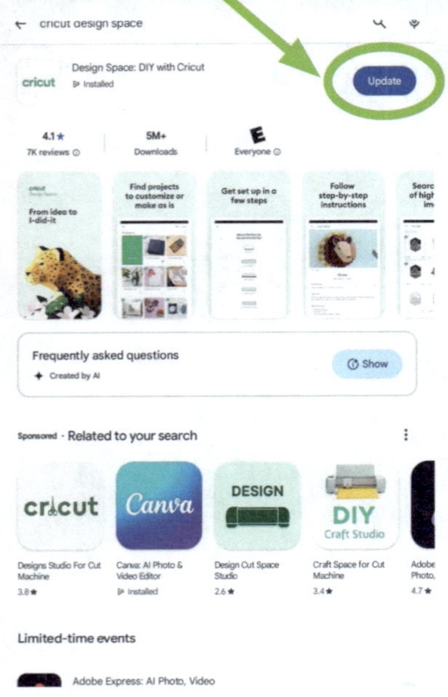

Step 3: Wait for the Cricut Design Space app to update, usually just a few minutes.

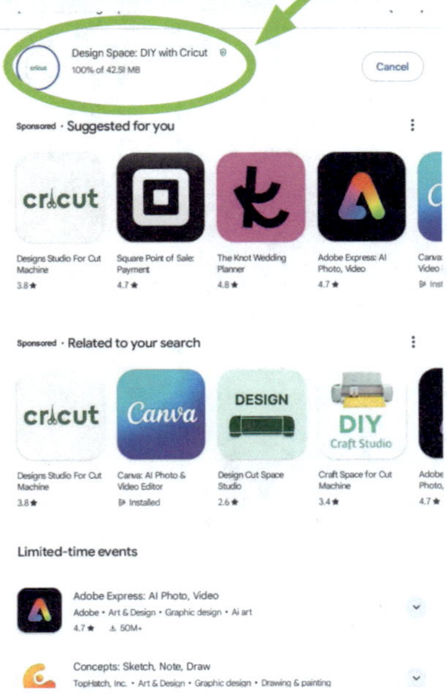

Step 4: Tap Open to launch the updated version of the Cricut Design Space app.

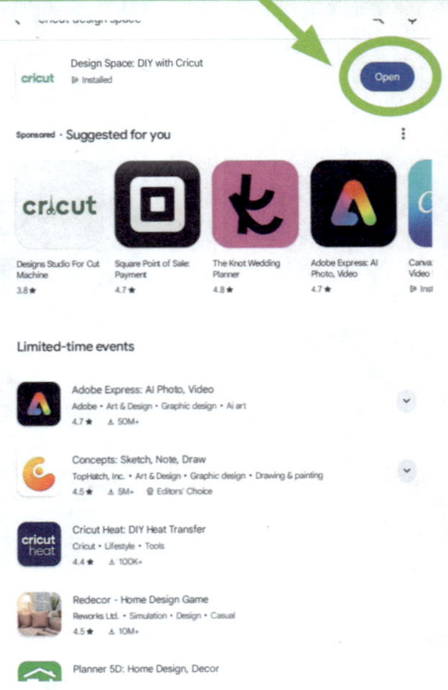

Android

HOW TO TROUBLESHOOT DESIGN SPACE PROBLEMS

Your ability and willingness to troubleshoot problems is a high factor in your success with your Cricut (and really, most things in life). Problems happen, but you CAN solve them. Here are the steps I take when I encounter problems with Cricut Design Space:

Cricut Design Space is acting weird or not working at all.

Is it down?

- Yes → Watch for it to come back.
  - Still having problems?
    - Yes → Do you have a strong Internet connection?
    - No → Have fun and make something awesome!
- No → Is it installed and up-to-date?
  - Yes → Have fun and make something awesome!
  - No → Install and/or update!
    - Are you still having problems?
      - Yes → Do you have a strong Internet connection?
      - No → Have fun and make something awesome!

Do you have a strong Internet connection?

- Yes → Keep the app with Design Space open and don't move away while cutting.
- No → Connect to Internet & move your Cricut and device closer to router.

Are you still having problems?

- Yes → Close any other apps running on your device.
- No → Have fun and make something awesome!

Are you still having problems?

- Yes → Make sure your Cricut is actually connected via Bluetooth.
- No → Have fun and make something awesome!

Are you still having problems?

- Yes → Disconnect your Cricut, restart your device, and reconnect your Cricut.
- No → Have fun and make something awesome!

Are you still having problems?

- Yes → Contact Cricut Member Care. Cricut Member Care is very helpful!
- No → Have fun and make something awesome!

Having different problems? Here are more solutions:

Machine problems:
Check the Cricut site at help.cricut.com

Cutting problems:
Check my ideas at jennifermaker.com/cricut-cutting-problems-tips-cleaner-cuts

Mat problems:
Check my mat tips at jennifermaker.com/cricut-cutting-mats-sticky

Blade problems:
Check my blade tips at jennifermaker.com/cricut-blades-cutting-tips

TROUBLESHOOTING

WANT THE ULTIMATE DESIGN EXPERIENCE?

WITH JENNIFERMAKER
ADVANCE

This is a special program for ALL skill levels — I can help you advance from new to beginner or advanced to pro, and everything in between!

Do you love making things, but wish you could put your own unique spin on the design to create memorable, one-of-a-kind results? Are you tired of searching over and over for just the right design that fits your needs and spending all your money on files? Are you frustrated by your results when you try to customize something on your own?

Find out more at
jennifermaker.com/advance

BUILD A SOLID BUSINESS PLAN WITH THE MAKER MARKETPLACE

Have you heard people say, "Wow! You could sell this!" when they look at your crafts? Have you ever thought about selling your handiwork?

Have you been daunted by the prospect of what it takes to start a successful business selling your crafts? **It's no quick and easy task, but I'm here to help!**

The Maker Marketplace handbook explores the many aspects of starting and running a handmade crafts business, **from the very beginning thoughts about why you'd like to start a business to evaluating your existing business.**

Find out more at

makeracademy.com/maker-marketplace-handbook

SUBLIMATION MADE SIMPLE

EVERYTHING YOU NEED TO KNOW ABOUT SUBLIMATION

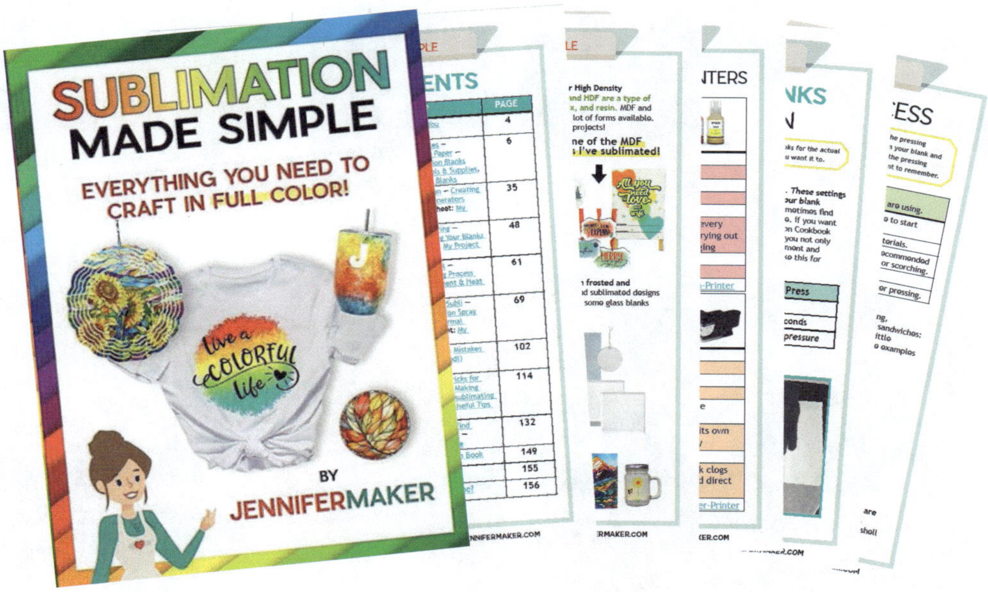

From what materials you need and what programs you can use to create designs, to how to use “hacks” and solve common issues, everything you need to do in order to create sublimation projects can be found in this book!

Want to create vividly colorful personalized matching tote bags for a family vacation to the beach? Interested in creating colorful ornaments to decorate a Christmas tree? Thinking about making yourself a personalized tumbler decorated with images of your pets? With sublimation, you can!

Find out more at

jennifermaker.com/sublimation-made-simple

CRAFT A LIFE YOU LOVE

Visit me at JenniferMaker.com regularly for inspiration, help, and projects!

Made in United States
Troutdale, OR
11/05/2026

56950744R00077